# ZAGATSURVEY®

# 2003

# SAN FRANCISCO BAY AREA RESTAURANTS

Local Editor: Meesha Halm

Local Coordinator: Maura Sell

Editor: Troy Segal

Published and distributed by
ZAGAT SURVEY, LLC
4 Columbus Circle
New York, New York 10019
Tel: 212 977 6000
E-mail: sanfran@zagat.com
Web site: www.zagat.com

# Acknowledgments

We'd like to thank Antonia Allegra, Laurie Armstrong, Mark Carter, Sarah Cummings, Heidi Cusick, Jon and Olive Poe Fox, D.K. Jackson, Michelle Anna Jordan, Vincent and Conor Logan, Mary Orlin, Laura Reiley and Willow Waldeck.

This guide would not have been possible without the hard work of our staff, especially Reni Chin, Anna Chlumsky, Jeff Freier, Jessica Gonzalez, Katherine Harris, Diane Karlin, Natalie Lebert, Mike Liao, Dave Makulec, Laura Mitchell, Rob Poole, Robert Seixas, Yoji Yamaguchi and Sharon Yates.

# Contents

What's New ............................ 5
About This Survey .................... 6
Key to Ratings & Symbols ............ 7
Most Popular Places ................. 9

**TOP RATINGS**
By Food; Cuisines, Features, Locations ...... 10
By Decor; Outdoors, Romance, Rooms, Views 15
By Service ........................... 17
Best Buys ........................... 18

**RESTAURANT DIRECTORY**
Names, Addresses, Phone Numbers,
Ratings and Reviews .................. 19

**INDEXES**
Cuisines ............................. 184
Locations ........................... 198
Special Features .................... 211
  Breakfast ......................... 211
  Brunch ........................... 211
  Buffet Served ..................... 212
  Business Dining ................... 212
  Catering .......................... 213
  Celebrity Chefs ................... 214
  Child-Friendly .................... 215
  Critic-Proof ...................... 216
  Dancing ........................... 216
  Delivery/Takeout .................. 216
  Dining Alone ...................... 218
  Entertainment ..................... 219
  Fireplaces ........................ 220
  Historic Places ................... 221
  Hotel Dining ...................... 222
  "In" Places ....................... 224
  Jacket Required ................... 225
  Late Dining ....................... 226
  Meet for a Drink .................. 226
  Microbreweries .................... 227
  Noteworthy Newcomers .............. 227
  Offbeat ........................... 228
  Outdoor Dining .................... 228
  People-Watching ................... 232
  Power Scenes ...................... 232
  Pre-Theater Menus ................. 233
  Private Rooms ..................... 233
  Prix Fixe Menus ................... 237
  Quiet Conversation ................ 238
  Raw Bars .......................... 238
  Romantic Places ................... 239

Senior Appeal . . . . . . . . . . . . . . . . . . . . . . . 240
Singles Scenes . . . . . . . . . . . . . . . . . . . . . . 241
Sleepers. . . . . . . . . . . . . . . . . . . . . . . . . . . 242
Tasting Menus. . . . . . . . . . . . . . . . . . . . . . 242
Tea Service . . . . . . . . . . . . . . . . . . . . . . . . 243
Teen Appeal . . . . . . . . . . . . . . . . . . . . . . . 243
Theme Restaurants. . . . . . . . . . . . . . . . . . 244
Valet Parking. . . . . . . . . . . . . . . . . . . . . . . 244
Views. . . . . . . . . . . . . . . . . . . . . . . . . . . . . 245
Visitors on Expense Account . . . . . . . . . . . 246
Wine Bars . . . . . . . . . . . . . . . . . . . . . . . . . 247
Winning Wine Lists. . . . . . . . . . . . . . . . . . 247
Worth a Trip . . . . . . . . . . . . . . . . . . . . . . . 249
**Wine Chart** . . . . . . . . . . . . . . . . . . . . . . . . . 252

# What's New

There's no denying that the local recession and a drastic decrease in tourism since 9/11 have clouded the Bay Area restaurant scene this year: while profits were down, closures were up (the 12-year-old Cypress Club was a notable casualty). Still, we can't help but point out some silver linings for you, the customer. It's easier to snag reservations at hot spots, and many places have lowered prices or come up with other ways to coax diners out of their dens.

**There's No Place Like Home:** One winning formula is to provide comfort food (of any ethnicity) conveniently and at easy-to-swallow prices. The Moroccan Aziza, the Italian Incanto and the American Julia have all set up modest shop in residential neighborhoods. Even existing establishments have embraced gemütlichkeit – for example, that old swinger Johnfrank has gone Home, offering in its reincarnated form simple American favorites at half the cost.

**Steak Your Claim:** Perhaps it was this desire for the familiar that caused San Franciscans to embrace meat, as proffered by newcomers Acme Chop House, Daily Grill, FlatIron Grill and Izzy's. Restaurateur Pascal Rigo spearheaded the Gallic equivalent (steak frites) at Marinette, which leads a beefy bistro brigade that includes Chez Papa Bistrot, Jeanty at Jack's and Le Zinc.

**Small Budgets, Small Plates:** The proliferation of little-dish dining continues: Rocco's Seafood Grill re-emerged as F.I.G.S., featuring small plates from France, Italy, Greece and Spain, and Zuzu touts tapas from Latin America. Even traditional establishments like Hawthorne Lane have doubled the number of their appetizers, acknowledging that the graze craze is here to stay.

**News From Napa:** Once the sleepy stepchild of the wine country, the town of Napa is undergoing a major revitalization. The momentum began with the new COPIA Center and its flagship Julia's Kitchen, a refined Californian–New French named for museum trustee Julia Child; it continues with Uva, a trattoria turned Southern Italian scenster.

**Luxe Redux:** For those who still have the means, the sky's still the limit at several swanky French *arrivistes,* such as chef George Morrone's Redwood Park and Fleur de Lys, triumphantly risen from the ashes of a fire. There's also Gary Danko, the *Survey*'s new No. 1 for Food – edging out by a decimal place the longtime champ French Laundry. Of course, these spots will run you more than San Francisco's average meal cost of $33.03 – but you've got to indulge sometimes. Besides, spending stimulates the local economy.

San Francisco, CA                           Meesha Halm
August 6, 2002

# About This Survey

For 24 years, Zagat Survey has reported on the shared experiences of diners like you. Here are the results of our *2003 San Francisco Bay Area Restaurant Survey,* covering some 935 restaurants. This marks the 17th year we have covered restaurants in the Bay Area, extending from the wine country to the Monterey Peninsula.

By regularly surveying large numbers of avid local restaurant-goers about their collective dining experiences, we hope to have achieved a uniquely current and reliable guide. For the first time this year, we conducted the Bay Area survey entirely online. More than 3,600 people participated. Since the participants dined out an average of 3.1 times per week, this *Survey* is based on roughly 590,000 meals annually.

Of our surveyors, 52% are women, 48% men; the breakdown by age is 19% in their 20s, 33% in their 30s, 18% in their 40s, 19% in their 50s and 11% in their 60s or above. Possibly as a result of surveying online, the average age of our surveyors has declined this year, from 45 to 42.

Of course, we are especially grateful to our editor, Meesha Halm, a cookbook author and Internet producer, and to our coordinator, Maura Sell, a professionally trained chef and specialty food industry consultant.

To help guide our readers to the Bay Area's best meals and best buys, we have prepared a number of lists. See Most Popular (page 9), Top Ratings (pages 10–17) and Best Buys (page 18). To assist the user in finding just the right restaurant for any occasion, without wasting time, we have also provided 46 handy indexes and have tried to be concise.

As companions to this guide, we also publish the *San Francisco Nightlife Survey* and the *Los Angeles/So. California Restaurant Survey,* as well as *Zagat Surveys* and Maps to more than 70 other markets around the world. Most of these guides are also available on mobile devices and at **www.zagat.com,** where you can also vote and shop.

To join our next **San Francisco Bay Area Survey** or any of our other upcoming *Surveys,* all you need to do is register at zagat.com and select the *Survey* in which you'd like to participate. Each participant will receive a free copy of the resulting guide when it is published.

Your comments, suggestions and even criticisms of this guide are also solicited. There is always room for improvement with your help. You can contact us at sanfran@zagat.com or by mail at Zagat Survey, 4 Columbus Circle, New York, NY 10019. We look forward to hearing from you.

New York, NY
August 6, 2002

Nina and Tim Zagat

# Key to Ratings/Symbols

**Name, Address & Phone Number**

**Zagat Ratings**

**Hours & Credit Cards**

| F | D | S | C |
|---|---|---|---|

Tim & Nina's  ◑🅂⊅  ▽ 23 | 9 | 13 | $15

*9999 Mission St. (The Embarcadero), 415-555-7233*

◪ Open "more or less when they feel like it", this bit of Embarcadero ectoplasm excels in seafood with an Asian-Argentinian-Australian twist; the staff seems "fresh off the boat", even if the fish isn't, and while the view of the garbage barges is "a drag", no one balks at the bottom-feeder prices ("the older the entrée, the cheaper the bill").

**Review, with surveyors' comments in quotes**

Restaurants with the highest overall ratings and greatest popularity and importance are printed in CAPITAL LETTERS.

Before each review a symbol indicates whether responses were uniform ■ or mixed ◪.

**Hours:** ◑ serves after 11 PM
 🅻 open for Lunch
 🅂 open on Sunday
 🅼 open on Monday

**Credit Cards:** ⊅ no credit cards accepted

**Ratings:** Food, Decor and Service are rated on a scale of **0** to **30.** The Cost (C) column reflects our surveyors' estimate of the price of dinner including one drink and tip.

| F Food | D Decor | S Service | C Cost |
|---|---|---|---|
| 23 | 9 | 13 | $15 |

| | |
|---|---|
| **0–9** poor to fair | **20–25** very good to excellent |
| **10–15** fair to good | **26–30** extraordinary to perfection |
| **16–19** good to very good | ▽ low response/less reliable |

For places listed without ratings or a cost estimate, such as an important **newcomer** or a popular **write-in,** the cost is indicated by the following symbols.

| | | | |
|---|---|---|---|
| **I** | $15 and below | **E** | $31 to $50 |
| **M** | $16 to $30 | **VE** | $51 or more |

# Most Popular

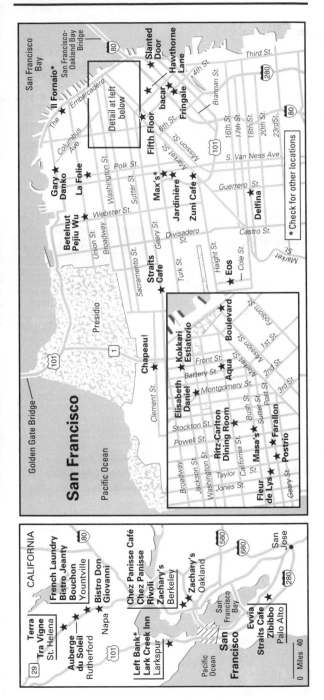

# Most Popular

Each of our reviewers has been asked to name his or her five favorite restaurants. The places most frequently named, in order of their popularity, are:

| | |
|---|---|
| 1. Boulevard | 21. Kokkari Estiatorio |
| 2. French Laundry | 22. Fifth Floor |
| 3. Gary Danko | 23. Max's |
| 4. Aqua | 24. Ritz-Carlton Dining Rm. |
| 5. Chez Panisse | 25. Bistro Don Giovanni |
| 6. Slanted Door | 26. Left Bank |
| 7. Chez Panisse Café | 27. Masa's |
| 8. Bistro Jeanty | 28. Fleur de Lys |
| 9. Delfina | 29. Lark Creek Inn |
| 10. Farallon | 30. Fringale |
| 11. Jardinière | 31. Betelnut Pejiu Wu |
| 12. Hawthorne Lane | 32. Auberge du Soleil |
| 13. Postrio | 33. Bouchon |
| 14. Il Fornaio | 34. Elisabeth Daniel* |
| 15. Evvia | 35. Rivoli |
| 16. Tra Vigne | 36. Straits Cafe* |
| 17. Zuni Cafe | 37. Eos Restaurant |
| 18. Zachary's Pizza | 38. Zibibbo |
| 19. bacar | 39. Terra |
| 20. La Folie* | 40. Chapeau! |

It's obvious that many of the restaurants on the above list are among the San Francisco area's most expensive, but if popularity were calibrated to price, we suspect that a number of other restaurants would join the above ranks. Given the fact that both our surveyors and readers love to discover dining bargains, we have added a list of 80 Best Buys on page 18. These are restaurants that give real quality at extremely reasonable prices.

* Tied with restaurant directly above it

# Top Ratings

Top lists exclude restaurants with low voting.

## Top 40 Food Rankings

| | |
|---|---|
| **29** Gary Danko | Bistro Jeanty |
| French Laundry | Cafe Jacqueline |
| **28** Sierra Mar | Rivoli* |
| Masa's | Hana Japanese |
| Ritz-Carlton Dining Rm. | Cafe La Haye |
| Chez Panisse | Domaine Chandon |
| **27** La Folie | Koi Palace |
| Sushi Ran | Rest. at Stevenswood |
| Chez Panisse Café | Delfina |
| Aqua | Fresh Cream |
| Boulevard | Swan Oyster Depot |
| Emile's | Jardinière |
| Acquerello | Slanted Door |
| Erna's Elderberry Hse. | Elisabeth Daniel |
| Terra | Tastings Restaurant |
| La Toque | Gayle's Bakery |
| Fleur de Lys | Kabuto Sushi |
| Le Poisson Japonais | Auberge du Soleil |
| **26** Le Papillon | **25** Zachary's Pizza |
| Charles Nob Hill | Campton Place |

## Top Food by Cuisine

**American (New)**
29 Gary Danko
   French Laundry
26 Cafe La Haye
   Tastings Restaurant
25 Chez TJ

**American (Traditional)**
27 Boulevard
25 Lark Creek Inn
24 Dottie's True Blue Cafe
22 Buckeye Roadhouse
   Mama's/Washington Sq.

**Bakeries/Delis**
26 Gayle's Bakery
25 Downtown Bakery
24 Emporio Rulli
23 Liberty Cafe & Bakery
21 JZ Cool

**Barbecue**
24 Foothill Cafe
   Koryo Wooden Charcoal
23 Brother's Korean
21 Bo's Barbecue
   Flint's Barbecue

**Cajun/Creole/Southern**
20 PJ's Oyster Bed
21 Catahoula Restaurant
   Kingfish
17 Elite Cafe
   Nola

**Californian**
28 Sierra Mar
   Chez Panisse
27 Chez Panisse Café
   Erna's Elderberry Hse.
26 Charles Nob Hill

**Chinese**
25 Ton Kiang
24 Great Eastern
   Yank Sing
   R & G Lounge
23 Tommy Toy's Cuisine

**Continental**
26 Rest. at Stevenswood
22 Caprice
20 Dal Baffo
   Maddalena's & Café Fino
19 Bella Vista

---

\* Tied with restaurant directly above it

## Dim Sum
**26** Koi Palace
**25** Ton Kiang
**24** Yank Sing
**23** Restaurant Peony
Fook Yuen

## Eclectic/International
**24** Firefly
**23** Restaurant Umunhum
Montrio
**21** Wappo
Andalu

## French (Bistro)
**26** Bistro Jeanty
**25** Syrah
Chapeau!
Fringale
**24** L'Amie Donia

## French (Classic)
**27** Emile's
**26** Cafe Jacqueline
Fresh Cream
Auberge du Soleil
**25** Campton Place

## French (New)
**28** Masa's
Ritz-Carlton Dining Rm.
**27** La Folie
Terra
La Toque

## Fusion
**25** House
Roy's at Pebble Beach
Eos Restaurant
**22** Straits Cafe
**21** Brix

## Hamburgers
**24** Taylor's Automatic
**20** Mo's Burgers/Grill
Burger Joint
**18** Barney's
**17** Balboa Cafe

## Indian
**25** Vik's Chaat Corner
**24** Amber India
Shalimar
Indian Oven
**22** Pakwan

## Italian
**27** Acquerello
**26** Delfina
**25** Tra Vigne
Merenda
**24** Pane e Vino

## Japanese
**27** Sushi Ran
Le Poisson Japonais
**26** Hana Japanese
Kabuto Sushi
**25** Kirala

## Latin American
**22** Destino
Charanga
**21** Alma
**19** Miramonte
Cha Cha Cha

## Mediterranean
**26** Rivoli
**25** Bay Wolf
**24** Lalime's
Chez Nous
Zax

## Mexican
**24** Doña Tomás
Pancho Villa Taqueria
La Taqueria
**22** Maya
Taqueria Cancun

## Middle Eastern/Greek
**25** Evvia
**24** Kokkari Estiatorio
**23** Maykedah
Truly Mediterranean
**19** La Mediterranée

## Pizza
**25** Zachary's Pizza
**24** Tommaso's
Postrio
Pauline's Pizza
**23** Pazzia

## Seafood
**27** Aqua
**26** Koi Palace
Swan Oyster Depot
**25** Pisces
**24** Farallon

## Spanish
**22** César
Zarzuela
Zuzu
**20** B44
**19** Iberia

## Steakhouses
**24** House of Prime Rib
**23** Harris'
Morton's of Chicago
Ruth's Chris
**22** Alfred's Steak House

# Top Food

### Tapas/Small Plates
**25** Isa
**24** Chez Nous
**23** À Côté
**22** Destino
César

### Thai
**25** Thep Phanom
**24** Yukol Place
Marnee Thai
**23** Manora's
**21** Royal Thai

### Vegetarian
**29** French Laundry
**27** Fleur de Lys
**24** Roxanne's*
**23** Greens
**22** Millennium

### Vietnamese
**26** Slanted Door
**25** Thanh Long
**23** Three Seasons
**22** Ana Mandara
**21** Golden Turtle

# Top Food by Special Feature

### Breakfast**
**24** Dottie's True Blue Cafe
Oliveto Cafe & Rest.
**23** Café Fanny
**22** Mama's/Washington Sq.
Jimmy Bean's

### Brunch
**24** Ritz-Carlton Terrace
Postrio
**23** Wente Vineyards
Zuni Cafe
**21** Andalu

### Hotel Dining
**28** Masa's
Hotel Vintage Court
Ritz-Carlton Dining Rm.
Ritz-Carlton Hotel
**25** Campton Place
Campton Place Hotel
Fifth Floor
Hotel Palomar
Pacific
Pan Pacific Hotel

### Late Night
**24** Great Eastern
Koryo Wooden Charcoal
**23** Brother's Korean
Bouchon
**22** Taqueria Cancun

### Newcomers/Rated
**25** Julia's Kitchen
Village Pub
Merenda
Redwood Park
**24** Dry Creek Kitchen

### Newcomers/Unrated
Acme Chop House
Chez Papa Bistrot
Chez Spencer
D'Asaro
Julia

### People-Watching
**27** Boulevard
**26** Jardinière
**25** Evvia
Village Pub
**23** Zuni Cafe

### Tasting Menus
**29** Gary Danko
French Laundry
**28** Masa's
Ritz-Carlton Dining Rm.
**27** La Folie

### Wine Bars
**25** Eos Restaurant
**23** Liberty Cafe & Bakery
**21** bacar
**17** First Crush
**14** Hayes & Vine

### Worth a Trip
**29** French Laundry
Yountville
**28** Chez Panisse
Berkeley
**27** Erna's Elderberry Hse.
Oakhurst
Terra
St. Helena
La Toque
Rutherford

---

\* Low votes
** Other than hotels

# Top Food by Location

## Berkeley
*28* Chez Panisse
*27* Chez Panisse Café
*26* Rivoli
*25* Zachary's Pizza
    Kirala

## Castro/Noe Valley
*25* Ma Tante Sumi
*24* Firefly
*22* Destino
    Hamano Sushi
    2223 Restaurant

## Chinatown
*24* Great Eastern
    R & G Lounge
*23* Hunan Home's
*21* Yuet Lee
    House of Nanking

## Civic Center/Hayes Valley
*26* Jardinière
*23* Zuni Cafe
*22* Millennium
    Hayes Street Grill
*21* Bistro Clovis

## Cow Hollow/Marina
*25* Merenda
    Isa
*24* Pane e Vino
    Yukol Place Thai
    PlumpJack Cafe

## Downtown
*28* Masa's
*27* Aqua
    Fleur de Lys
*26* Elisabeth Daniel
*25* Campton Place

## Embarcadero
*27* Boulevard
*23* Ozuma
*22* One Market
*21* Lapis
*20* Town's End

## Fisherman's Wharf
*29* Gary Danko
*23* Grandeho's Kamekyo
*22* Ana Mandara
*20* Scoma's
*19* Mandarin

## Haight-Ashbury/Cole Valley
*25* Eos Restaurant
    Thep Phanom
*24* Indian Oven
*23* Boulange de Cole Valley
    Grandeho's Kamekyo

## Mendocino County
*26* Rest. at Stevenswood
*25* Cafe Beaujolais
    Albion River Inn
*24* Rendezvous Inn
    St. Orres

## Mission
*26* Delfina
    Slanted Door
*24* Watergate
    Slow Club
    Woodward's Garden

## Monterey/Carmel
*28* Sierra Mar
*26* Fresh Cream
*25* Roy's at Pebble Beach
*24* Pacific's Edge
*23* Stokes Restaurant

## Napa/Sonoma Valley
*29* French Laundry
*27* Sushi Ran
    Terra
    La Toque
*26* Bistro Jeanty

## Nob Hill/Russian Hill
*28* Ritz-Carlton Dining Rm.
*26* Charles Nob Hill
*25* Frascati
*24* Ritz-Carlton Terrace
    Ristorante Milano

## North Beach
*26* Cafe Jacqueline
*25* House
    Jianna
*24* Helmand
    Tommaso's

## Oakland
*25* Zachary's Pizza
    Bay Wolf
*24* Citron
    Doña Tomás
    Oliveto Cafe

# Top Food

## Pacific Heights/Japantown
**25** Cafe Kati
**24** Maki
    Meetinghouse
    Chez Nous
**22** Garibaldis

## Palo Alto
**27** Le Poisson Japonais
**25** Evvia
**24** L'Amie Donia
    Bistro Elan
**23** Higashi West

## Richmond
**26** Kabuto Sushi
**25** Chapeau!
    Ton Kiang
**24** Clémentine
**22** Straits Cafe

## San Jose
**27** Emile's
**26** Le Papillon
**25** La Forêt
**24** La Taqueria
**23** A.P. Stump's

## SoMa
**25** Fringale
**24** Kyo-Ya
    Hawthorne Lane
    Yank Sing
**23** Manora's

## South Beach/Pac Bell Park
**21** South Park Cafe
**18** Butler & The Chef Cafe
**16** Infusion Bar & Rest.
**15** MoMo's
**14** Paragon

## Sunset
**25** House
    Thanh Long
**24** Ebisu
    Marnee Thai
**20** PJ's Oyster Bed

## Van Ness/Polk
**27** La Folie
    Acquerello
**26** Swan Oyster Depot
**24** House of Prime Rib
**23** Harris'

# Top 40 Decor Rankings

*29* Garden Court
*28* Ahwahnee Dining Room
Sierra Mar
Erna's Elderberry Hse.
*27* Ana Mandara
Farallon
Auberge du Soleil
Julius' Castle
Jardinière
Shadowbrook
*26* Ritz-Carlton Dining Rm.
Fleur de Lys
Pacific's Edge
Domaine Chandon
Chateau Souverain Café
Martini House
Mikayla at Casa Madrona
Ozumo
Gary Danko
El Paseo

French Laundry
Kokkari Estiatorio
Grand Cafe
Dry Creek Kitchen
La Forêt
Masa's
*25* Aqua
Fifth Floor
Boulevard
Roy's at Pebble Beach
Le Colonial
Rest. at Meadowood
Ondine
Madrona Manor
Tra Vigne
John Ash & Co.
Lapis Restaurant
Cetrella Bistro & Café
La Toque
Carnelian Room

## Outdoors

Auberge du Soleil
B44
Bistro Don Giovanni
Bistro Elan
Bistro Jeanty
Boulange de Cole Valley
Brix
Cafe Bastille
Cafe Flore
Casanova
Chaya Brasserie
Cool Café
Domaine Chandon

Foreign Cinema
Isa
John Ash & Co.
Julia's Kitchen
La Note
Lark Creek Inn
Left Bank
Marché aux Fleurs
Plouf
Ritz-Carlton Terrace
Sociale
Tra Vigne
Wente Vineyards

## Romance

Acquerello
Aziza
Cafe Jacqueline
Chez TJ
Dal Baffo
Elisabeth Daniel
El Paseo
Erna's Elderberry Hse.
Flea St. Café
Fleur de Lys
Jardinière

Jianna
Khan Toke Thai House
MacCallum House
Maddalena's & Café Fino
Maharani
Manka's Inverness Lodge
Ritz-Carlton Dining Rm.
Slow Club
Terra
Woodward's Garden
Zaré

# Rooms

Ahwahnee Dining Room
Ana Mandara
Aqua
Asia de Cuba
Azie
BIX
Boulevard
Dry Creek Kitchen
Evvia
Farallon
Fleur de Lys
Garden Court
Grand Cafe

Hawthorne Lane
Jardinière
Jeanty at Jack's
Kokkari Estiatorio
La Toque
Le Colonial
Le Poisson Japonais
Martini House
Postrio
Ritz-Carlton Dining Rm.
Roxanne's
St. Orres
Trader Vic's

# Views

Albion River Inn
Auberge du Soleil
Beach Chalet Brewery
Bella Vista
Caprice
Carnelian Room
Cityscape
Cliff House
Domaine Chandon
Fresh Cream
Greens
Guaymas
Julius' Castle

Ledford House
Little River Inn
Mikayla at Casa Madrona
Mistral
Moss Beach Distillery
Navio
Nepenthe
Ondine
Pacific's Edge
Roy's at Pebble Beach
Sierra Mar
Valhalla
Waterfront Restaurant

# Top 40 Service Rankings

**29** Erna's Elderberry Hse.
**28** Gary Danko
    French Laundry
**27** Ritz-Carlton Dining Rm.
    Sierra Mar
    Masa's
    Acquerello
**26** Charles Nob Hill
    Fleur de Lys
    Chez Panisse
    Campton Place
    La Toque
    La Folie
    La Forêt
**25** Le Papillon
    Terra
    Elisabeth Daniel
    Auberge du Soleil
    Domaine Chandon
    Ritz-Carlton Terrace

    Fresh Cream
    Chapeau!
    Emile's
    Applewood Inn & Rest.
    Plumed Horse
    Albion River Inn
    Redwood Park
    Chez TJ
    Frascati
**24** Chez Panisse Café
    Boulevard
    John Bentley's
    Merenda
    Rest. at Stevenswood
    Fifth Floor
    Aqua
    Cafe La Haye
    Flying Fish Grill*
    Albona Ristorante Istriano
    El Paseo

---

\* Tied with restaurant directly above it

# Best Buys

## Top 40 Bangs for the Buck

List derived by dividing the cost of a meal into its ratings.

1. Jay's Cheese Steak
2. Pancho Villa Taqueria
3. La Cumbre Taqueria
4. Taqueria Cancun
5. El Balazo
6. Emporio Rulli
7. La Taqueria
8. Boulange de Cole/Polk
9. Downtown Bakery
10. Burger Joint
11. Truly Mediterranean
12. Cactus Taqueria
13. Picante Cocina
14. Taylor's Automatic
15. King of Thai
16. Jimmy Bean's
17. Butler & The Chef Cafe
18. Café Fanny
19. Vik's Chaat Corner
20. Pork Store Cafe
21. Gayle's Bakery
22. Frjtz Fries
23. Chloe's Cafe
24. Bette's Oceanview Diner
25. Mama's Royal Cafe
26. Jimtown Store
27. Mario's Bohemian Cigar
28. Mo's Burgers/Grill
29. Dottie's True Blue Cafe
30. Lovejoy's Tea Room
31. East Coast West Deli
32. Axum Cafe
33. Asqew Grill
34. Cafe 817
35. Kate's Kitchen
36. Pomelo
37. It's Tops Coffee Shop
38. Mama's/Washington Sq.
39. Citrus Club
40. Hotei

## Other Good Values

À Côté
Alma
Andalu
Antica Trattoria
Bouchon
Cafe Gibraltar
César
Cha Cha Cha
Chapeau!
Charanga
Chez Nous
Chez Panisse Café
Chez Papa Bistrot
Destino
Firefly
Helmand
House
Hyde Street Bistro
Isa
Julia
JZ Cool
La Luna
L'Amie Donia
Le Charm French Bistro
Liberty Cafe & Bakery
L'Osteria del Forno
Luna Park
Merenda
Pane e Vino
Pesce
Pizzetta 211
PlumpJack Cafe
Shalimar
Slow Club
Sociale
Swan Oyster Depot
Ti Couz
Tommaso's
Tu Lan
Vivande Porta Via

# Restaurant Directory

# San Francisco

|  | F | D | S | C |
|---|---|---|---|---|

**Absinthe** ●LS      20 | 23 | 19 | $40
*398 Hayes St. (Gough St.), 415-551-1590*
■ There's never an absinthe of customers (garbed in everything from "tuxedos to overalls") at this "dramatic", "dark" and "alluring" French bistro, the "hub of action in Hayes Valley"; although the "reminiscent-of-Paris" classics are served all day (and during a "yummy weekend brunch"), expect a "mad dash" "before or after the opera, symphony or ballet"; the service may "lag behind" at those times, but "top-shelf" "vintage cocktails" help "numb" any discomfort.

**Ace Wasabi's** SM      22 | 14 | 15 | $31
*3339 Steiner St. (bet. Chestnut & Lombard Sts.), 415-567-4903*
◪ "Imaginative" "sushi concoctions" and "kicky sake mixed drinks" lure "Marina babes" and J. Crew–clad twentysomething guys to this "packed-to-the-gills" "hip Japanese" "sweat box"; although ear-shattering "funky rock-'n'-roll reverberating throughout" makes "you think you've crashed a Tri Delt party" (complete with "daunting lines"), nightly "bingo helps you win $20 off your meal."

**Acme Chop House** SM      – | – | – | M
*24 Willie Mays Plaza (bet. King & 3rd Sts.), 415-644-0240*
Traci Des Jardins lends her Midas touch to this modern-day chophouse and grill near Pac Bell Park, made kinder and gentler by her commitment to naturally raised meats and poultry, organic produce and locally caught fish; even the dining room has been renovated in a socially responsible way, with cork flooring, certified sustainable mahogany tabletops and non-toxic upholstery.

**À Côté** ●LS      23 | 21 | 20 | $32
*5478 College Ave. (Taft St.), Oakland, 510-655-6469*
◪ This "French-style tapas place" ("love the mussels in Pernod") reigns supreme as "the scene" in "hip, yuppie Rockridge"; "come with a crowd to share" chef/co-owner Chris Rossi's (also of next door's Citron) *petit plats* on the "terrific terrace" (to escape the "noisy front") or join the fracas at the "fun communal table" inside; admittedly, "the wait can get out of hand", but the "creative cocktails" and "great selection of wines" help "keep you happy."

**ACQUERELLO**      27 | 23 | 27 | $60
*1722 Sacramento St. (bet. Polk St. & Van Ness Ave.), 415-567-5432*
■ It's no wonder this "fine-dining Northern Italian" "hidden" off Polk Street "is "still numero uno" in the hearts and minds

of most surveyors, what with chef Suzette Gresham's "sublime combinations" ("foie gras truffle pasta to die for"), her co-owner/maitre d' Giancarlo Paterlini's "classic old-world service" and "impeccable wine list" and the room's "beautiful vaulted ceiling"; true, it's "very pricey" and "more formal" than its trendy brethren, but the refined regulars like it that way.

### AHWAHNEE DINING ROOM, THE 🄻🅂🄼          19 | 28 | 20 | $47

*The Ahwahnee Hotel, 1 Ahwahnee Rd., Yosemite National Park, 209-372-1489*

☑ Eating in this "spectacular", "beautiful dining room in the midst of Yosemite Valley" with "views of the waterfalls" and El Capitan through "the ceiling-high windows" is "like dining in an Ansel Adams photograph"; admittedly, neither the "overpriced" hearty Californian dinners nor the service "can compete with the atmosphere" – but hey, "you have to cut the waiters some slack when you realize most live in tents"; so while it's "not a true foodie destination, it's definitely a treat in the wild."

### Ajanta 🄻🅂🄼          21 | 17 | 18 | $24

*1888 Solano Ave. (bet. The Alameda & Colusa Ave.), Berkeley, 510-526-4373*

■ "Chef-owner Lachu Moorjani's monthly newsletter for customers" describing his "rotating menu" is "just one indication of the serious approach" of this "adventurous" Indian whose "ecstatic curries" and "incredible mango lassies" (yogurt drinks) "stand above the crowds of its buffet-style" Berkeley brethren; delighted Delhi devotees declare "if the spicy food doesn't send you spinning, the erotic wall paintings will."

### Alamo Square 🅂🄼          20 | 17 | 18 | $26

*803 Fillmore St. (bet. Fulton & Grove Sts.), 415-440-2828*

☑ If you're looking for "all the essence of a French eatery with none of the pretense", then remember the Alamo, where "you get to choose the kind of fish you want, how you want it cooked and with what sauce"; whatever you pick, you'll enjoy it in a "cute, cramped space" at "palatable prices" declare defenders; antagonists argue that while it's a "great concept, the execution's not up to the hype" or the "worth the effort" to get to the Western Addition.

### Albion River Inn 🅂🄼          25 | 24 | 25 | $46

*3790 Shoreline Hwy./Hwy. 1 (Albion Airport Rd.), Albion, 707-937-1919*

■ "Romance rules" at this "incomparable" address "overlooking the Pacific" that "blends a relaxed North Coast [character] with exquisite attention to detail"; it's a perennial "top pick in Mendocino County" thanks to "delightfully presented", "out-of-this-world" Californian fare and a "knowledgeable staff" that suggests "worthwhile pairings" from a wine list "heavy on the local good stuff"; "complete your meal with a single malt from the endless list of scotches" and stay over in one of the "luxury cabins."

### Albona Ristorante Istriano  23 | 15 | 24 | $39 |

*545 Francisco St. (bet. Mason & Taylor Sts.), 415-441-1040*

■ Trekking to this "intimate", "well-kept secret" in North Beach "is like visiting your uncle" overseas: "chatty host Bruno Viscovi will charm you with his exuberance and love for his native Istrian food", which "borrows flavors and cooking techniques from Northern Italy and Central Europe" ("just different enough to make it unique"); P.S. the "free valet parking is greatly appreciated."

### Alcatraces L S M  ∇ 21 | 17 | 23 | $28 |

*4042 24th St. (bet. Castro & Noe Sts.), 415-401-7668*

■ "In a previously doomed location", this "new place in Noe Valley" seems to be "making a saucy go of it" thanks to the "delicious combinations of Cajun" and Californian creations of chef Glenn 'Gator' Thompson, "a boisterous and welcoming host" who "comes out to chat with the customers" amid the voodoo-chic "kitschy decor"; no reservations are taken, but you're welcome to wait at the bars next door.

### Alegrias, Food From Spain S M  18 | 15 | 18 | $29 |

*2018 Lombard St. (Webster St.), 415-929-8888*

◪ For a sense of being "transported to a little family-owned restaurant in Spain", simply travel to the "trendy Marina" for the "tempting tapas and great sangria" offered by this Iberian with a "cozy", if "sort of cheesy, decor"; the jaded jibe it's "nothing to write home about" (especially when the "service is up to you to initiate"); still, "a nice back room" makes it a "great place to go with friends."

### Alexis Baking Company L S M  20 | 11 | 13 | $17 |

(aka ABC)

*1517 Third St. (School St.), Napa, 707-258-1827*

■ Co-chef/owner "Alexis Handelman holds court" at her "funky" bakery-oriented American cafe "in the thick of unpretentious Napa city proper"; "for what she does" – mostly "superb breakfasts", boxed lunches and "killer cakes" (especially for weddings) – "she does it well"; just "count on waiting", because it's an "institution" among "local winemakers and vineyard managers."

### Alfred's Steak House L S M  22 | 18 | 21 | $43 |

*659 Merchant St. (bet. Kearny & Montgomery Sts.), 415-781-7058*

◪ This "decidedly old-school" "unapologetic steakhouse" boasts "big leather booths and big chandeliers" reminiscent "of a Rat Pack hangout"; but while boosters "bypass the chains" for the "amazing cuts" of beef and "the best Caesar salad in town" (prepared tableside), malcontents mutter about the "dark, musty" atmosphere and attitude, finding the whole affair "worn, like an old man."

### Alice's 🄻🅂🄼　　　　　　　20 | 16 | 17 | $19
*1599 Sanchez St. (29th St.), 415-282-8999*
■ "Tasty, healthy and fresh" "Californian-ized Chinese" cuisine makes this "off-the-beaten-path" place a favorite among Noe Valley neighbors; while the "addictive dishes", "fabulous glass and orchid collection" and even the sometimes "hectic service" are all "in the same vein" as (unrelated) competitors Eliza's and Eric's, it lacks their "long lines" claim converts who "can't stop going back."

### Alioto's 🄻🅂🄼　　　　　　　16 | 15 | 17 | $35
*8 Fisherman's Wharf (The Embarcadero), 415-673-0183*
🄴 Nostalgists name this "a classic place to take out-of-towners" to "watch the sunset over the Golden Gate Bridge" or the "seals playing near the fishing boats" while tucking into "typical" "Wharf seafood" and "Sicilian specialties"; but lachrymose locals warn "you're paying for the history" – the "family-owned and -operated" business dates from 1926 – and suggest you just "stop by the bar for a couple of drinks", leaving the dining to "the touristas."

### Allegro 🅂🄼　　　　　　　▽ 20 | 16 | 18 | $37
*1701 Jones St. (Broadway), 415-928-4002*
■ "A definite place to be seen among" the city's "illustrious and famous political clientele" ("Democrats only") and "Russian Hill swells" – who keep it a "well-hidden" secret – this "intimate", "basic" "old-style Italian" garners votes for the "best gnocchi in SF" and its signature chicken under the brick.

### All Season's
### Cafe and Wine Shop 🄻🅂🄼　　　　23 | 18 | 23 | $31
*1400 Lincoln Ave. (Washington St.), Calistoga, 707-942-9111*
■ "What could be better than browsing a well-stocked, fairly priced wine shop, walking two feet with your purchase and ordering great food to drink it with?" ask fans who frequent this "kooky but adorable" "diner-like" cafe "in the heart of Calistoga"; a "new chef" (a Thomas Keller protégé) whips up "great seasonal" Californian–New French fare that's deemed the "perfect après–mud bath meal."

### Alma 🄼　　　　　　　　　21 | 18 | 18 | $34
*1101 Valencia St. (22nd St.), 415-401-8959*
■ "Check it out, amigos": chef-owner Johnny Alamilla "captures the soul of Nuevo Latino cuisine" amid the "cool atmosphere" of his new "trendy" Mission digs; "a mix of cultures" jams into the "loud" environs to sample the

"scrumptious" "interesting flavors" (especially "awesome selection of seviches") and the small but "adventurous wine list", handily explained by the "friendly and knowledgeable servers"; best of all, it's "not too hard on the pocketbook."

### Amber India 🅛🅢🅜  24  17  17  $26

*Olive Tree Shopping Ctr., 2290 W. El Camino Real (Rengstorff Ave.), Mountain View, 650-968-7511*

◪ "Throngs of spice-hungry enthusiasts" disregard a Mountain View "mini-mall exterior" for what they claim is the "best Indian food outside India or London" (especially the "melt-in-your-mouth butter chicken") – "although it's priced that way"; dissenters deem "the decor lacking" and say "the staff must have trained at Indifference University", but as "the line outside" at lunchtime testifies, the food "is so worth it."

### Amici's East Coast Pizzeria 🅛🅢🅜  18  9  15  $18

*2033 Union St. (Buchanan St.), 415-885-4500*
*790 Castro St. (Church St.), Mountain View, 650-961-6666*
*226 Redwood Shores Pkwy. (Twin Dolphin Dr.), Redwood Shores, 650-654-3333*
*69 Third Ave. (San Mateo Dr.), San Mateo, 650-342-9392*
*1242 Fourth St. (C St.), San Rafael, 415-455-9777*

■ Proffering "the closest thing to real pizza an East Coast transplant will find in the Bay Area" ("without the New York attitude"), this "relatively high-priced" chain wins plaudits for its "deliciously thin crust" pies and "fast delivery" – even if single-serving seekers snipe "no slices? what's with that?"

### ANA MANDARA 🅛🅢🅜  22  27  20  $44

*Ghirardelli Sq., 891 Beach St. (Polk St.), 415-771-6800*

◪ "Like dining on a movie set" ("Disney meets Hanoi") is how most starstruck surveyors summarize investors Don Johnson and Cheech Marin's "sexy", "fancy French-Vietnamese" "peaceful refuge" "buried in the touristy Fisherman's Wharf area"; a "dressed-to-impress, sassy crowd" waits in the "very cool upstairs bar" (serenaded by live jazz Thursday–Saturday), but a handful of critics pans the "small portions", which they call "overpriced."

### Andalu 🅜  21  19  18  $31

*3198 16th St. (bet. Guerrero & Valencia Sts.), 415-621-2211*

◪ Though named for the birthplace of Spanish small plates, this "up-and-comer" actually serves "super, tasty tapas" and entrées "from all over the globe"; it's fast become "the new hot spot" for "trendy but not insufferable" groups, thanks to "easy-on-the-wallet" prices, "a nonstop fun" (read: "noisy") vibe and "fantastic white sangria" ("to help you forget you are in the heart of the gritty Mission") – all of which compensates for the sometimes "spotty service."

### Angkor Borei L S M        ▽ 18 | 9 | 18 | $18
*3471 Mission St. (Cortland Ave.), 415-550-8417*
■ "Good, fast, cheap – you can have all three" at this "secret place" in an admittedly "seedy area" of lower Bernal Heights; insiders instruct "never mind the decor" (an "oddly shaped narrow room"), just go for the "consistently interesting Cambodian food" and "friendly staff."

### Angkor Wat L S M        20 | 15 | 20 | $24
*4217 Geary Blvd. (bet. 6th & 7th Aves.), 415-221-7887*
☑ "Tasty", "subtle Cambodian cuisine" and "beautiful dancers on weekends" sum up this "popular spot in the Inner Richmond"; but while enthusiasts note "hey, the Pope ate here", foes wonder "was he disappointed too?" citing "tired and worn" decor and "very slow, if gracious, service."

### Anjou L        23 | 18 | 21 | $37
*44 Campton Pl. (bet. Post & Sutter Sts.), 415-392-5373*
■ Entering this "well-hidden secret" "jewel box" of a bistro is like leaving "the maddening crowds" of Union Square and "stepping into a little Paris"; everything is "French-inspired", from the "always fabulous food" to the "no-nonsense service" that's "lax in that special Parisian way" to the "cramped" seating; still, the "ladies who lunch" and "pre-theater" crowds know a "good value for the money" when they see it.

### Antica Trattoria S        22 | 17 | 20 | $35
*2400 Polk St. (Union St.), 415-928-5797*
■ "You'd think you were in Italy" or the movie *Big Night* at this "loud but fun", "jumping" Polk Street trattoria ("don't even bother trying to go without reservations"); "you can taste the passion that chef" Ruggero Gadaldi and his "accommodating" staff have for the "simple, rustic" yet "*molto bene*" "monthly changing menu", prompting patrons to proclaim "if this place were any better, I'd move in."

### Anton & Michel Restaurant L S M        ▽ 22 | 24 | 23 | $52
*Mission St. (bet. Ocean & 7th Aves.), Carmel, 831-624-2406*
☑ Carmel's "classic" Continental "old standby" garners a generation gap; its plethora of proponents posit the "peaceful spot", replete with "romantic" "gardens and fountains", "hasn't missed a step in all these years" and is still the place to "go when you really want to feel pampered"; however, young'uns yowl this kind of dining "went out of style in the 1960s" and can't compete with the "trendy up-and-comers" in town.

### Anzu L S M        20 | 19 | 18 | $45
*Hotel Nikko, 222 Mason St. (O'Farrell St.), 415-394-1100*
■ "Who would have thought" that the "best place to have superb sushi and melt-in-your-mouth steak under one

roof" would be at a "hip, moderne" Downtown "luxury hotel" (with prices to match); its central location means "massive migration to the theater" at 8 PM, but if you've got the time, "do have a sake martini chaser"; P.S. "don't miss the liveliest Sunday brunch" featuring a KKSF live jazz broadcast.

### Aperto L S M   19 | 15 | 18 | $28
*1434 18th St. (Connecticut St.), 415-252-1625*
■ "If you're casting about for a good meal in Potrero Hill", hone in on this "casual" trattoria that "fits the familiar feel of the neighborhood"; the "homemade pasta is to drool for", but regulars "always look at the specials on the chalkboard" before ordering; true, "it's crowded, it's loud and it's busy", but it's "a great standby, particularly for lunch."

### Applewood Inn & Restaurant   24 | 23 | 25 | $42
*13555 Hwy. 116 (River Rd.), Guerneville, 707-869-9093*
■ Boasting a "balcony overlooking a courtyard" and a "perfect setting" "right on the Russian River", this little-known, "very pink villa" sets a Californian–New French table that emphasizes "local ingredients and wines" (e.g. pork loin cooked in house-pressed apple cider); since it's also a "nice place to stay", this "Guerneville treasure" is "easily worth the drive – and the calories."

### A.P. Stump's L M   23 | 23 | 20 | $48
*163 W. Santa Clara St. (bet. Almaden Blvd. & San Pedro St.), San Jose, 408-292-9928*
☑ "Even during a slump, tech titans" and Compaq Center–goers admit they'd be "stumped to find a better restaurant in San Jose" than this "hopping", "glamorous" "expense-accounter" noted for its "adventurous" New American–Californian fare, "outstanding wine list" and "wonderful outdoor dining in back"; "hit-or-miss service" is the only slight stumbling block.

### AQUA L M   27 | 25 | 24 | $64
*252 California St. (bet. Battery & Front Sts.), 415-956-9662*
☑ Chef/co-owner "Michael Mina's masterpiece" – a "glittering Downtown" destination that "drips with beautiful people" – "continues to perform swimmingly", with "floral arrangements as spectacular" as the "staggeringly good" seafood and "cutting-edge wine list"; while "professional" but "holier-than-thou" service and being "squeezed in" like sardines "dampen" some spirits, most "food sharks" willingly "mortgage the house" to power-dine here: when the "fish is this fantastic, you can put up with anything."

### A. Sabella's S M   19 | 17 | 18 | $36
*2766 Taylor St. (Jefferson St.), 415-771-6775*
☑ Those wishing for that "traditional Wharf experience" find this 82-year-old "family-owned classic" is "always a

safe bet", as you can fill up on "fresh seafood" (from the 1,000-gallon tank up front) and "crusty sourdough" while "watching the sun set over the Golden Gate Bridge"; although "you're taxed for that view", the "remodeled" "Jetsons-meets-Chanel" interior is a cut above the other "tourist traps", and markups on the "superb wine list" are considerably lower.

### Asia de Cuba ●LSM   18   23   17   $55
*Clift Hotel, 495 Geary St. (Taylor St.), 415-929-2300*

◪ "Remember to don your Manolo Blahniks" before entering co-owner Ian Schrager's "fashion-forward" Downtowner, the epitome of "disco dining at its best and worst"; the chic croon the Chino-Latino cuisine "served family style" in "gargantuan portions" is "fabulously different", but the "velvet-roped" "superficiality", "bank heist"–priced bills and "blaring techno music" "seem more show than go" to the unimpressed; still, "this is as hip as it gets for SF" – just dig the "peekaboo wall cutout" into the Redwood Room bar.

### AsiaSF SM   16   18   19   $34
*201 Ninth St. (Howard St.), 415-255-2742*

■ This "campy, outrageous" SoMa nightclub is "always a drag" – literally, thanks to the "gender illusionists" who "catwalk down the bar" nightly in a "down-and-dirty" cabaret show; "it's just the right place" for a "girls' night out" or out-of-towners seeking "a good intro into SF culture"; while the "Asian-Cal tapas" "are an afterthought", they're "surprisingly" "edible", and "transvestite service with a smile makes up for the puny portions."

### Asqew Grill LSM   18   11   15   $14
*1607 Haight St. (Clayton St.), 415-701-9301*
*3348 Steiner St. (Chestnut St.), 415-931-9201*

■ The "clever concept" of "everything-on-a-stick" – you "play the pairing game" of "mixing and matching" "delicious grilled kebabs" with starches – makes this Californian couple in the Haight and the Marina a great "place to grab a quick bite before heading out for the evening"; expect "no-frills" decor and "self-service", but for what it is – "quick, simple" and "cheap" – "you can't beat it."

### A Tavola LSM   19   19   18   $34
*716 Laurel St. (bet. Cherry & Olive Sts.), San Carlos, 650-595-3003*

◪ This "convivial" "lively spot" "on San Carlos' trendy Laurel Street" (by the folks who run Mistral and Kingfish) attracts a "young professional crowd" that "tries not to overdo the bread and olive oil" before tucking into the "competent" Italian–New American fare; "upscale decor" and a "fun bar" give it a sophisticated "city feel", but critics complain the "amateur service" "can't seem to rise to a level commensurate with the ambiance."

## AUBERGE DU SOLEIL L S M  26  27  25  $66
*Auberge du Soleil Inn, 180 Rutherford Hill Rd. (Silverado Trail), Rutherford, 707-967-3111*

■ Dining at this "magnificent" Rutherford "romantic" is "like making it into heaven" – and not simply because it's got "one hell of a view" "overlooking the valley" and vineyards; chef Richard Reddington's "exquisite version" of French-Med fare "makes it nearly impossible to choose" and the international wine list (1,250 labels rich) "isn't bad either" – plus, there's "top-notch service" "to match"; although the place is "stiffly priced", the "view is the same, and much cheaper, at lunch."

## Autumn Moon Cafe L S M  19  16  16  $23
*3909 Grand Ave. (Sunnyside Ave.), Oakland, 510-595-3200*

☑ You'd think "these women invented brunch" ("didn't they?") judging from the "super French toast, omelets and pancakes" consumed at this "slightly trendy Oakland scene"; mornings are clearly "where it's at" (especially on the "pleasant patio"), but the kitchen prepares American "comfort food with a twist" "all times of the day"; however, the impatient warn "you'll be howling at the moon waiting for a seat" and dealing with the "glacial service."

## Avenue 9 L S M  19  13  17  $28
*1243 Ninth Ave. (bet. Irving St. & Lincoln Way), 415-664-6999*

☑ Some call this "neighborhood treasure" "tucked into the Sunset's" "restaurant row" a "bargain Boulevard" for its "competent versions of trendy" Californian fare at "great prices" and "without all the Downtown attitude"; critics who make the crosstown trek tut-tut about the "crowded" seating and "really funky setting", to which regulars retort, fine – "stay away so it remains easy to get a table."

## Axum Cafe S M  21  8  13  $14
*698 Haight St. (Pierce St.), 415-252-7912*

☑ Just "Axum about Ethiopian food" and disciples will direct you to this spot in the "funk of Lower Haight", insisting it serves the "best in the city"; the "spicy fare" (both meat and vegetarian) "fills your stomach without emptying your wallet" and "makes up for the lack of ambiance" and "spotty service"; just "don't be afraid to get your fingers dirty."

## Azie S M  21  23  18  $51
*826 Folsom St. (bet. 4th & 5th Sts.), 415-538-0918*

☑ "The way cool" scene (think "dark lighting, curtained booths") is "worth the price of admission" at this "stunning", "sensual" SoMa spot that features "artfully presented" Asian–New French dishes meant to be shared "family-style" and "timely service"; although "teensy-weensy portions" ("the Nine Bites [sampler] is more like 4.5 bites") are a drawback, "prices have been lowered now that the bloom is off the dot-com rose."

### Aziza ⑤Ⓜ    22 | 21 | 20 | $38
*5800 Geary Blvd. (22nd Ave.), 415-752-2222*

■ Armed with his "mother's recipes", "gracious service" and "wine savvy", chef-owner Mourad Lahlou has happily relocated his Marrakech-inspired Marin outpost to outer Richmond; while the meal begins with a "ritual hand-washing with rose water" and features the requisite belly dancer, the "creative" modern "takes on the favorites" are arguably "better than the food served in Morocco" and the "sensual, sexy setting" transcends "the usual tacky" *Arabian Nights* decor.

### BACAR ◐Ⓛ⑤    21 | 24 | 20 | $49
*448 Brannan St. (bet. 3rd & 4th Sts.), 415-904-4100*

☑ "A nexus of activity", this New American with an "EOS heritage" (same chef) but "tempered by a bit of SoMa attitude" is where oenophiles and "dot-commers who can still afford it" go to "gush over" the "towering glass-fronted" "floor-to-ceiling wine cellar" and the "stunning" "three-tiered setup"; however, grouchy gourmands grouse "the good but not awesome food" is not yet "on par with" the "grape squeezings" and say service can be "either superb or flighty."

### Baker Street Bistro Ⓛ⑤    18 | 14 | 17 | $27
*2953 Baker St. (bet. Greenwich & Lombard Sts.), 415-931-1475*

■ Street-smart surveyors swoon that this "adorable little bistro" in Cow Hollow is the best way to take "a trip to France without the cost or the jet lag"; the food represents "a delicious slice of Paris" at "phenomenal prices", while the owner and "the most agreeable French waiters ever known" "will lavish you (and your date) with attention"; sure, "it's cramped" and "parking is impossible", but "*c'est la vie.*"

### Balboa Cafe Ⓛ⑤Ⓜ    17 | 16 | 17 | $31
*3199 Fillmore St. (Greenwich St.), 415-921-3944*

☑ While it's known as a "good ole" Cow Hollow "meat market" "jam-packed" with "SF glitterati", preppies and "lecherous divorcees", "people eat here too" – albeit "the only item" on the American menu "worth eating is" the famous "Balboa Burger on a baguette"; although social critics call it a "disaster on weekend evenings without even enough room to change your mind", it's "saved by its professional staff."

### Baldoria ⑤Ⓜ    19 | 19 | 19 | $29
*2162 Larkin St. (Green St.), 415-447-0441*

■ "Forget North Beach" instruct insiders and "catch a cab" to this "cute neighborhoody Italian" off Van Ness; what with "attentive, flirtatious waiters", "really fresh homemade pastas" and "surprisingly low prices" (the "wine list is a steal"), "what's not to like?"

### Barbara's Fishtrap ⓁⓈⓂ⌿   18 | 11 | 15 | $21
*281 Capistrano Rd. (Hwy. 1), Princeton by the Sea,*
*650-728-7049*

☑ Fin fans flock to this "down-home" "greasy spoon" "built on a pier", "where the locals eat"; "the facility could use some sprucing up", but you can't beat "the best fish and chips around", damn "good chowda" and the "Princeton by the Sea harbor view."

### Barney's Gourmet Hamburger ⓁⓈⓂ   18 | 10 | 12 | $15
*3344 Steiner St. (Chestnut St.), 415-563-0307*
*4138 24th St. (Castro St.), 415-282-7770*
*1600 Shattuck Ave. (Cedar St.), Berkeley, 510-849-2827* ⌿
*1591 Solano Ave. (Tacoma Ave.), Berkeley,*
*510-526-8185* ⌿
*5819 College Ave. (Chabot Rd.), Oakland, 510-601-0444* ⌿
*4162 Piedmont Ave. (Linda Ave.), Oakland, 510-655-7180* ⌿

☑ You won't see any purple dinosaurs at this local burger empire, but you will find "this-ain't-McDonald's" "killer" patties with "variations up the wazoo" (including portobello and soy) that are "best eaten outside on a nice day" ("it's kind of depressing inside"); drawbacks include "ketchup-like service", a "cash-only policy" (at most locations) and the fact that you have to "order your fries separately" – but order them you must: "they almost upstage" the main event.

### Basil ⓁⓈⓂ   20 | 17 | 18 | $25
*1175 Folsom St. (bet. 7th & 8th Sts.), 415-552-8999*

■ This "competitively priced" SoMa Siamese has "all the right spices" and all the right moves; from the Thai food that's decidedly "more interesting than the usual" to the "understated IKEA atmosphere" that "attracts a young, hip crowd (the young staff looks just as hip)", it's a "godsend in an otherwise desolate location."

### Basin, The Ⓜ   ▽ 18 | 20 | 21 | $40
*14572 Big Basin Way (5th St.), Saratoga, 408-867-1906*

☑ "Martinis and meatloaf" sums up this little-known New American Saratoga spot, which specializes in "unusual combinations of old-time favorites" and has a staff that excels at "catering to personal peccadilloes"; fueled by a "unique drink menu", "it's a fun place, but expensive for what you get" sniff skeptics, who add it "loses something in an effort to be trendy."

### Basque Cultural Center ⓁⓈ   ▽ 20 | 14 | 20 | $26
*599 Railroad Ave. (bet. Orange & Spruce Aves.),*
*South San Francisco, 650-583-8091*

■ "If you're Basque, you're in heaven – this is your place", where "old men in berets drink" and young men play "handball in the adjacent court"; luckily for the rest of us, the expats "share with any who are willing to venture" to

South SF for the "generous amounts of authentic" "yummy food"; it's all "cheap" enough that you can actually afford to "bring the family", even if the actual digs "leave something to be desired."

### Battambang L M　　　18 | 12 | 17 | $18
*850 Broadway (9th St.), Oakland, 510-839-8815*
☑ "Saigon comes to Oakland" via this "awesome little Cambodian" whose "food is street-vendor zesty", service "considerate" and prices an "excellent value"; pals plead "don't let the grim interior stop you" from enjoying it.

### Bay Wolf L S M　　　25 | 21 | 23 | $41
*3853 Piedmont Ave. (Rio Vista Ave.), Oakland, 510-655-6004*
■ Oakland native "Jack London would have enjoyed" this ("if he could have afforded it") determine devotees of this "venerable" establishment "frequented by foodies" for over 25 years; a meal here is "like visiting a good friend who happens to be a great cook" thanks to chef/co-owner Michael Wild's "beautifully prepared" Cal-Med cuisine ("duck is a specialty, but everything is good"), "waiters who seem proud to serve it" and the "casual" elegance of the "lovely old house", a converted Victorian manse.

### Beach Chalet Brewery L S M　　　11 | 18 | 11 | $26
*1000 Great Hwy. (bet. Fulton St. & Lincoln Way), 415-386-8439*
☑ This "historic" "oceanfront building" perched at the tip of the outer Richmond is "an awesome place to watch" "the sun dive into the Pacific Ocean" and study the 1930s "unique murals downstairs"; but dubious diners warn the "house-brewed beer with great SF names" "is far better than" "the overpriced, unimaginative" American eats, "clueless" service and "interminable waits"; so "have an appetizer", but "look elsewhere for a real" meal.

### Bella Trattoria L S M　　　21 | 17 | 20 | $30
*3854 Geary Blvd. (3rd Ave.), 415-221-0305*
■ Inner Richmond residents say this "inexpensive" "local haunt" offers "a taste of Little Italy in the Avenues" with the same "panache" as "its sister restaurant Baldoria"; go for "*molto buono*" "homemade pastas", a "warm atmosphere" and "flirty waiters" "who treat you as if you are their long lost cousin from the old country."

### Bella Vista M　　　19 | 23 | 21 | $46
*13451 Skyline Blvd. (5 mi. south of Rte. 92), Woodside, 650-851-1229*
☑ Perched "high on a ridge overlooking the Bay" and Santa Cruz foothills, this "secluded", "romantic restaurant" in Woodside appeals to the "Italian sports car" set who appreciate its "first-class service", "old-world atmosphere" and "strong wine list"; but be sure to "get a table with a

view" – otherwise the "overpriced", "tired Continental cuisine" might not be worth "the long, twisty drive."

### BETELNUT PEJIU WU L S M   | 22 | 21 | 16 | $34 |

*2030 Union St. (Buchanan St.), 415-929-8855*

◪ "It's best to go with a group and sample as much of the menu as you can" at this Cow Hollow "Chinese beer house" for Caucasians that touts "sensational" "tapas gone Asian, plus funky island drinks" and brews "to go with them"; true, the rollicking "bar scene amounts to a modern-age Studio 54" for the "Union Street crowd" and "the staff seems far too hip to be bothered with customers", but Betel nuts note it "is certainly worth the abuse" – just be sure to reserve (or else plan to "wait three hours").

### Bette's Oceanview Diner L S M   | 20 | 15 | 16 | $16 |

*1807 Fourth St. (Hearst Ave.), Berkeley, 510-644-3230*

■ "Don't take the 'ocean view' in the name literally" and you won't be disappointed in this "classic diner with a Berkeley twist" that's always "bursting" with activists, academics and "the *This Old House* crowd", who happily endure "marathon waits" for "incredible soufflé pancakes" amid an art deco "kitsch atmosphere"; the impatient groan "if only the space were as generous as the helpings", but "you can always shop while waiting", or Bette-r yet, "try her take-out shop next door."

### B44 L M   | 20 | 17 | 19 | $35 |

*44 Belden Pl. (bet. Bush & Pine Sts.), 415-986-6287*

■ "If you can't get to Barcelona, head to this" "great Catalan" cafe "in a tiny winding alley" near Union Square; chef-owner "Daniel Olivella brings the best of Spain to SF" – "an amazing variety of paellas" and "outstanding authentic tapas" (think fish cheeks and blood sausage) proffered by "chatty", accented waiters; if the "very modern" dining room is "too noisy", snag a seat outside and "prepare your palate" with a "glass of sherry."

### Big Four L S M   | 21 | 24 | 22 | $51 |

*Huntington Hotel, 1075 California St. (Taylor St.), 415-771-1140*

■ Supping at this "hilltop retreat for the rich (and want-to-be rich)" in the Huntington Hotel is "like dining with the descendants of Nob Hill's [original] Big Four" tycoons thanks to the "old-time SF posh gentleman's club atmosphere" and "the service that goes with it"; while it's still "where stock deals and society galas are planned", "you have to pin a medal on chef Gloria Ciccarone-Nehls" for cooking such "remarkably modern", "consistent" New American fare.

### Bissap Baobab S   | 19 | 19 | 17 | $20 |

*2323 Mission St. (19th St.), 415-826-9287*

■ "Escape to the warm trade winds of Western Africa" at this "funky-in-all-the-right-ways" Mission hideaway; it features an "inexpensive", "sparse" Senegalese menu ("flavorful" "grilled meats, salads and couscous"), but "beautiful multiculti" "imbibers" insist that the "fabulous fresh fruit cocktails" "are the highlight"; after dinner, "head around the corner for bumpin' beats at Keur Baobob Bar" (located in the restaurant's original space on 19th Street).

### Bistro Aix 🆂Ⓜ 21 | 17 | 19 | $32
*3340 Steiner St. (bet. Chestnut & Lombard Sts.), 415-202-0100*
■ Although it's a "charming Marina staple for dates and small groups", the Aix-cited avow this "graciously inviting" spot "feels like a bistro in Provence"; the "excellent" Mediterranean menu and "large wine bar" offer an "unbeatable value" (especially the "midweek prix fixe"), enhanced by "impeccably friendly service"; however, "definitely sit on the heated, quaint back patio", as "the interior can be quite noisy."

### Bistro at Glen Ellen Ⓛ🆂Ⓜ ▽ 15 | 15 | 13 | $31
*13740 Arnold Dr. (Rte. 12), Glen Ellen, 707-996-4401*
■ Though the ratings don't yet fully reflect it, "new chef" Brian Sinnott (ex mc²) is "getting it right" with his Eclectic–New American cooking at this Glen Ellen eatery that offers a choice between a "charming creekside" patio seat or a "romantic table by the fireplace" inside; "reasonable prices" help "make it a good spot to end your day in Sonoma."

### Bistro Clovis Ⓛ🆂Ⓜ 21 | 17 | 18 | $36
*1596 Market St. (Franklin St.), 415-864-0231*
■ While this Hayes Valley "sleeper" is located in a slightly "seedy part" of Market Street – strategically close to "the opera and the symphony" – when you "walk through that door, suddenly you are in Dijon"; those "bitten by the love bug" swoon it's "what a small French bistro should be", with "all the classics": tarte Tatin, "terrific wine tastings" and, *bien sûr*, "sassy" Gallic service.

### BISTRO DON GIOVANNI Ⓛ🆂Ⓜ 24 | 22 | 22 | $40
*4110 St. Helena Hwy./Hwy. 29 (bet. Oak Knoll & Salvador Aves.), Napa, 707-224-3300*
■ Although its "non-pretentious Italian" menu is "not as exotic as at the other famed restaurants" in Napa, there's a reason "wine industry" folk (don't be surprised to "see Robert Mondavi") and "smart locals" migrate to this "casual, festive" trattoria situated "among the vineyards": the "unparalleled pastas", "excellent selection" of vino and "friendly service" all "guarantee a good time."

### Bistro Elan Ⓛ 24 | 18 | 21 | $41
*448 California Ave. (El Camino Real), Palo Alto, 650-327-0284*
☑ "Why doesn't everybody know about this place?" demand discoverers of this "fabulous" destination "far from the

[Palo Alto] crowds and beautiful Valley people"; the "superb" "Californian translation of French bistro" fare ("they really know what to do with foie gras"), "well-chosen wine list" and "attentive service" make it "suitable for a romantic meal with your honey or a place to impress your VC"; "the only drawback" is the din "of the crowded room."

### BISTRO JEANTY ●ⓁⓈⓂ    26  21  23  $43
*6510 Washington St. (Mulberry St.), Yountville, 707-944-0103*
■ Chef-owner Philippe Jeanty's "eponymous" French even "out-bistros Paris", because "it's friendlier" and you only have to drive to Yountville to savor it; "food purists" who "make regular pilgrimages" insist the combination of "luscious" "hearty fare" ("no nouvelle or diets here"), "charming" "rustic decor" and "unpretentious" ambiance (including a "fantastic community table") is "worth every decibel" and dollar – though actually the reasonable prices are pretty "*incroyable.*"

### Bistro Liaison ⓁⓈⓂ    22  18  19  $31
*1849 Shattuck Ave. (Hearst Ave.), Berkeley, 510-849-2155*
☑ "Ooh-la-la" fawn Francophiles over this "lively entrée into the Berkeley bistro scene"; it offers a touch of the Left Bank for left-wingers, "complete with sidewalk seating" and "excellent" New French fare that "stirs up memories of Paris"; a few fault the "frazzled service", but most covetous commuters still "wish it were in my neighborhood."

### Bistro Ralph ⓁⓂ    21  16  21  $38
*109 Plaza St. (Healdsburg Ave.), Healdsburg, 707-433-1380*
■ After 10 years, palates still tingle at chef-owner Ralph's "lively" New American located "on the picturesque square in Healdsburg"; although the "limited menu" changes weekly, you can always count on the "same ole, same ole" "favorite chicken livers and great Liberty duck" confit and the "outstanding offering of Sonoma County" "wines by the glass"; drinkers deem "the bar seating" much better than the dining room's "cramped quarters."

### Bistro Vida ⓁⓈ    19  21  19  $34
*641 Santa Cruz Ave. (El Camino Real), Menlo Park, 650-462-1686*
■ From the "very Parisian setting" ("burgundy walls" and "the requisite big framed posters") "to the steak frites", "you'd think you were in Saint-Germain" instead of this Menlo Park "neighborhood cafe"; even though there are "no fireworks in the food" (expect "standard bistro fare"), habitués holler huzzahs over the fact that "you're not seated, you're welcomed" at this "great drop-in" spot.

### Bix ⓁⓈⓂ    20  24  20  $48
*56 Gold St. (bet. Montgomery & Sansome Sts.), 415-433-6300*
■ "When you want a sexy, feel-good evening", go to this "Downtown back alley" that exudes "film noir atmosphere";

"the well-prepared American fare" and the "consummate martinis", "outstanding jazz quartet" and "professional waiters in white dinner jackets" "go a long way to make up for the loud" (yet "dazzling") bar jammed with "locals in-the-know" and the "trolling" thirty- and fortysomething "jet set."

### Bizou L M
21 | 18 | 20 | $40

*598 Fourth St. (Brannan St.), 415-543-2222*

☑ Gallic-oriented gourmets "can't get enough of this" "longtime SoMa staple"; chef-owner Loretta Keller's "unusual" "plate-licking" "bistro comfort food" is "the real deal" – "the kind you imagine eating in France" (beef cheeks and fried *haricots verts* "are a must" when they're on the menu); although the "spartan interior" is "not the most inviting" or quiet, the staff is "friendly and accommodating" and the entire effort feels straight "from the heart."

### Black Cat ◗ M
16 | 18 | 15 | $39

*501 Broadway (Kearny St.), 415-981-2233*

☑ "The new incarnation" of über-chef Reed Hearon's North Beach "swinging place" with its "revamped French bistro menu" and "art deco interior" is an "improvement over last year" some patrons purr; but others snipe the "clueless service" and "overpriced" fare suggest "this cat has used all nine of its lives"; P.S. the Blue Bar downstairs "shares the kitchen but has the added value of live blues and jazz."

### Blackhawk Grille L S M
21 | 24 | 20 | $44

*The Shops at Blackhawk, 3540 Blackhawk Plaza Circle (Camino Tassajara), Danville, 925-736-4295*

☑ You wouldn't guess that this Danville Californian lodged "in a mall" would boast such a "beautiful, tranquil setting" "overlooking the water"; "the pond is artificial", but "the food is real", and real "good", thanks to "the current chef who has taken it to a new level"; it's a spot for "sophistication in the suburbs" – though the hawk-eyed note "prices have gone up" and huff over "hetchy-catchy service."

### Bloo S
– | – | – | M

*400 Haight St. (Webster St.), 415-252-5862*

With its unadorned white walls, baby-blue bucket seats and low-hanging light fixtures, this cool-bloo newcomer feels like an anachronism in the Lower Haight; however, the two California Culinary grads who oversee the Eclectic comfort-food menu (which runs the gamut from veggie moussaka to fried chicken and waffles) are betting that nicely priced entrées will lure hipsters to this sketchy stretch.

### Blowfish, Sushi To Die For L S M
21 | 20 | 15 | $36

*2170 Bryant St. (20th St.), 415-285-3848*

☑ If you like "erotic" "Japanese *anime*" and "thumping techno blaring from overhead" "with your edamame", then join the "hipsters vying for seating" at this "hot, happening" Mission warehouse that pumps out "a huge variety" of "creative rolls", "fish so fresh you might have caught it yourself" and unbeatable sake cocktails; however, cynics carp about "uneven service" and "overblown" prices – "I'm not sure I would die for it."

### Blue Nile S
18 | 15 | 14 | $19

*2525 Telegraph Ave. (Dwight Way), Berkeley, 510-540-6777*

◪ Diners dig "diving right in" to "family plates" of "perfectly spiced" "finger-lickin' good" Ethiopian fare, "scooping it all up with a piece of *injera*" and washing it down with "heavenly honey wine" at this "dirt-cheap" Berkeley joint that always warrants a "wait on line"; while the "dark, moody" "decor is a little worse for wear", Romeos report "the private booths with Greg Brady bead curtains are the most romantic you can get on a student's budget."

### Blue Plate, The M
22 | 16 | 18 | $27

*3218 Mission St. (29th St.), 415-282-6777*

■ Judging from the Cal-American menu at this "low-key joint" in Bernal Heights, you might think "mom took a kitchen job", but it's actually run by two "young foodies who love what they do"; it's that "collective good vibe", along with a DJ who plays "cool vinyl" and a "young neighborhood feel", that attracts "city hipsters" and makes this arguably the "best of the many fancy comfort-food restaurants in SF" (a jump in the Food score agrees).

### Bocca Rotis S M
18 | 15 | 17 | $26

*1 W. Portal Ave. (Ulloa St.), 415-665-9900*

◪ Although "it's not a destination place", West Portal patrons praise this purveyor of French-Italian fare for its three Rs – "reliable, reasonable and always room to drop in" (plus a fourth, "wonderful rotisserie meats"); all that "makes up for drawbacks like the noise and lack of imaginative decor" (hint: ask for a "booth in the back").

### Boonville Hotel S M
▽ 22 | 22 | 22 | $42

*14050 Hwy. 128 (Lambert Ln.), Boonville, 707-895-2210*

■ Situated in quirky inland Boonville, this upscale roadhouse is much more than a "terrific way station on a long drive" up the Mendocino coast; intrepid travelers insist the "creative" "often-changing" Cal–New American menu that "uses lots of fresh, local produce (much of it grown on the premises)" is "well worth" the commute but nonetheless urge "spend the night" in the newly renovated Shaker-chic hotel.

### Bo's Barbecue L M
21 | 9 | 16 | $17

*3422 Mount Diablo Blvd. (Brown Ave.), Lafayette, 925-283-7133*

■ While most folks visit this down-home rib joint in Lafayette for the "fantastic" "falling-off-the-bone" ribs, insiders insist "the real secret is the melt-in-your-mouth brisket";

whichever your fancy, "a heavy dose of Bo" McSwine's (appropriate name, huh?) personality makes up for the otherwise "simple dining area."

**BOUCHON ◑ L S M**    23 | 23 | 21 | $43 |
*6534 Washington St. (Yount St.), Yountville, 707-944-8037*
✍ "Another killer Thomas Keller winner" hail habitués of this "bustling" "Parisian bistro" that's an affordable "consolation prize" for "not getting into its sister, French Laundry"; expect "fantastically authentic food", "stunning" Montparnasse decor (including sidewalk seating) and a "great wine selection (what else can be expected?)", but "bring your earplugs" and be prepared to "love thy neighbor, because you'll be sitting in his lap"; happily, it "stays open late (not many in Napa Valley do)."

**Boulange de Cole Valley L S⊭**    23 | 18 | 14 | $13 |
*1000 Cole St. (Parnassus St.), 415-242-2442*
**Boulange de Polk L S⊭**
*2310 Polk St. (Green St.), 415-345-1107*
**Marinette L S**
*3352 Steiner St. (Chestnut St.), 415-614-2941*
■ This team of *très charmants* New French bakery/cafes owned by Bay Bread Boulangerie's Pascal Rigo features "authentic pastries" ("the most delicious cannelles"), "tasty baguette sandwiches" and big "bowls of latte"; both "can be overcrowded", so do as the Francophiles do: order at the very "slooow" "self-service counter", then "dine alfresco" and "admire the scene"; N.B. new *cousine* Marinette is unrated.

**BOULEVARD L S M**    27 | 25 | 24 | $54 |
*1 Mission St. (Steuart St.), 415-543-6084*
■ "Find the money, find the time" to "stroll down this Boulevard", the *SF Survey*'s six-time Most Popular; "it epitomizes all that you'd ever want", from Nancy Oakes' "sublime" American cuisine to Pat Kuleto's "splendid" "recreation of an art nouveau hangout" to a "staff intent on making your experience outstanding"; if you're not "lucky enough to get a window" table over the Embarcadero, "sit at the counter and watch the chefs."

**Brandy Ho's L S M**    18 | 10 | 14 | $21 |
*217 Columbus Ave. (bet. Broadway & Pacific Ave.), 415-788-7527*
✍ "Go for the smoke and fire or go somewhere else" dare disciples of this "Caucasian-catering" "Chinese in Chinatown" known for its fiercely fiery "Hunan flavor" that "really spices up an evening"; however, critics cry "the ambiance is nonexistent and the service is bordering on hostile", arguing that "if you have to put this much sauce on the food, something is very, very wrong."

### Brannan's Grill ⃞⃞⃞　　18　21　19　$33
*1374 Lincoln Ave. (bet. Cedar & Washington Sts.), Calistoga, 707-942-2233*
☑ A "well-done interior" "sets the tone" for this "fantastic Craftsman" "Calistoga dining room" replete with "high-polish fern bar" and "big booths"; its location "right in town" near the spas is a boon to "tourons", who can "enjoy that glass of wine" and New American fare "so much better knowing that bed is just steps away"; however, locals grouse about "wine-country prices" for the "nowhere-as-creative menu" since the departure of the chef last year.

### Brava Terrace ⃞⃞　　▽ 17　18　14　$36
(fka Brazio)
*The Shops at Blackhawk, 3241 Blackhawk Plaza Circle (bet. Camino Tassajara & Crow Canyon Aves.), Danville, 925-736-3000*
☑ Ratings may not reflect chef-owner Fred Halpert changing this Danville destination from an Italian steakhouse to a French bistro (named for his now-defunct St. Helena spot); those who have visited the new version report "they are still working out some of the service kinks", but the "food is straightforward, the portions are hearty" and it remains a "relaxing place to sit next to water and watch ducks."

### Brazen Head ◑⃞⃞≠　　20　18　19　$34
*3166 Buchanan St. (Greenwich St.), 415-921-7600*
■ This "relatively unknown" Cow Hollow classic with "no awning or sign out front" (hint: "find it by the string of Christmas lights") lures brazen buffs with "pretty good" American "updated meat and potatoes", "a serious drinking bar" and "lots of character" – "dark wood", "private nooks" and "candlelight romance"; the no-reservations spot is also packed "in the wee hours" with chefs, "since the kitchen stays open till 1 AM."

### Breads of India & 　　21　8　14　$18
### Gourmet Curries ⃞⃞⃞≠
*2448 Sacramento St. (Dwight Way), Berkeley, 510-848-7684*
☑ "If there were such a thing as Cal-Indian fare, this would be its zenith" marvel masala mavens over this Berkeley "hole-in-the-wall" that draws kudos for its "superlative" "curries from different regions" and naan-a from heaven; although the "long waits on the sidewalk" and the "curt waiters'" demands that you "be seated with another group" make it "feel like a *Seinfeld* episode", consensus is "the food makes it well worth it."

### Bridges Restaurant ⃞　　22　23　21　$50
*44 Church St. (Hartz Ave.), Danville, 925-820-7200*
☑ This "top spot in Downtown Danville" "tries to be a big-city" destination, and boosters believe that with the "beautifully presented" "Californian-Asian–influenced

cuisine", "luxurious" decor ("we love dining alfresco") and "excellent service", "it almost does it"; however, dubious diners declare it's located a bridge too far – and grouse you "pay SF prices" for "the hype, thanks to its [featured role in] *Mrs. Doubtfire*."

### Britt-Marie's  L S ⬭          ▽ 17  12  20  $22
*1369 Solano Ave. (bet. Carmel Ave. & Ramona St.), Albany, 510-527-1314*

■ This "funky" "venerated institution" (since 1981) functions as the quintessential "meeting place" for Solano Avenue "local people"; the "friendly service", "warm European atmosphere" and "good Eclectic cafe food" make it a "fine" choice when "you want to stay in the neighborhood."

### Brix  L S          21  21  20  $42
*7377 St. Helena Hwy./Hwy. 29 (Washington St.), Napa, 707-944-2749*

☑ Sojourners swoon that "the vineyard views", "strolls through the gardens" and "train chugging by at sunset all enhance a great dining experience" at this "elegant" Napa source for "creative" Cal cuisine with "an Asian influence" (slightly tweaked since ushering in a "new chef") and a "well-done wine list"; however, skeptics sniff it's "somewhat inconsistent", warning with so "many other restaurants in the area", "they better tighten up on service."

### Brother-in-Law's Bar-B-Que  L S  20  2  8  $14
*705 Divisadero St. (Grove St.), 415-931-7427*

☑ "It's definitely a hole-in-the-wall, best suited to takeout", but ask "people who are particular" about barbecue and you'll be led to this "funky, finger-licking, burns so good" spot in the Western Addition; "be patient if you go, you're on BBQ time here", but when those 'cue cravings hit, you too will start asking o brother, where art thou?

### Brother's          23  4  13  $22
### Korean Restaurant  L S M
*4128 Geary Blvd. (bet. 5th & 6th Aves.), 415-387-7991 ◗*
*4014 Geary Blvd. (bet. 4th & 5th Aves.), 415-668-2028*

☑ "As the crowds of Asians will attest", this Inner Richmond set of "do-it-yourself BBQ" places smokes the competition by delivering some of the "best" "authentic Korean food with all the fixin's" (never mind that "the decor is less than nothing"); insiders indicate that 4014 Geary "is just as good without the long wait", but "jet-lagged or late-night people" should "hit the main branch", which serves (and "is packed") "into the wee hours."

### Bruno's  S          13  20  16  $29
*2389 Mission St. (bet. 19th & 20th Sts.), 415-648-7701*

☑ Boasting "more lives than a cat", "Bruno's is back" (again), only this time it's slinging "reasonably priced rustic Italian fare for the new economy"; "the retro decor" remains, and it's still a "swanky" spot to "go for cocktails and to catch some good live jazz" in the Mission, but naysayers weary from "too much turnover" report that "the food has really gone downhill" since its heyday.

### Buca di Beppo 🖲Ⓜ    15  17  17  $24
*855 Howard St. (bet. 4th & 5th Sts.), 415-543-7673* Ⓛ
*Pruneyard Shopping Ctr., 1875 S. Bascom Ave. (Campbell Ave.), Campbell, 408-377-7722*
*643 Emerson St. (bet. Forest & Hamilton Aves.), Palo Alto, 650-329-0665*
◪ "Spunky staffers" ply "rambunctious groups" with "tons o' Americanized Southern Italian" grub ("meatballs the size of Barry Bonds' homers") at this "loud and crazy", "fun family-style" trio covered ceiling to floor "with kitsch galore" ("a bust of the Pope on a lazy Susan", "fake grape vines"); critics cry "check it out once" but fuhgeddabout returning – even "the Sopranos would be disappointed" by the "Chef Boyardee food" and "atrocious lines."

### Buca Giovanni 🖲    20  20  20  $34
*800 Greenwich St. (Mason St.), 415-776-7766*
◪ Loyalists laud this off-the-beaten-path Italian's "yummy" "Tuscan menu" ("the rabbit is an excellent choice"), "wonderful" "intimate environment" and "congenial service" as "a welcome change from the rest of the North Beach tourist traps"; but dissenters declare this 20-year-old has "outlived the reputation" built by the "previous owner."

### Bucci's ⓁⓂ    20  18  17  $27
*6121 Hollis St. (bet. 59th & 61st Sts.), Emeryville, 510-547-4725*
■ Also known as "Emeryville's token fancy restaurant", "welcoming" co-owner Amelia Bucci's "industrial-chic" cafe is "a pleasant meeting place"; although the kitchen garners kudos for "wonderful" thin-crust pies, partisans insist "it's way more than a pizza place", as evidenced by the "solid" Cal-Med menu and "dependable wine list."

### Buckeye Roadhouse Ⓛ🖲Ⓜ    22  22  20  $39
*15 Shoreline Hwy./Hwy. 1 (west of Hwy. 101), Mill Valley, 415-331-2600*
■ A "great hunting-lodge" "atmosphere complete with raging fireplace" makes this "updated roadhouse" a comfy place to tear into "classy ribs" and other "hearty American" "comfort food" "gone expensive"; reservations are a must, however, as the milieu's "always mobbed" with "married, middle-aged, martini-sipping Mill Valley" minglers.

### Buck's Ⓛ🖲Ⓜ    14  20  15  $21
*3062 Woodside Rd. (Cañada Rd.), Woodside, 650-851-8010*
◪ This Woodside cafe is "known more for its Sand Hill Road venture capitalist gatherings" ("would you like a

term sheet with that?") and its "kitschy" "cowboy clutter collection" than for its cuisine; although ratings for "usual American coffee shop fare" have slid along with dot-commers' prospects ("the fun atmosphere doesn't make up for disappointing food"), this "landmark place" remains "crowded with an eclectic mix of technology wunderkinds, breakfasting bicyclists and local gentry."

**Burger Joint** L S M  20 | 12 | 15 | $12
*700 Haight St. (Pierce St.), 415-864-3833*
*807 Valencia St. (19th St.), 415-824-3494*
■ "A beacon of Americana in the Mission" and the Lower Haight, this "*Jetsons* retro-futurist" "burger joint" draws crowds for its organic "Niman Ranch beef", which "allows you the confidence" to indulge your "red-meat fix"; "the service is quick" and the "fries fresh-cut", making it "a handy stop" for "late-night snacking"; N.B. there's a to-go branch at SFO.

**Butler & The Chef Cafe, The** L M  18 | 20 | 18 | $16
*155A South Park St. (bet. 2nd & 3rd Sts.), 415-896-2075*
■ This "hidden" "little French sandwich shop" "located in hip" South Park could just as easily "be at home on the south bank of the Seine"; although it offers an "authentic" "Continental breakfast" and hybrid lunch offerings (think "hot dog on a baguette"), it's really the "charming Parisian decor" (furnished from its affiliated antique store, and for sale) that makes Francophiles marvel "*magnifique!*"

**butterfly** ◖ S  16 | 20 | 12 | $38
*1710 Mission St. (bet. Duboce Ave. & 14th St.), 415-864-8999*
◪ A "sort of utopia under Highway 101 in the Mission", this supper club with a "fun design" lures lots of "beautiful people" with its "wonderful cocktails" and "cool live jazz and DJ" scene, but the "small plates" of "Asian-Cal fusion" food and "careless service" (in decline since our last *Survey*) just don't fly with pessimists who predict that, "like the dot-com" biz, it's got "more buzz than substance."

**Cactus Taqueria** L S M  20 | 12 | 13 | $12
*1881 Solano Ave. (The Alameda), Berkeley, 510-528-1881*
*5642 College Ave. (Keith Ave.), Oakland, 510-547-1305*
■ Berkeley benefits from the "damn good", "ultra-fresh" "selection of meat- and non-meat filled" burritos, etc. pumped out by this "consistent, cheap" taqueria, which manages to be "cheerful" despite the "self-serve cafeteria setting"; P.S. "Rockridge weeps from being deprived so long" of its branch, scheduled to reopen in summer 2002.

**Cafe Bastille** L M  17 | 15 | 15 | $28
*22 Belden Pl. (bet. Bush & Pine Sts.), 415-986-5673*
◪ Francophiles fawn over this "tiny" "tucked away" Downtowner that "puts the French in french fry" (just

witness "the crowds that storm this Bastille" for the July 14 street party); even if the "authentic" Parisian fare is "not the best in the city" and the "sexy waiters" seem *un peu* "impolite", when you're "sitting on a street that looks like a Hollywood stage set and sipping Pastis, who cares?"

### Cafe Beaujolais 🆂 Ⓜ          25 | 19 | 23 | $48
*961 Ukiah St. (School St.), Mendocino, 707-937-5614*

■ This venerable "expensive-but-worth-it" dinner house "right in Downtown Mendocino" continues to maintain the "perfect" recipe "for a romantic weekend" – "quaint Victorian" charm and "creative" Cal-French "food that warms your soul in the cool, crisp weather"; though "the founders have been gone for some time", "the homemade breads" and "same friendly servers" are "as unforgettable as ever", prompting out-of-towners to lament, "it's tragically unfair that something this good is so far away."

### Cafe Citti 🅻🆂Ⓜ          21 | 13 | 16 | $24
*9049 Sonoma Hwy./Hwy. 12 (Shaw Ave.), Kenwood, 707-833-2690*

■ Citti folk "would prefer to keep" this "roadside" trattoria in an "unassuming corner" of Kenwood "a secret, but it's too late" – word has already seeped out that the "hearty" Northern Italian food at "reasonable prices" makes it a "great place for lunch when winery hopping" or for a "casual dinner"; so "ignore the deli decor and dig into" "awesome rotisserie chicken and super Caesar salad."

### Café Claude 🅻Ⓜ          17 | 16 | 15 | $27
*7 Claude Ln. (bet. Grant Ave. & Kearny St.), 415-392-3515*

◪ Those on "small-town budgets" who want a big City of Lights atmosphere hoof it to this Downtown cafe – replete with zinc bar and "accented waiters" – that's "frequented by so many French people" it'll "make you think you're on the Left Bank"; *hélas,* while the bistro fare is "much cheaper than a plane ticket to Paris", it's nothing to write home about, and the same goes for the "insolent" service.

### Cafe Cuvée 🆂          20 | 13 | 16 | $27
*2073 Market St. (14th St.), 415-621-7488*

■ Castrolites claim this "charming" "neighborhood favorite" "where the owner is also the chef" "never disappoints" "with a cozy atmosphere and an updated [monthly] International menu that always offers something worth trying"; while "everything is made with love and creativity" (and organic ingredients when possible), "it's really about the unbelievable brunch"; the staff is a bit "relaxed", "but that's ok if you want to be leisurely."

### Cafe 817 🅻Ⓜ          21 | 15 | 14 | $17
*817 Washington St. (bet. 8th & 9th Sts.), Oakland, 510-271-7965*

■ "A swell spot" in Downtown Oakland "for cutting work" and pretending to be in Tuscany, this "tiny" "urban cafe" specializes in "simple" but "good breakfast and lunch" ("don't miss the poached eggs atop polenta"); while it boasts "comfortable Euro" decor, "eating alfresco at a sidewalk table" provides the ultimo "Italianissimo" experience.

### Cafe Esin ◼    ▽ 27 | 13 | 22 | $44

*2416 San Ramon Valley Blvd. (Crow Canyon Rd.), San Ramon, 925-314-0974*

◼ "Not your usual strip-mall offering", "everyone's favorite in San Ramon" "is like eating at a friend's house except" "the incredible Med-American meals could fit the bill in any SF" establishment; the "staff treats you like an old friend as well", and whatever you do, don't miss the "excellent selection of desserts", "all made by" co-owner Esin deCarion herself.

### Café Fanny ◼ⓈⓂ    23 | 12 | 15 | $15

*1603 San Pablo Ave. (Cedar St.), Berkeley, 510-524-5447*

◪ At this "Berkeley standby" (or should we say 'stand-up', since often "you literally stand" to sip "ridiculously" "big bowls" of "café au lait" while "balancing your food in another hand"), "foodies", "poseurs and hipsters" happily "line up for their Fanny fix" of "fantastic" ("I'd expect nothing else from [co-owner] Alice Waters") French–Northern Italian breakfasts and lunches; however, the locale "overlooking a parking lot", paired with "premium pricing", causes cynics to call this a "yuppie truck stop."

### Cafe Flore ◼ⓈⓂ⊘    14 | 17 | 13 | $15

*2298 Market St. (Noe St.), 415-621-8579*

◼ This "Castro icon" (aka "Cafe Hairdo") is "a success because it's perfectly located and doesn't try too hard"; while the sun-drenched, "flower-sheltered" patio is "more like a command post" where "cute gay boys" "catch up on last night's gossip" and watch the "moving scenery" than a place to "chow down", the American fare "isn't bad."

### Cafe For All Seasons ◼ⓈⓂ    18 | 13 | 18 | $25

*150 W. Portal Ave. (bet. 14th Ave. & Vicente St.), 415-665-0900*

◼ Serving "homey American cuisine with a modern spin", this West Portal "perennial favorite" "is the quintessential neighborhood restaurant" "where nothing really changes (even the specials have been specials for years)"; but judging from the long "waits for a table" in the "noisy, crowded" dining room, we suspect the "granny crowd and families" "feel comfortable" with that.

### Cafe Gibraltar ⓈⓂ    ▽ 28 | 18 | 24 | $37

*171 Seventh St. (Hwy. 1), Montara, 650-728-9030*

◼ This unassuming "local" haunt known for its "artistically crafted" "Mediterranean food with a tasty twist" in a "simple" room and "super-friendly staff" is "a poorly kept secret" that's turned into a "wonderful coastal find" for the rest of us; N.B. at press time, it was scheduled for an autumn move to larger digs at 425 Alahambra Avenue, El Grenada.

### CAFE JACQUELINE S    26 | 18 | 19 | $41

*1454 Grant Ave. (bet. Green & Union Sts.), 415-981-5565*
◪ Specializing in "soufflés, soufflés and soufflés" for two, this "little cafe tucked away in North Beach" is arguably "the most romantic restaurant, period" ("don't go if you don't want to propose"); cynics gripe the dining room "is very charming, but it had better be, since you'll be spending so much time there" dealing with "snooty service" and "prices that, like the food, are overinflated"; but most feel watching chef-owner "Jacqueline Marguiles in the back with eggs everywhere, whipping up those masterpieces" is "worth it."

### Cafe Kati S    25 | 18 | 21 | $45

*1963 Sutter St. (bet. Fillmore & Webster Sts.), 415-775-7313*
◪ "East meets West, and neither one ever tasted this good" at this "jewel tucked between Japantown and Pacific Heights", where "vertical-food innovator" Kirk Webber's Cal-Eclectic creations are "as pleasing to the palate as to the eye" (and, admittedly, "much more engaging than" the "rather nondescript room"); armed with a "well-informed staff with a knack for suggesting great combinations of wine" and courses, this "great little spot" "certainly competes with the big boys."

### CAFE LA HAYE S    26 | 17 | 24 | $38

*140 E. Napa St. (bet. 1st & 2nd Sts.), Sonoma, 707-935-5994*
■ Say hey to this "tiny restaurant with an even tinier kitchen" whose "consistently" "well-executed" regional New American fare "pays attention to freshness and flavor" while its "personable owner" pays attention to his customers; "coupled with a central location" on the square and "excellent art shows", you'll see why it's considered "the pride of Sonoma" and packed with locals and visitors "unwinding at the end of a long day of winery hopping."

### Cafe Lolo L M    25 | 17 | 21 | $39

*620 Fifth St. (bet. D St. & Mendocino Ave.), Santa Rosa, 707-576-7822*
■ This "Santa Rosa landmark hasn't been discovered by tourists, but locals love it" and are "rather glad" to keep the secret, as "it's not very big" and enough folks already cram the "cozy" space for chef/co-owner Michael Quigley's "superb" American "gourmet comfort food"; "service is sometimes slow", but "terrific area wines" compensate.

### Cafe Lucy Le Petit Bistro L    ▽ 24 | 12 | 20 | $23

*1408 Clay St. (Jefferson St.), Napa, 707-255-0110*
■ "What kept you guys so long in finding out about this gem?" marvel in-the-know Napans who "keep coming back" for the namesake chef-owner's "terrific" "eclectic

mix" of Cal-Provençal cuisines; true, there are "no interior-decorating statements here" (though you can "eat outside under the vines") – "just delicious, unpretentious" fare and a "courageously offbeat wine list", making it a great "getaway from the high-priced restaurants" of the area.

### Café Marcella ⬛🅂　　　23　18　20　$41
*368 Village Ln. (Santa Cruz Ave.), Los Gatos, 408-354-8006*
◪ This "see-and-be-seen" spot for the Los Gatos and "Saratoga set" gets hyped for its "ample portions" of "consistently fabulous" "rustica" French-Italian "fare done with class" and its "knowledgeable owners" who are "always there" to navigate the "top-notch wine list" (no surprise, as they own the wine shop next door); however, the "way-too-noisy", "crowded conditions" necessitate that diners "learn to lip-read in order to communicate with the waiter – and each other."

### Cafe Marimba ⬛🅂🅼　　　20　17　12　$25
*2317 Chestnut St. (bet. Divisadero & Scott Sts.), 415-776-1506*
*908 Fourth St. (bet. A St. & Lootens Pl.), San Rafael, 415-459-7696*
◪ "If you're in the mood for a fun fiesta" head to this "wild" Marina Mexican; "you'll be hard-pressed to find better guacamole", "killer moles" and "not-your-typical-rice-and-beans" Oaxacan specialties than what's served up amid a "colorful" "crowded" atmosphere; too bad the "overwhelmed", "model-quality waitresses" don't act as quickly as the "tasty margaritas"; N.B. the new San Rafael branch is unrated.

### Café Niebaum-Coppola ⬛🅂🅼　　　13　19　13　$30
*916 Kearny St. (Columbus Ave.), 415-291-1700*
*473 University Ave. (bet. Cowper & Kipling Sts.), Palo Alto, 650-752-0350*
◪ Now playing in a city near you (provided it's North Beach or Palo Alto), this team of "lovely looking" cafes/bars with "movie posters, Italian tchotchkes", "traditional Neapolitan pizza" and flights of Francis Ford's vino offers a "wine-tasting break without the Napa-size headache of wine-country traffic" acolytes attest; but the disappointed demur this duo's "making me an offer I *can* refuse" – "Coppola directs films better than he directs restaurants", with particular pans for the "staff that lacks social grace."

### Cafe Prima ⬛🅂🅼　　　▽ 18　19　15　$28
*124 E. Laurel St. (bet. Franklin & Main Sts.), Fort Bragg, 707-964-0563*
◪ The Ivory Coast meets the North Coast at this "unusual" African where the eats are "different without being weird"; the few intrepid travelers who've discovered it declare Kenyan-born chef Raymond Thoya "is a magician" at "co-mingling the foods of his native country" with the "Californian cuisine" sensibility of Fort Bragg ("the samosas

are worth their weight in ivory"); however, complaints surface about "inconsistent service" and hours.

### Cafe Pro Bono LSM 19 14 20 $32
*2437 Birch St. (California Ave.), Palo Alto, 650-326-1626*
■ "Stanford professors" and "power-lunching" Palo Altoids bring clients to this "delicious" Ital-Med "to seal the deal", especially if they order the signature cheese-and-almond sauce ravioli to seal the meal; though perhaps "no longer hip", it remains "one of the singular bargains in the South Bay" thanks to a "bustling-yet-attentive staff."

### Cafe Riggio SM 16 15 17 $29
*4112 Geary Blvd. (bet. 5th & 6th Aves.), 415-221-2114*
◪ You can't miss the "enormous clown painted on the storefront" and the crowds lining up outside this "friendly trattoria" that's kept many Richmonders happy "for 23 years"; more irritable Italophiles, however, question why fool around with "tired and heavy food" "when there are so many great" places elsewhere?

### Café Rouge LSM 19 19 18 $33
*Market Plaza, 1782 Fourth St. (bet. Hearst Ave. & Virginia St.), Berkeley, 510-525-1440*
◪ Hailed for its "fancy burgers" and mean martinis served at the "beautiful zinc bar" is "Marsha-Knows-Meat" McBride's split-level French bistro – even if "the retail charcuterie" and hanging chickens "would terrify a vegan"; the savvy "escape the noise by sitting upstairs", but the sensitive turn rouge with anger at the often "arrogant service."

### Café Tiramisu LM 20 15 19 $35
*28 Belden Pl. (bet. Bush & Pine Sts.), 415-421-7044*
■ "Everyone leaves with a smile" after the "excellent cuisine" – dessert devotees declare "they do have the best" you-know-what – and "friendly service" at this "jam-packed, lively" "little trattoria", the lone Italian stallion on Frenchy Belden Alley; since the "space is somewhat cramped", the wine cellar or "outdoor seating is definitely recommended."

### Caffe Centro LM ▽ 17 12 13 $18
*102 South Park St. (bet. 2nd & 3rd Sts.), 415-882-1500*
■ This "buzzing" Cal-"European–style shop that's the heart of SF's South Park" supplies "incredibly good sandwiches" and "amazing salads" to dot-com worker bees; its grand centro location means this "pint-size place gets pretty packed during lunch hour", so better "take it to go."

### Caffe Delle Stelle LSM 16 13 16 $26
*395 Hayes St. (Gough St.), 415-252-1110*
◪ Symphony-goers "looking for basic Northern Italian without out-of-this-world prices" know this "crowded" trattoria in Hayes Valley "is the place to go before of after

the sounds of music"; the "fun, energetic atmosphere", "free bubbly water" and "friendly" (at least after the curtain goes up), accented waiters "hit a high note" for many; however, foes feel this long-playing but less-than-stellar number "is not a destination in its own right."

### Caffè Greco ◗ⓁⓈ Ⓜ ⇆　　∇ 20 | 16 | 16 | $12
*423 Columbus Ave. (bet. Green & Vallejo Sts.), 415-397-6261*
■ "A must for those wanting a North Beach cappuccino/gelato/cheesecake experience", this Italian sidewalk cafe hawks "*buono caffe e espresso*" and "excellent people-watching"; "stop by after dinner" or try one of their focaccia sandwiches at lunchtime and "feel like you're in Firenze."

### Caffe Macaroni Ⓜ⇆　　　　18 | 10 | 16 | $28
*59 Columbus Ave. (Jackson St.), 415-956-9737*
☑ "If you're in the mood for" "pretty good" (albeit not great) "old-world" Southern Italian fare and want to escape "the North Beach madness", this pizza "pie-shaped" "dive" that "reeks with authentic atmosphere" is your spot; a Decor score drop indicates "the cramped setting" and "low ceilings make some feel claustrophobic, but the flirty waiters" – the kind "who are not afraid to insist you change your order" – "ensure a lively time."

### Caffè Museo ⓁⓈ Ⓜ　　　　16 | 14 | 9 | $18
*San Francisco Museum of Modern Art, 151 Third St. (bet. Howard & Mission Sts.), 415-357-4500*
■ This upscale cafeteria makes a "superb stop-off" for a "mid-museum" Med munch after marveling at the Matisses and Manets; granted, "there's no other reason to go" if you're not visiting SF MOMA, but the food's "surprisingly good" – just ask the culture vultures lining up for the "pricey panini and espresso drinks."

### Caffe Sport Ⓛ⇆　　　　　16 | 15 | 13 | $31
*574 Green St. (bet. Columbus & Grant Aves.), 415-981-1251*
☑ "The tacky decor" – "picture an explosion in an Italian junk shop [that leaves] half the inventory sticking to the walls" – and the "rude rep" of the waiters are "part of the charm" at this North Beach "tourist trap", serving "family-style dinners" since 1969; good sports say "lots of fun can be had" here, but spoilsports sniff the sassy "Sicilian scene" doesn't "make up for the shortcomings" in the grub.

### Calistoga Inn
### Restaurant & Brewery ⓁⓈ Ⓜ　　18 | 19 | 18 | $34
*1250 Lincoln Ave. (Cedar St.), Calistoga, 707-942-4101*
■ "Conveniently located on Calistoga's main drag", this "budget-minded" brewery offers a laid-back spot to "lounge on the large patio" and "enjoy a house brew" (that is, if "you can still drink after all that wine tasting") and "good, if not overwhelming", grilled American fare.

**Cambodiana** L S ▽ 23 | 10 | 19 | $20

*2156 University Ave. (bet. Oxford St. & Shattuck Ave.), Berkeley, 510-843-4630*

■ "Unique flavors", "sauces that sing" and a "friendly" staff make this a "must", especially for the "fabulous lamb"; perhaps the dining room could use "a coat of paint", but hey, a trip here is "cheaper than a flight to Phnom Penh" and "makes a fine prequel to your next Berkeley Rep play."

**Campton Place** L S M 25 | – | 26 | $60

*Campton Place Hotel, 340 Stockton St. (bet. Post & Sutter Sts.), 415-955-5555*

■ "Come well dressed" and be prepared to "get pampered" at this "elegant sophisticate" "tucked in an alley near busy Union Square"; a post-*Survey* renovation of the "luxurious" intimate dining room has raised it to the level of chef Laurent Manrique's "refined" yet "soulful" Gascon- and Basque-influenced cooking, but you can count on the same "absolutely perfect service", in charge of an "incredible cheese" tray and a new foie gras cart; true, "it's very pricey, but you get what you pay for" (so rare in this life).

**Capellini** L S M 19 | 20 | 18 | $33

*310 Baldwin Ave. (B St.), San Mateo, 650-348-2296*

◪ "Yuppies flock" to this "stylish" San Mateo mainstay known for its "wonderful pizzas", "consistent pastas" and bustling bar; trendoids aren't exactly tripping over "the very traditional Northern Italian menu that never changes" and "very noisy" scene, but "the place is always packed, so they must be doing something right."

**Capp's Corner** L S M 14 | 14 | 17 | $24

*1600 Powell St. (Green St.), 415-989-2589*

◪ "Before going to see *Beach Blanket Babylon*", "step back in time" and into this "old-time joint" where "AARP waitresses" serve "plenty" o' "classico *famiglia* style" Italian eats; the "three-course prix fixe" "hasn't changed in [42] years", and while the food's "merely" "mediocre", at least it's a "bargain" for our recessionary times.

**Caprice, The** S M 22 | 25 | 21 | $49

*2000 Paradise Dr. (Mar West St.), Tiburon, 415-435-3400*

◪ The "tempting" Continental "food is secondary" at this tip of Tiburon's waterfront; the capricious carp it's "extremely expensive", but Bay boosters bleat they'd gladly "pay city prices for the killer views" "of Angel Island and SF" and the "good service"; it's one of those "special-occasion" spots where "a window table is a must."

**Carême Room** L M – | – | – | E

*California Culinary Academy, 625 Polk St. (Turk St.), 415-292-8229*

If you're willing to eat somebody's homework, then this historic dining room at the California Culinary Academy, where toques-in-training take turns preparing and serving Asian eats at lunch, French fare at dinner, is for you; willing guinea pigs find the banter at the Thursday and Friday buffets "always amusing", even if stern graders find it "hard to believe the folks cooking will someday be chefs."

### Carnelian Room §Ⓜ　　16　25　19　$51
*Bank of America Ctr., 555 California St., 52nd fl. (bet. Kearny & Montgomery Sts.), 415-433-7500*
☑ "Out-of-town visitors" will feel like they're on "the top of the world" at this "formal" Downtown aerie "perched atop the 52-story Bank of America" building; "it's all about the view" – a "dazzling" "360-degree vista of SF and the Bay" – but "the service is polished" too, unlike that of other "tourist traps"; however, a nosedive in the Food score suggests the "pricey" Californian fare "does not reach the same heights", so perhaps stick to a "skillfully made cocktail."

### Carneros Ⓛ§Ⓜ　　▽ 22　19　18　$40
*The Lodge at Sonoma, 1325 Broadway (Leveroni Rd.), Sonoma, 707-931-2042*
■ "All hotel eating should be this good" crow Carneros-vores after sampling the "absolutely delicious", "finely crafted menu" at The Lodge at Sonoma; the Cal-Med menu employs only regional cheeses, breads and produce, and the 100 percent Sonoma wine list (heavily weighted with the in-house bottlings) is "one of the most educational you'll see"; "cool local art" and "excellent service" round out a most "enjoyable" experience.

### Carrara's ⓁⓂ　　▽ 19　16　17　$24
*2735 Broadway (27th St.), Oakland, 510-663-2905*
■ Longtime cafe chef-owner Paul Carrara's "charming bistro" transplanted to this "out-of-the-way" Oakland location delivers "surprisingly good" "inventive" Med fare "in an . . . auto dealership?"; although backseat drivers honk "getta location", most designated diners declare it's "a refreshing change of pace" – just beware, lest you "feel like buying a car."

### Carta Ⓛ§Ⓜ　　16　14　18　$34
*1760 Market St. (bet. Gough & Octavia Sts.), 415-863-3516*
☑ Intrepid diners "like the surprise and challenge" of the "monthly changing menu" at this International moving target on Upper Market; guests are "always treated like a king" (or sultan or prime minister, depending on the week), but the culinary roulette creations can be "hit or miss" – because "how can one chef be a master of all?"

### Casanova Ⓛ§Ⓜ　　23　23　20　$46
*Fifth Ave. (bet. Mission & San Carlos Sts.), Carmel, 831-625-0501*
☑ You'll feel like a regular Casanova at this "ultra-romantic" "perennial favorite" that evokes "a visit to Provence" thanks

to "beautiful garden patios", an "outstanding" French–Northern Italian menu, a "mean wine list" and a "dedicated staff"; a handful of spurned surveyors snap "it's overpriced and overdone" but concede "that's Carmel."

### Casa Orinda 🆂🅼  18 | 18 | 19 | $31
*20 Bryant Way (Moraga Way), Orinda, 925-254-2981*
■ Saddle up to this "friendly" "Orinda institution that hasn't changed since the '50s", with a "cowboy atmosphere" ("guns on the wall, etc.") that "transports you back to when cattle ranches ruled in this area"; although it offers "reliable food and drink of the Old West and a bit of Italy", "don't get anything but the fantastic fried chicken and biscuits" (arguably "the best in the territory") and "you'll be happy."

### Catahoula
### Restaurant & Saloon 🅻🆂🅼  21 | 18 | 20 | $39
*Mount View Hotel, 1457 Lincoln Ave. (bet. Fair Way & Washington St.), Calistoga, 707-942-2275*
■ "Big Daddy" "Jan Birnbaum is still knocking 'em dead" with his "truly terrific" "down-home Southern cooking" ("tasty rooster gumbo", "soft, sexy grits") at this "lively", "casual" Calistoga hangout that's packed with "locals and tourists alike"; it's "not for dieters", but "adventurous diners" say "it's a nice change of cuisine" (even if it does – horrors! – "require beer in the heart of the wine country"), and definitely "worth the drive."

### Celadon 🅻🅼  23 | 18 | 20 | $35
*1040 Main St. (bet. 1st & Pearl Sts.), Napa, 707-254-9690*
■ "You'll have to search for the entry to [owner] Greg Cole's hideaway", but fans insist the "consistently tasty" "imaginative" Med–New American menu is "worth the trouble"; the "intimate surroundings" make for a "cozy atmosphere", but sun seekers say the "ambiance is best when you can sit outside"; Napa natives are green with envy that the crowd is "now mostly non-locals"; N.B. at press time it was scheduled for a move to the Napa Mill complex (500 Main Street).

### Central Park 🅻🆂🅼  – | – | – | M
*181 E. Fourth Ave. (San Mateo Dr.), San Mateo, 650-558-8401*
This Fourth Avenue fusion specialist (backed by vets from San Carlos' Ristorante Piachere and Belmont's Vivace) is fast becoming the darling of San Mateo with an Eclectic menu that ranges from coconut prawns to paella; huge photos of flowers decorate the modernistic decor.

### César 🆂🅼  22 | 20 | 17 | $27
*1515 Shattuck Ave. (bet. Cedar & Vine Sts.), Berkeley, 510-883-0222*
■ "One of the only grown-up bars" and "places to get food after 9 PM in Berkeley", this "fun, fun, fun" "authentic

Spanish" spot in the "Gourmet Ghetto" is packed with "graying ponytails and multiple piercings" (and "people waiting to get into Chez P" next door) grazing at "communal tables"; the "super-tasty tapas" are bested only by the "bartenders who know everything there is to know about the extensive wine and drinks list"; just prepare to "deal with the din" and "the waits."

### Cetrella Bistro & Café 🆂Ⓜ | 22 | 25 | 18 | $40 |
*845 Main St. (Monte Vista Ln.), Half Moon Bay, 650-726-4090*
◪ "Wonderful food and a spacious room with roaring fireplaces" "recall the warmth of the Mediterranean" at this ambitious upstart; add to that weekend jazz combos, tempting tapas "in the bar" and an "excellent wine list" and you understand why it's being dubbed the "best thing that's ever happened to Half Moon Bay"; however, snipes about "inexperienced staffers" and some "inconsistent" cooking indicate it's "still feeling the pains of a new eatery."

### Cha Am Thai Ⓛ🆂Ⓜ | 20 | 12 | 15 | $19 |
*701 Folsom St. (3rd St.), 415-546-9711*
*1543 Shattuck Ave. (Cedar St.), Berkeley, 510-848-9664*
### Cha Am Thai Express Ⓛ Ⓜ⇆
*307 Kearny St. (Pine St.), 415-956-8241*
◪ Surveyors are certainly not tongue-Thai-ed to express their opinions about this set of Siamese straddling both sides of the Bay (plus an express take-out spot Downtown); Berkeley boosters boast their "tropical-looking" branch is "one of the best" in the suburbs; however, underwhelmed Moscone Center conventioneers cry "everything tastes the same" and lament "the in-and-out mentality of the service" in SoMa.

### Cha Cha Cha Ⓛ🆂Ⓜ | 19 | 16 | 13 | $23 |
*1801 Haight St. (Shrader St.), 415-386-5758*
### Cha Cha Cha @ Original McCarthy's 🆂Ⓜ
*2327 Mission St. (bet. 19th & 20th Sts.), 415-648-0504*
◪ These hangouts are "a cross between a college frat party and a joint in Jamaica", and we're not sure which is "louder" – the "voodoo-like" decor or the decibel level; be it in the Haight or the Mission, expect packs of "pickled yuppie chicks" and their dates "quaffing" "dangerously good sangria" and "sopping up sauce" from the "scrumptious" "Pan-Caribbean tapas"; there are "lines longer than for Disneyland rides" and the servers are on island time, so "be prepared to drink and wait, wait and drink."

### Chantilly ⓁⓂ | ▽ 20 | 20 | 20 | $53 |
*3001 El Camino Real (Selby Ln.), Redwood City, 650-321-4080*
◪ This "*très, très cher*" Redwood City retreat (actually near Atherton) caters to "rich venture capitalists" and regulars with its "pampering, professional" staff, "traditional French–Northern Italian menu" and "great wine list";

however, the nouveau riche are rankled by "unimaginative food" and "overdone decor", likening the experience to "eating on an octogenarian's cruise ship."

## CHAPEAU! S
| 25 | 17 | 25 | $44 |

*1408 Clement St. (15th Ave.), 415-750-9787*

■ "Who wouldn't take their hats off to this terrific little" bistro buried in the recesses of the Richmond? – despite the "loud, bustling, cramped" dining area, the "fantastic, carefully prepared French food" rivals "any top room on the swankiest side of town" (the "prix fixe dinners" offer "champagne tastes at beer prices") ; aided by a "seemingly psychic staff", the owners "couldn't be friendlier", whether navigating the exceptional wine list or proffering "the classic two-cheek kiss on your way out."

## Charanga
| 22 | 14 | 18 | $24 |

*2351 Mission St. (bet. 19th & 20th Sts.), 415-282-1813*

■ "Charanga is to Cha Cha Cha what *The Facts of Life* was to *Diff'rent Strokes* – a few more women and lots of character" hypothesize metaphor-mixing diners of this "refreshingly unpretentious" Mission hideaway; as a surge in the Food score suggests, chef/co-owner Gabriela Salas cooks a mean "treasure" trove of tapas spanning the Caribbean, while her "friendly" partner Rita Abraldes does a great job rolling out the welcome mat.

## Charcuterie L S M
| 20 | 14 | 17 | $33 |

*335 Healdsburg Ave. (Plaza St.), Healdsburg, 707-431-7213*

■ There are "pigs, pigs everywhere" but not a drop to eat (save the signature pork tenderloin) at this wee-wee-wee Healdsburg cafe that once was "a real charcuterie" but now is simply an "unpretentious but satisfying" "Cal-French bistro" with "reasonable prices" and "lighthearted service"; while the "whimsical" "porcine-themed decor" offers "tons to look at", surveyors snort "it's not exactly pretty."

## CHARLES NOB HILL S
| 26 | 24 | 26 | $75 |

*1250 Jones St. (Clay St.), 415-771-5400*

■ "Words like over-the-top, pampered and scrumptious come to mind" when describing this "polished diamond" that "didn't miss a step when" a new chef assumed the reins; go ahead, "play Nob Hill for a day" and "splurge" on the "Bacchanalian adventure" of "the two-hour tasting menu", in which the "highly professional staff seems to intuit your every need" as you sample bite after bite of the "sumptuous" Californian–New French creations in "one of the most elegant" – some say "stuffiest" – "rooms in town."

## Charlie's L S M
| 16 | 16 | 14 | $38 |

*1838 Union St. (bet. Laguna & Octavia Sts.), 415-474-3773*

☑ A "major scene and meat market" for "super-yuppies" "in heat", this Cow Hollow hangout "feels more like a bar than a restaurant"; while some "thirty- and fortysomething" swingers say "the Californian food is better than expected", skeptics are sick of "the attitude they exude", snapping sorry, Charlie – your "15 minutes are up."

### Chateau Souverain Café at the Winery L S M
| 22 | 26 | 21 | $45 |

*400 Souverain Rd. (Hwy. 101, Independence Ln. exit), Geyserville, 707-433-3141*

◪ You might "go for the wine" but you'll "stay for the Californian-French food" suggest smitten surveyors about this "gorgeous" "winery restaurant" "set among the vineyards" in Geyserville; "when you drive up you feel like you're going to eat at a palace" and the service keeps up the illusion, though it's "a bit arch" for some tastes, who also note the cuisine is not "as perfect as the surroundings"; still, this is "the perfect place for a summer lunch", served alfresco until 5 PM.

### Chaya Brasserie L S M
| 20 | 22 | 18 | $44 |

*132 The Embarcadero (bet. Howard & Mission Sts.), 415-777-8688*

◪ This Embarcadero Asian "succeeds in striking a very difficult balance", featuring both raw fish that "can't get any more fresh" and "inventive French food" in a "dramatic" "modern" dining room that affords "fabulous views of the Bay Bridge"; but fashionistas fret that the scene is "not as trendy as that of the LA branch" ("what is in SF?"), while the "service, or rather a lack thereof" and premium prices are just as bad – though there's "excellent value during sushi happy hour" on weekdays.

### Chaz Restaurant S
∇ | 23 | 19 | 22 | $40 |

*3347 Fillmore St. (bet. Chestnut & Lombard Sts.), 415-928-1211*

◼ Considered "one of the secret treasures of the SF dining scene", chef-owner Charles Salomon's Marina home is one of those rare places "where you can dine on superb food" ("brilliant" New French–New American in this case) and "carry on a conversation without yelling"; given all that, plus "excellent service" and a "convivial", "neighborly feel", it's a wonder "not more people know about it."

### Chef Chu's L S M
| 20 | 14 | 18 | $25 |

*1067 N. San Antonio Rd. (El Camino Real), Los Altos, 650-948-2696*

◪ *In Style* meets Shanghai at this "pricey" Los Altos "institution" "adorned with photos" of celebrity chef/cookbook author Lawrence Chu posing with "famous personalities"; since 1970 its extensive menu has been "the standard by which South Bay Chinese is defined, and though mavericks may mutter "yesterday's chic" tastes "a little tired" today and "badly needs a face-lift", they're shouted down by the starstruck, who swoon over the "real treat of meeting Chef Chu" himself.

## Chenery Park ⑤Ⓜ 22 20 20 $32

*683 Chenery St. (Diamond St.), 415-337-8537*

■ "You'll think you've died and gone to comfort-food heaven" at this "great New American" "neighborhood spot that [presents] food like the fancy places" ("what else would you expect from Boulevard alums?") in a "casual yet elegant" multilevel dining room; toss in a "friendly, down-to-earth staff" and down-to-earth prices and you'll see why it's "put Glen Park on the culinary map"; P.S. there's a special children's menu on Tuesdays.

## Chez Nous Ⓛ⑤ 24 15 18 $30

*1911 Fillmore St. (bet. Bush & Pine Sts.), 415-441-8044*

☑ "Three cheers for Pascal Rigo" for "raising tapas to an art form" cry converts to his Upper Fillmore bistro; "come prepared to share" the "excellent Med" eats and see why this place is known as "small-plate heaven"; unfortunately, the bill and "waits on the sidewalk" (no reservations) are quite sizable, and less is not more when it comes to the "cramped dining room" and mini wine list; still, the staff is "incredibly accommodating", so overall, "it's worth it."

## CHEZ PANISSE Ⓜ 28 24 26 $71

*1517 Shattuck Ave. (bet. Cedar & Vine Sts.), Berkeley, 510-548-5525*

■ "Who knew that heaven was just a trip across the Bay" ask pilgrims who "come to this Berkeley holy spot to "worship at the feet of Alice Waters"; the flock reports that eating the "flawless" "market-based" Cal-Med cuisine in a "Craftsman cathedral" with "well-orchestrated service" is a "seemingly religious experience"; although "the simplicity" of it all causes a few heretics to hiss about the "emperor's new clothes", most feel "it's worth every penny to be one step closer to nirvana."

## CHEZ PANISSE CAFÉ ⓁⓂ 27 23 24 $41

*1517 Shattuck Ave. (bet. Cedar & Vine Sts.), Berkeley, 510-548-5049*

■ Luckily for "common people" "with gourmet tastes and student budgets", "Chez Panisse Jr." "is a lot like" the "acclaimed" "temple downstairs", only at "half the price"; the Cal-Med menu "still has that incomparable Alice Waters touch", "paired with a welcoming staff", but the atmosphere is "more fun", the bookings are "a little easier to get" (though it's recommended to "call exactly one month in advance") and, free-choice advocates rejoice, "you can order what you like" "without being tied into that day's menu."

## Chez Papa Bistrot Ⓛ⑤Ⓜ – – – M

*1401 18th St. (Missouri St.), 415-824-8210*

Plouf owner Jocelyn Bulow hopes to find his thrill on Potrero Hill with this latest project, a 38-seat Provençal bistro; chef Ola Fendert (ex Plouf) proffers such classics as seafood pot-au-feu, *pissaladière* (a pizza-like tart) and charcuterie and cheese plates in a classic Gallic setting replete with racy red walls, a zinc bar and sidewalk tables.

### Chez Spencer L S M  – | – | – | M
*82 14th St. (Folsom St.), 415-864-2191*
Laurent Katgely (ex Foreign Cinema) is back at the stoves at this hip Mission supper club; Continental breakfast fare and to-go lunches are available weekdays, while the dinner menu features inventive French creations; thanks to co-owner (and wife) Erin's music connections, the bar area will showcase jazz performers nightly, including swing icon Lavay Smith on Wednesdays.

### Chez TJ  25 | 24 | 25 | $69
*938 Villa St. (bet. Castro St. & Shoreline Blvd.), Mountain View, 650-964-7466*
■ "South Bayers need not drive to SF for a magical dining experience" when they can be pampered by "subtle and attentive" servers while supping on "outrageously good" New French–New American fare "in a charming little Victorian house"; just "wear loose pants" because "only [four- or six-course] set menus are available", accompanied by "nice wine tastings"; you'll "want to savor every morsel" (since you're paying "expensive" prices for each one).

### Chloe's Cafe L S M ⇗  21 | 13 | 17 | $15
*1399 Church St. (26th St.), 415-648-4116*
■ "Noe Valleyans love to wait for food" and this "cute"-as-a-bug (and "tiny" as one too) American gives the "weekend mob" plenty of reasons – the "fluffiest eggs, kick-ass pancakes" and "creative lunch sandwiches" – to "spend half their sunny mornings on the sidewalk"; luckily, the "service is fast and good", so the "line moves fast."

### Chow L S M  18 | 14 | 17 | $20
*215 Church St. (Market St.), 415-552-2469*
### Park Chow L S M
*1240 Ninth Ave. (bet. Irving & Lincoln Sts.), 415-665-9912*
◪ "Usually an everything-but-the-kitchen-sink menu is a bad sign", but "it works" at this pair of "always hopping" "chow-on-the-cheap" neighborhood Eclectics, making them a "faithful" "fallback" for "groups or kids"; the Castro and "hip Inner Sunset" branches have the same menu, but the former is "quite loud" and the latter's "cozier", thanks to a fireplace and "protected upstairs deck"; consensus is "you get what you pay for", and while most "mean that in a good way", serious foodies opt to "say ciao."

### Christophe L S  24 | 18 | 23 | $29
*1919 Bridgeway (Spring St.), Sausalito, 415-332-9244*
■ Christopher Columbus! – while this "sleeper" Sausalito bistro has been proffering "great food, mood and service"

since 1978, a surge in the Food score indicates that the hiring of a "new chef" plus a gentle remodel have paid off; only question is, how do they manage, because with the "unbelievably low-priced" "excellent four-course, early-bird menu", "they're practically giving it away."

### Citizen Cake L S  19 | 16 | 16 | $30
*399 Grove St. (Gough St.), 415-861-2228*

☑ Patriots "pledge allegiance" to this Hayes Valley haunt, arguably "SF's greatest pâtisserie", where the sweets "will knock your socks (or diet) off"; and since the savory Cal "food sometimes reaches the heights" of the "architectural" cakes, it's a good spot "to have a bite before the opera or ballet" as well; however, conscientious objectors protest the "cold", "arty atmosphere" and "colder service."

### Citron S M  25 | 20 | 22 | $44
*5484 College Ave. (bet. Lawton & Taft Aves.), Oakland, 510-653-5484*

■ "In a neighborhood that has more restaurants than parking spaces", this "cozy" "storefront" bistro in Rockridge "still stands alone" thanks to chef-owner Chris Rossi's oft-"changing French menu" (don't worry, the "consistently" "distinct, clear flavors" are always "worth the gamble"); in addition, the "service sparkles", there's a "lovely patio out back" and it boasts "one of the best wine lists in the Bay Area"; so "if you can't get into [sister] A Côté next door", "this hidden gem" is still, thankfully, accessible.

### Citrus Club L S M  18 | 11 | 14 | $15
*1790 Haight St. (Shrader St.), 415-387-6366*

☑ "Retreat from the chaos of the Haight" at this Asian noodle house, where the big bowls of "hot, delicious nutrient-filled soups" at "down-to-earth prices" "are just what you want on a cold, foggy evening"; the proprietors also kick out some "kick-ass spring rolls" and "sake martinis to top it all off", which, judging from the "pretty long lines", seem to make up for "hole-in-the-wall decor and service."

### Cityscape ◕ S M  ▽ 20 | 25 | 21 | $44
*Hilton San Francisco, 333 O'Farrell St. (bet. Mason & Taylor Sts.), 415-923-5002*

■ "As the name implies", this American perched atop Downtown's Hilton hotel commands "spectacular city views in all directions" – so "beautiful" that the "very good food" seems "secondary"; surveyors suggest "bring the tourists" to the "pricey" jazz and champagne Sunday brunch, when they can be doted on by the "excellent" staff.

### Clémentine S  24 | 20 | 23 | $40
*126 Clement St. (bet. 2nd & 3rd Aves.), 415-387-0408*

■ Take your darling to this "charmer" in the Inner Richmond that's the quintessential Gallic bistro, complete with "friendly service" and "fabulous food" "without the usual fanfare"; sure, the "tables are close together and it can get quite noisy" but you want "authentic", *n'est-ce pas?*; P.S. "it's not an expensive place, but don't tell your date."

### Cliff House ⓛⓢⓜ   13 | 20 | 15 | $34

*1090 Point Lobos Ave. (bet. Balboa St. & 48th Ave.), 415-386-3330*
☒ For most tourists, "there's no visit to SF without a visit to" this 139-year-old "waterfront" landmark whose "large picture windows" allow "diners to get up-close-and-personal with the raging seas"; however, locals lament "you can't chew the scenery or the American food" and suggest "have an Irish coffee, enjoy the view and then go somewhere else" to eat; P.S. pleas for "some refreshing" will be heeded come fall, when this Richmonder is scheduled for major rehabilitation while remaining open.

### Club XIX ⓢⓜ   – | – | – | VE

*The Lodge at Pebble Beach, 17 Mile Dr. (Hwy. 1), Pebble Beach, 831-625-8519*
Consulting chef Hubert Keller (Fleur de Lys) helped inspire the "great", lighter-than-usual New French fare at this "classy part of The Lodge at Pebble Beach" that, as befits a jacket-required place, offers "attentive service"; attempt to dine before dark because "you can't beat the view" of the legendary golf links afforded from the outdoor patio.

### Cobalt Tavern ⓢⓜ   21 | 19 | 20 | $38

*1707 Powell St. (Union St.), 415-982-8123*
■ Die-hard habitués of North Beach "never thought the ghost of the Washbag could be exorcised" but concede chef-owner Guy Ferri and his "wonderful cast of employees" have "done it" with this New American ("try the skate, you won't be [treading] on thin ice"); "although the blue-on-blue interior can be a bit tiresome", it's "livened by the great jazz band" that provides "not-too-noisy" "background music"; P.S. the kitchen "stays open" till midnight on weekends, "a rarity" in this town.

### Cole's Chop House ⓢⓜ   21 | 21 | 21 | $49

*1122 Main St. (bet. 1st & Pearl Sts.), Napa, 707-224-6328*
☒ "Chicago meets Napa" at this "two-tier" steakhouse offering the "absolute best red-meat fix in the valley"; while the "dry-aged steaks are to die for", they're "priced as if they were in Manhattan", a downer "considering you have to order the sides" separately; while the house remains "lively" and "crowded", a drop in ratings across the board suggests it might be losing some of its chops.

### Compass Rose ⓛⓢⓜ   ▽ 14 | 26 | 18 | $33

*Westin St. Francis Hotel, 335 Powell St. (Geary St.), 415-774-0167*
☒ Whether you're looking for the "perfect place" to enjoy "fabulous high tea" "after a day of shopping" or an "old-

time cocktail lounge" to "sip champagne" and soak up a "wonderful cross section of people", you just can't beat the "ambiance and elegance" of this "beautiful" grand salon Downtown, where "the teapot is consistently full", the staff consistently "accommodating" and the live jazz always "tops" – all of which "more than makes up" for the "pricey, mundane" Asian-Continental cuisine.

### Cool Café **L S** ▽ | 20 | 18 | 14 | $18 |
*Stanford University Cantor Arts Ctr., 328 Lomita Dr. (Museum Way), Palo Alto, 650-725-4758*

■ Chef-owner Jesse Cool successfully blends the culinary and visual arts at her "fab" Cantor Arts Center cafe where you can consume "creative (and delicious) organic fare" "while sitting outside" and "looking at the stunning" "Rodin Sculpture Garden"; although the Californian lunches (served Wednesday–Saturday) "primarily" attract "long lines" of museum-goers, "it's open to the public" too, spurring the savvy to swoop down Thursday nights for dinner and cool cosmopolitans.

### Coriya Hot Pot City ●**L S M** | 14 | 7 | 9 | $18 |
*852 Clement St. (10th Ave.), 415-387-7888*

◪ Amateur chefs hotfoot it over to this "all-you-can-eat and all-you-can-cook" Taiwanese "pig-out" palace in the Inner Richmond where you "can fill your stomach without emptying your wallet"; "how good the food is depends on" "how well you can barbecue and mix sauce", and so while fans find it "interactive fun", killjoys call the concept "tiring", dis the decor (mainly "raw meats and seafood on display") and sniff "you'll go home smelling like dinner."

### Cosmopolitan Cafe **L M** | 20 | 19 | 19 | $43 |
*Rincon Ctr., 121 Spear St. (bet. Howard & Mission Sts.), 415-543-4001*

■ The spell of a "previously cursed location" has been broken by this "plush" SoMa bi-level outpost with a dual identity: by day, it's a "businessperson's dining haven" thanks to the "well-presented" "comfort food with a contemporary twist"; by night, it's a "highly active Gen-X scene" fueled by "the best" you-know-whats "in town"; cosmopolites find the New American cuisine "worth the clamor of the bar scene", though maybe not worth the "friendly" but "fumbling service."

### Costeaux
### Bakery and Cafe **L S M** ▽ | 20 | 14 | 14 | $14 |
*417 Healdsburg Ave. (bet. North & Piper Sts.), Healdsburg, 707-433-1913*

■ This "fabulous" family-owned and -operated "working bakery" (since 1923) is "good to drop into for coffee", "out-of-this-world pastries" and "fantastic" "French onion soup"; alternatively, you can get boxed "sandwiches for picnics", featuring their signature sourdough breads, before heading on through Healdsburg; N.B. closes at 5 PM.

### Cozmo's Corner Grill 🆂🅼    16  17  16  $31
*2100 Chestnut St. (Fillmore St.), 415-351-0175*
◪ Chef Steven Levine's "neighborhood-scale sibling of the Cosmopolitan Cafe" offers "more casual food and gentler prices" on this "prime corner spot in the Marina"; the large buzzing bar may be the next "meet market of choice among the trendy set", while foodies suggest sharing "small plates" of the Californian comestibles; just be warned, the din "forces dinner conversation to be shouted" and the staff could be "better trained."

### Crustacean 🅻🆂🅼    22  16  18  $40
*1475 Polk St. (California St.), 415-776-2722*
◪ At this Asian crustacean with "weird '80s decor (the neon sign says it all)" in a Polk Street strip mall, "everyone will tell you to get the" "sinfully good" "whole roasted garlic crab" and "those heavenly garlic noodles" – "and you should"; critics carp about the "outrageously expensive" prices that are "a little too stiff for getting your hands messy" and "inconsistent service" ("I thought ripping off people waslimited to Fisherman's Wharf"), but happy high-rollers just "splurge and crack away."

### Cucina Paradiso 🅻🆂🅼    ▽ 25  17  24  $31
*Golden Eagle Shopping Ctr., 56 E. Washington St.*
*(Petaluma Blvd.), Petaluma, 707-782-1130*
◼ The nondescript "strip-mall location" of this "authentic little trattoria" belies the "light-handed finesse" of its *cucina*; armed with "a good selection of Italian and Californian wines" and an "attentive staff", it's considered "one of the better places in the North Bay" by locals, and while "the decor ain't everything", "eating alfresco on warm nights" is as close to paradise in Petaluma as you're gonna get.

### Cucina Viansa 🅻🆂🅼    ▽ 17  17  13  $25
*Sonoma Plaza, 400 First St. E. (Spain St.), Sonoma,*
*707-935-5656*
◼ Situated right on the Sonoma Plaza, this "very casual" Northern Italian is "a great place to stop for a sandwich or nice salad" "en route to the wine country"; the bar is also primo for tasting the bottlings of its parent Viansa Winery, particularly on Fridays and Saturdays, when you can sip and be serenaded by a rotating variety of "live music."

### Curve Bar & Restaurant 🅻🆂🅼    ▽ 10  8  13  $26
*747 Third St. (King St.), 415-896-2286*
◪ This "nice little sports bar" with "close proximity to Pacific Bell Park" is a "terrific place to have drinks before [or after] a Giants game", thanks in large part to owner and celebrity bartender Johnny Love, who imbues it with "a

twinkle of fun"; however, most sports fans agree "don't bother" outside baseball season, as the Traditional American fare strikes out.

### Daily Grill 🄻🅂🄼     – | – | – | M |
*347 Geary St. (Powell St.), 415-616-5000*
This clubby behemoth of a grill (with 14 national branches) has set its sights on Union Square; the American menu is pointedly predictable (think crab cakes, steak tartare, New York cheesecake), as are the generous portions for modest prices; it's all housed in a setting reminiscent of SF's historic eateries – so settle in, pretend you're Sam Spade and sink your teeth into that 20-ounce T-bone.

### Dal Baffo 🄼     20 | 20 | 24 | $56 |
*878 Santa Cruz Ave. (University Dr.), Menlo Park, 650-325-1588*
◪ This "decidedly traditional" Menlo Park institution offers all the aspects of a "special-night-out place" – "service to rival the best Persian carpet salesman", a "wine list the size of a dictionary" and "elegant" Continental–Northern Italian fare; however, while your "glass will never be less than half-full of fancy mineral water", the overall experience seems half-empty to the "under-70" set, who snipe "the interior needs a makeover", as does the "passé food."

### D'Asaro 🄻🅂🄼     – | – | – | M |
*1041 Middlefield Rd. (bet. Jefferson & Main Sts.), Redwood City, 650-995-9800*
Chef Christopher Fernandez (ex Stars Seattle) is back in the Bay Area and cooking up his unique brand of pan-regional Italian cuisine such as braised lamb shanks and housemade sweet-pea-and-mascarpone ravioli at this wood-beamed rustic trattoria down in Redwood City; the wine list, naturally, emphasizes vino from The Boot.

### Deep Sushi ●🄼     ▽ 22 | 18 | 18 | $31 |
*1740 Church St. (29th St.), 415-970-3337*
■ Despite the absence of signage (hint: "look for the glowing yellow box"), this "smaller-than-a-shoebox" newcomer in "sleepy" outer Noe Valley is fast becoming the 'it' place for the "hipper-than-thou" set; with sushi chefs rolling out "unorthodox, gravity-defying dishes" from behind an opalescent bar, a "jumpsuit-sporting" "funky, urban youth staff" and DJs spinning electronica on the weekends, this late-night spot is clearly not your average Japanese.

### Delancey Street 🄻🅂     17 | 16 | 21 | $27 |
*600 The Embarcadero (Brannan St.), 415-512-5179*
◪ "Only in SF" can you find a "socially conscious" eatery, a foundation-owned non-profit staffed by "those who attended the school of hard knocks" and "filled with suits" from the Embarcadero financial district; while initially folks come "for the cause, not the cuisine" ("straightforward"

American eats), the "great views of the Bay" and the "friendliest service" ensure they return "with pleasure."

### DELFINA S M — 26 | 19 | 22 | $38

*3621 18th St. (bet. Dolores & Guerrero Sts.), 415-552-4055*

☑ "If you're wondering where to have your last supper, look no further" than this "little treasure" "in the Mission"; it offers an "amazing blend of a phenomenal", "ever-evolving menu", served by "tattooed hotties" "that are slacker in appearance only", and a bill that's "half of other restaurants of its caliber"; although "it's hard to say which is more difficult – getting a reservation or finding a parking spot" – and the room is as loud as "an airport runway", to many it's "simply the best Italian in SF."

### Della Santina's L S M — 20 | 19 | 19 | $33

*133 E. Napa St. (1st St.), Sonoma, 707-935-0576*

■ Although it's located "right off the square" in Sonoma, "dinner in the garden on a sunny day" at this stalwart "transports you back to Italy"; "there's no pretense in the menu – just food like mama makes", if you were lucky enough to grow up "in Lucca" (think rabbits cooked on a rotisserie and the "best gnocchi you've ever had"); "cozy atmosphere" and a "really wonderful staff" round out the appeal of this "old favorite."

### Desiree L M ⊘ — _ | _ | _ | I

*Film Society Bldg., 39 Mesa St. (Lincoln Blvd.), 415-561-2336*

Chef-owner "Anne Gingrass [ex Hawthorne Lane] does wonders with" the exceptionally small lunch menu at her postage-stamp Presidio cafe that's "a gem" "if you can find it" hidden away in the Film Society Building; the daily roster of sandwiches and salads (available to eat in or boxed up) is inspired by whatever her heart desired at the local farmers' market that week.

### Destino M — 22 | 21 | 19 | $32

*1815 Market St. (bet. Guerrero & Valencia Sts.), 415-552-4451*

■ Your destiny awaits at this "awesome South American", "a dark and delicious gem" that sparkles "with a sexy atmosphere" (fueled by the "flamenco and tango dancers" midweek) and the "intriguing flavors" of its signature ahi seviche and "not-your-ordinary tapas"; not surprising, it's "no longer a secret" in "the up-and-coming neighborhood" of the Upper Market.

### Deuce L S M — ∇ 20 | 17 | 20 | $36

*691 Broadway (Andrieux St.), Sonoma, 707-933-3823*

■ "It's worth going a few blocks off the Sonoma square" to find this "family-owned" 1890 house sporting a "charming" "patio for alfresco dining"; but don't let the "old-fashioned ambiance" fool you – the Deuce's wild yet "excellently prepared" New American menu is 21st-century "hip" (specials include "anything from ostrich to alligator"), with a "great wine list" from the county to accompany it.

### Dine Ⓜ
21 | 17 | 18 | $42

*662 Mission St. (Annie Alley, bet. New Montgomery & 3rd Sts.), 415-538-3463*
☑ Although there's been "a little drop in the food since [founding chef] Julia McClaskey left", many still count on "great Dine-ing" at this "chic, simple" "respite in the midst of busy Mission Street" that delivers "great homey American fare in an urban warehouse setting"; it remains a "reliable member of the happening SoMa set" – you still "have to shout to be heard" over "the hopping bar scene."

### Dipsea Cafe, The Ⓛ Ⓢ Ⓜ
18 | 14 | 15 | $19

*200 Shoreline Hwy./Hwy. 1 (Tennessee Valley Rd.), Mill Valley, 415-381-0298*
*2200 4th St. (West Crescent Dr.), San Rafael, 415-459-0700*
■ "Don't forget to wear your biking shorts" to fit in at this "post-workout mecca" in Mill Valley (and now San Rafael) that "defines breakfast in Marin"; "long lines and high prices don't seem to deter the hoards" from "lining up to chow down on" "inventive omelets with shrimp and avocado", pancakes (pumpkin, anyone?) and serious "rocket fuel" (aka coffee) in the "sunshiny" "homey, farm-decorated" room; N.B. open for lunch too.

### DOMAINE CHANDON Ⓛ Ⓢ
26 | 26 | 25 | $58

*1 California Dr. (Hwy. 29), Yountville, 707-944-2892*
■ There isn't a better "spot to go broke" than this "magical" Yountville winery restaurant situated "only a few stumbles from an outstanding champagne cellar"; visitors can tour the facility "and then sit down" "in the lap of luxury" to "absolutely fantastic" New French–Cal cuisine, proffered by "attentive and discreet" servers; those who want their kick without the hangover-inducing prices can sit on the "patio looking over the well-manicured grounds" and opt for the "sparkling-wine sampler" and appetizers.

### Doña Tomás
24 | 18 | 18 | $28

*5004 Telegraph Ave. (bet. 49th & 51st Sts.), Oakland, 510-450-0522*
■ "Mexico City is alive" and well at this Oakland outpost whose "devastating carnitas" and "to-die-for squash enchiladas" positively "jump with inspiration", offering a "nice spin on south-of-the-border" food; "on warm nights" snag a seat "on the outdoor patio by the fountain", but be warned "you won't want to linger because the hardwood chairs are [truly] hard wood."

### Dottie's True Blue Cafe Ⓛ Ⓢ Ⓜ
24 | 10 | 15 | $16

*522 Jones St. (bet. Geary & O'Farrell Sts.), 415-885-2767*
■ "A diamond in the rough" Tenderloin, this "funky" little American is exactly "what a breakfast joint should be",

offering "fresh-baked goods", the "hands-down best" flapjacks and "healthy" omelets served by a "friendly staff"; true, "you can always count on being approached by wackos while you wait in line", and "it closes early – but who needs pancakes after 3 PM anyway?"

### downtown ∎S  20 | 20 | 18 | $38
*2102 Shattuck Ave. (Addison St.), Berkeley, 510-649-3810*
☑ "From the owners of César", this young "swanky" Med seafooder "breaks the granola code" by "enlivening the theater district, keeping un-Berkeleyish hours" and offering "cool jazz" ("ask to be seated in the main room if you want to hear the live music, in the back room if you don't"), but while advocates are upbeat about this Downtowner, others balk at the "too-high prices" and "general inconsistency."

### Downtown
### Bakery & Creamery ∎S M⊅  25 | 11 | 17 | $13
*308A Center St. (Matheson St.), Healdsburg, 707-431-2719*
∎ "Who needs Krispy Kreme" when you can load up on the "amazing sticky buns, homemade ice-cream sandwiches" and delectable "little pizza breads" at this "old-timey" bakery in the center of Healdsburg; it's "strictly a takeaway" affair, so "sit on the bench out front and meet the locals and their dogs" or enjoy your sugar high "in the town square."

### Dragon Well ∎S  21 | 15 | 18 | $21
*2142 Chestnut St. (bet. Pierce & Steiner Sts.), 415-474-6888*
∎ This "very Marina-ish" pleaser is an "Americanized" "yuppie Chinese" "at its finest", from the "stylish, if spartan, decor" to the "fresh, light" menu that "covers all the classics and doesn't leave you with a hate-yourself-in-the-morning greasy aftertaste"; it's also "one of the few on this [trendy] street where the staff is eager to help"; small wonder it's always "filled with couples searching for a good value."

### Dry Creek Kitchen ∎S M  24 | 26 | 20 | $56
*Hotel Healdsburg, 317 Healdsburg Ave. (Matheson St.), Healdsburg, 707-431-0330*
☑ "Manhattan comes to Healdsburg in the best way" thanks to "the new star of Sonoma, Charlie Palmer", who "courts the upscale crowd" with "chic" decor, an all-local "wine list that could take you days to" read and "wonderfully prepared seasonal and regional food" in his New American kitchen; most welcome every aspect of the New York state of mind "except for the 'tude" of the staff, which is "almost too sophisticated for laid-back wine country"; P.S. "BYO" indigenous vintages "and they waive the corkage fee."

### Duarte's Tavern ∎S M  20 | 10 | 16 | $24
*202 Stage Rd. (Pescadero Rd.), Pescadero, 650-879-0464*
☑ "After a day at the beach", this "funky", "old" "locals' hangout" on the "backcountry coast side" of Pescadero

(aka "the middle of nowhere") is worth veering "the few miles off Highway 1" – provided, surveyors stress, you stick with the "awesome artichoke or green chile soups" (sopped up with "warm sourdough bread") and "their famous ollalieberry pie", skipping "the main courses, which are iffy at best."

### Duck Club ⓈⓂ    20 | 21 | 20 | $43

*Bodega Bay Lodge & Spa, 103 Coast Hwy. 1 (Doran Beach Rd.), Bodega, 707-875-3525*
*Lafayette Park Hotel, 3287 Mt. Diablo Blvd. (Pleasant Hill Rd.), Lafayette, 925-283-3700* Ⓛ
*Stanford Park Hotel, 100 El Camino Real (Sand Hill Rd.), Menlo Park, 650-330-2790* Ⓛ
*Monterey Plaza Hotel & Spa, 400 Cannery Row (Wave St.), Monterey, 831-646-1700*

◪ "The older crowd tends to enjoy this" chain of hotel eateries for – what else? – "to-die-for duck" and other "elegant New American eats" served in a "tranquil setting" (nary a "hint of duck blinds", but "lovely ocean views" in Monterey and Bodega Bay); "for what it is and where it is", it's "a solid choice", even if critics quack "you can do better for the price."

### Dusit Thai ⓁⓈⓂ    ▽ 20 | 8 | 18 | $18

*3221 Mission St. (bet. 29th & Valencia Sts.), 415-826-4639*

◪ "In an area dominated by taquerias and fast food", this Bernal Heights "hole-in-the-wall" offers an enticing alternative with its "excellent Thai" eats that are easy dusit on the wallet and "personalized, caring service"; "nothing special" decor means most "usually have it delivered."

### E&O Trading Co. ⓁⓈⓂ    20 | 21 | 16 | $33

*314 Sutter St. (bet. Grant Ave. & Stockton St.), 415-693-0303*
*96 S. First St. (San Fernando St.), San Jose, 408-938-4100*

◪ "Indiana Jones meets the Hard Rock Cafe" at this set of "good-time" Downtown and San Jose microbreweries resembling an "Orientalist's dream" with "trees and nets hanging over the bar"; "bring a group of beer-loving friends" or "exotic"-drink enthusiasts and "graze" on a menu of "interesting Asian appetizers"; the staff is dinged for "having too much fun being hip and trendy", but the throngs agree this duo's "got pow punch to it."

### E'Angelo Ⓢ⊘    19 | 8 | 19 | $22

*2234 Chestnut St. (bet. Pierce & Scott Sts.), 415-567-6164*

◪ Located in the Marina, this "old-time Northern Italian" is the kind of "checked-tablecloth" place where "they stuff the people into their tables and then stuff their bellies" with "homemade pasta"; though "long lines are the norm for the low-budget fare", the "very amusing [accented] waiters keep the place hopping"; so "what more could you ask for?" – well, perhaps a "nicely decorated environment."

### East Coast
### West Delicatessen L S M
*1725 Polk St. (bet. Clay & Washington Sts.),*
*415-563-3542*
21 | 12 | 18 | $16

■ "Such a deli" this Polk Street newcomer is, dishing out the "best and only" "authentic" "Jewish fare" in the city; mavens marvel "the delish corned beef, crispy pickles and wonderful whitefish salad" are "enough to make my grandmother kvell"; so maybe portions are "on the pricey side", but still it's a slice of "New Yawk – with less attitude."

### Eastside West S M
*3154 Fillmore St. (Greenwich St.), 415-885-4000*
17 | 18 | 16 | $30

☑ Cow Hollowers like to "bring a date" to this "sexy", "dark" eatery, kick back to the "live jazz" or DJ and maybe have some "stunningly fresh seafood" from the raw bar; however, the regional American menu is deemed "secondary" to the "neighborhood scene", which is "always hopping with beautiful people" lining up for "the best mojitos in town."

### Ebisu L S M
*1283 Ninth Ave. (Irving St.), 415-566-1770*
24 | 12 | 17 | $32

☑ "Poseur sushi chefs flirt their way to your stomach", employing sashimi "like buttah" and off-the-wall "off-the-menu rolls" as their secret weapons at this "nothing-fancy" yet "always crowded" Japanese in the Inner Sunset; although there's always a school of "carping critics" calling it "claustrophobic" and "overrated", for "fresh fish" it's "close to what you'll get in Tokyo" and "worth the interminable wait and parking hassles."

### El Balazo L S M
*1654 Haight St. (bet. Belvedere & Clayton Sts.),*
*415-864-8608*
19 | 12 | 11 | $10

■ "Although the prices will shock the Mission's faithful", this "brightly painted" "non-divey joint" "puts its own stamp on Mexican food" with "fresh-cactus-and-goat-cheese burritos" and a "salsa bar stocked with fresh cilantro" that's "worth the extra buck"; the Grateful Dead–inspired names – Jerry's Burrito, Super Bob's – "remind you" of the local "Haight Street riffraff", who shuffle in until 10:30 PM for a "late-night snack."

### Eldo's Grill and Brewery L S M   _ | _ | _ | M
*1326 Ninth Ave. (Irving St.), 415-564-0425*
Although this "new Inner Sunset" bierhaus, decked out with three carousel horses, spent its first two months "without a liquor license" ("kind of rough when you're a brewpub"), the kitchen has been keeping up its half with a blend of Californian and Southwestern fare; at press time, general manager and brewmaster Gordon Malcolm Boyd (ex Gordon Biersch) hoped to have his house-crafted suds on tap by summer 2002.

### ELISABETH DANIEL, RESTAURANT
26 | 22 | 25 | $84

*550 Washington St. (bet. Montgomery & Sansome Sts.), 415-397-6129*

◪ Disciples of this New French Downtown destination deem it "a temple to fine dining", offering a "glass-encased kitchen with the mystique of an altar", "austere" "decor that creates a reverential atmosphere" and "smooth-as-silk servers" "hovering" like angels; malcontents may moan that the "Internet-boom prices" "for micro-portions" "are going to kill me", but before they go, even they "want [chef-owner] Daniel Patterson to cook their last meal."

### Elite Cafe ⑤Ⓜ
17 | 19 | 15 | $34

*2049 Fillmore St. (bet. California & Pine Sts.), 415-346-8668*

◪ "Give me étouffée" or give me death exclaim elitists who crave the "consistent" Cajun-Creole classics, "strong Bloody Marys at Sunday brunch" and "Big Easy vibe" of this "convivial" "Fillmore pub" that offers "a bit of ole Orleans in SF"; they also dig the "deep booths of dark wood you can sink into and never be heard from again" – though that does risk being "forgotten" by "waiters who need a pep talk."

### Eliza's Ⓛ⑤Ⓜ
22 | 19 | 16 | $22

*2877 California St. (bet. Broderick & Divisadero Sts.), 415-621-4819*
*1457 18th St. (bet. Connecticut & Missouri Sts.), 415-648-9999*

◪ This Potrero Hill and Pacific Heights duo serving new "Chinois" cuisine (read: "not weighted down with oil") in an equally "nontraditional", "colorful" dining room boasting "blown-glass decor" are decidedly "not your parents' Chinese restaurants"; although they're mecca even "for those who usually don't like" Mandarin fare, no one has the stomach for the "impatient servers" who "practically hurl you out the door as you're finishing your last bite."

### Ella's Ⓛ⑤Ⓜ
20 | 14 | 16 | $21

*500 Presidio Ave. (California St.), 415-441-5669*

◪ "Even with an expanded space", this "legendary" Traditional American in Presidio Heights continues to attract "USSR ration–like lines" "on weekends" for its "orgasmically wonderful brunches"; unfortunately, the "service is as slow as the thick maple syrup that you pour on the French toast" and on weekdays the "upscale diner food for dinner" often doesn't live up to the morning menu – two additional reasons to "go early."

### El Palomar Ⓛ⑤Ⓜ
14 | 16 | 14 | $21

*Palomar Hotel, 1336 Pacific Ave. (Soquel Ave.), Santa Cruz, 831-425-7575*

◪ Expect "moles, margaritas and a meat market" at this often-"packed" cantina "in strollable Downtown Santa

Cruz"; maybe "the food's average", but the "beautiful old Spanish decor" of "the main dining room" "transports you to a beautiful hacienda in Mexico"; "if you're pressed for time and cash", head to the "informal taco bar in the back" where the corn "tortillas are handmade to order."

### El Paseo S  21  26  24  $51
*17 Throckmorton Ave. (bet. Blithedale & Miller Aves.), Mill Valley, 415-388-0741*

■ "Hidden" down the cobblestone passageway for which it's named, this Mill Valley "favorite" is the preeminent "destination for a romantic dinner" for Marin's "older crowd"; with its warren of "steeped-in-charm" rooms, "old-fashioned French food with no apologies" (and a few Cal touches), "impeccable service" and "overwhelming wine list", it's the sort of place where "every visit you expect to see a man on his knees", proposing.

### EMILE'S  27  21  25  $55
*545 S. Second St. (bet. Reed & William Sts.), San Jose, 408-289-1960*

■ This "hallowed institution" "put San Jose on the map 30 years ago" thanks to its "exquisite, old-fashioned French" food fused with "Swiss culinary artistry", owner Emile Mooser's "personal, attentive" "Continental service" and that "marvelous" wine list; if the "sedate atmosphere" and "prohibitive prices" seem "a little stifling" in the 21st century, the "adventurous specials" and "to-die-for soufflés" "more than make up for it."

### Emmy's Spaghetti Shack ●⑤Ⓜ⇗  15  15  13  $20
*18 Virginia Ave. (Mission St.), 415-206-2086*

◩ "There's a lot of fuss over this Italian on the cusp of Bernal Heights", "full of groovy ex-dot-commers trying to stretch a buck"; while the menu is "definitely not just spaghetti", the "inventive" specials sometimes "exceed [the kitchen's] grasp" and "service is on the ditzy side"; the "hip" owners are "not afraid to let a DJ loose" in the dining room.

### Emporio Rulli ⓁⓈⓂ  24  23  19  $15
*464 Magnolia Ave. (bet. Cane & Ward Sts.), Larkspur, 415-924-7478*

■ "If you're aching for Italy", a trip to this "opulently beautiful" bakery/cafe (aka "the Vatican of pastry") "in Downtown Larkspur" "will get you by"; unrulli respondents rave "it doesn't matter if you weren't headed" here – "grab a latte and something gooey and head for the [sidewalk seats] to watch life."

### Enrico's Sidewalk Cafe ●ⓁⓈⓂ  16  19  15  $34
*504 Broadway (Kearny St.), 415-982-6223*

◩ "The best mojitos outside of Havana" and "great people-watching from the sidewalk patio" are the primary "reasons to sit" at "this classic icon" "in the porn district of North Beach"; while the Cal-Med munchies are simply "so-so" and the "service is sloppy", "live music and a hip bar scene" "give this staple its enduring charm."

### EOS RESTAURANT & WINE BAR 🆂Ⓜ
25 | 20 | 20 | $44

*901 Cole St. (Carl St.), 415-566-3063*

■ "Before there was bacar [its sister restaurant], there was Eos", a pioneer of "food-and-wine pairing" and "fusion" Asian fare that's "still making it work"; "the aesthetic presentation" on the plates (think "tall") "is reason enough to go" to Cole Valley, but don't miss "the trough of desserts" while you're there; "bad acoustics" in the "industrial chic" dining room prompt some to opt for the cozier "adjacent bar, which also offers the full menu" and "killer wine list."

### Eric's 🅛🆂Ⓜ
21 | 14 | 16 | $20

*1500 Church St. (27th St.), 415-282-0919*

◪ "If airfare gets any cheaper, even people from China will be coming" to this Outer Noe Valley haunt that offers an "addictive" formula – "creative" "killer" fare "at a bargain price"; although the "tasteful Victorian" setting "is a leap above" "the usual Chinatown decor", the "antsy service" is just as "brusque", making "takeout more satisfying."

### ERNA'S ELDERBERRY HOUSE 🆂Ⓜ
27 | 28 | 29 | $81

*48688 Victoria Ln. (Hwy. 41), Oakhurst, 559-683-6800*

■ Smitten surveyors who discover this "outstanding" Oakhurst wonder "on their way to Yosemite" "arrive exhausted and leave enchanted"; the "fairy-tale castle" makes an aptly "romantic" set for an "exciting food-and-wine-pairing" experience offered by the six-course Cal–New French prix fixe, with owner Erna Kubin-Clanin herself overseeing service (ranked the*Survey*'s No. 1) that "makes you feel both special and 'at home'"; N.B. tuckered-out travelers can stay at the related château next door.

### Esperpento 🅛🆂Ⓜ
18 | 16 | 13 | $24

*3295 22nd St. (Valencia St.), 415-282-8867*

◪ "Yummy sangria" and a "bustling atmosphere complete with a strolling mariachi band make" this "sweltering hot" "Spanish Mission joint feel like a trip to Barcelona" (though considerably "easier on your wallet"); however, despite "huge portions" of tapas and paella, skeptics sniff the overly "oily" "food lacks the flair of the flamenco show."

### Eulipia 🆂
20 | 18 | 19 | $36

*374 S. First St. (bet. San Carlos & San Salvador Sts.), San Jose, 408-280-6161*

◪ This "San Jose vet" has long been considered "perfect for an evening at the theater" nearby or a "celebratory meal" thanks to its "good New American–Californian cuisine", "low-key, friendly service" and "tranquil setting"; however, a contemporary crowd cries "the whole place reeks of the '80s" ("it was cool for my 8th-grade graduation"), sniffing there are now more exciting "choices Downtown."

### Everett & Jones Barbeque 🄻Ⓜ   19 | 10 | 13 | $16

*296 A St. (Myrtle St.), Hayward, 510-581-3222 ◑Ⓢ⊟*
*126 Broadway (2nd St.), Oakland, 510-663-2350 Ⓢ*
*2676 Fruitvale Ave. (bet. Davis & 27th Sts.), Oakland, 510-533-0900 Ⓢ⊟*
*3415 Telegraph Ave. (34th St.), Oakland, 510-601-9377 ⊟*

■ "Chow down, dogs" and "get ready to get messy", as this "rib-tickling BBQ" chain offers "heaven on a bone" along with other "authentic Southern grub" ("I dare you to order the hot sauce"); "outside of the Jack London Square location", these havens are absolute holes-in-the-wall" – and do "mostly takeout" – "but if you can get over the decor", you'll be rewarded with "three finger-lickin' goods."

### EVVIA 🄻ⓈⓂ   25 | 23 | 21 | $42

*420 Emerson St. (bet. Lytton & University Aves.), Palo Alto, 650-326-0983*

☑ "Greek meets West" at this "bustling" "Palo Alto haunt" serving "heavenly Hellenic cuisine" in a "warm setting" that feels "like eating in a country house" "in Athens"; order "anything roasted or grilled" (the "rack of lamb is absolutely divine"), pair it with an Adriatic wine and don't skip the stone-ground coffee heated over hot sand; while "the open fire lends a [homey] air", "don't be expecting a quiet evening" – the "noise is deafening."

### Fandango 🄻ⓈⓂ   23 | 23 | 21 | $39

*223 17th St. (Lighthouse Ave.), Pacific Grove, 831-372-3456*

■ With a "festive atmosphere" as evocative as the Spanish dance for which it's named, this "charming" "must-try in Pacific Grove" serves a "fabulous", "large" Med menu that ranges from puttanesca to porterhouse steak to paella that's "worth a trip on its own"; though the "variable service" stumbles a bit, most guests say a meal with "gracious host Pierre" Bain "makes you want to [get up] and sing."

### FARALLON 🄻ⓈⓂ   24 | 27 | 23 | $54

*450 Post St. (bet. Mason & Powell Sts.), 415-956-6969*

■ "All that's lacking is the mermaids" at Pat Kuleto's Downtown seafooder, "awash in a sea of glitz" (think "Jules Verne on acid"); fanciers "would swim upstream" for chef/co-owner Mark Franz's "unbeatable way with fish" (the seasonal "Maine lobster with truffle oil is total food sex"), which pairs well with the "stellar wine list" and "accurate, attentive service"; yes, it's "a bit Disney-esque" and the prices may leave you gasping for air, but most feel dining in "an octopus' garden" "can be divine."

## Farmhouse Inn & Restaurant, The S

▽ 22 | 21 | 23 | $41

*Farmhouse Inn, 7871 River Rd. (Wohler Rd.), Forestville, 707-887-3300*

■ This "wonderful" Forestville inn, located off the back roads of Sonoma's Russian River Valley, is turning heads since the new owners revamped the "restored country home"; while the same chefs are cranking out "sublime" California wine country–inspired fare (like the signature 'rabbit, rabbit, rabbit', in which the hare is prepared three ways), the newfound "superb service" and "excellent", souped-up wine list have diners "sorry we waited so long to try" it.

## FatApple's L S M

18 | 13 | 16 | $16

*1346 Martin Luther King Jr. Way (bet. Berryman & Rose Sts.), Berkeley, 510-526-2260*
*7525 Fairmount Ave. (bet. Colusa & Ramona Aves.), El Cerrito, 510-528-3433*

▨ "American comfort food at its best" has made this "inexpensive" Berkeley coffee shop a "Bay Area institution" "for over 30 years" (17 for its "more spacious" El Cerrito sibling); "retro-time burgers" appeal, "but the real thrill is" in the fat apple desserts ("forget about a slice – just get the whole damn pie"); "despite the cafeteria-like atmosphere and lengthy waits", it's a "parents' nirvana."

## Faz L M

15 | 18 | 15 | $32

*Crocker Galleria, 161 Sutter St. (bet. Kearny & Montgomery Sts.), 415-362-0404*
*600 Hartz Ave. (School St.), Danville, 925-838-1320*
*5121 Hopyard Rd. (bet. Gibraltar & Owens Drs.), Pleasanton, 925-460-0444* S
*1108 N. Mathilda Ave. (Moffett Park Dr., off Hwy. 237), Sunnyvale, 408-752-8000* S

▨ If ambiance were everything, then these "dramatic" Italian-Meds with "wonderful patios" and "live music" most nights would be sitting pretty; however, "while they still draw the [business] crowds", critics claim "the quality and creativity" of the kitchen's "has gone downhill" as the empire has expanded, and experiencing the "service is comparable to taking a slow boat to China."

## Feast L M

22 | 23 | 21 | $40

*714 Village Ct. (bet. Claremont Dr. & Patio Ct.), Santa Rosa, 707-591-9800*

■ "What [a difference] a new location" makes fawn fans as they feast their eyes on the "larger", more "comfy" and "contemporary" digs of this New American now located in Santa Rosa's Monterey Village (making it a "popular ladies' lunch spot"); a few folks feel "they need to grow into this new space", but chef/co-owner Jesse McQuarrie's "creative cooking" "ranks up there as some of SoCo's best."

### Felix & Louie's 🅢🅜　　14　17　16　$32
*106 Matheson St. (Healdsburg Ave.), Healdsburg, 707-433-6966*
◪ Brought to you by the chef-owner of nearby Bistro Ralph
and often "noisily" filled with its "overflow", this "fun"
"casual" spot is one of the best joints in Healdsburg to "drop
into for a drink" and hear "great jazz" ("every Wednesday
and Sunday") in the "huge bar area"; however, despite the
"prices and pedigree", the American-Italian menu is wildly
"inconsistent" ("wood-fired pizza is your best bet") and
the "service needs serious reconstruction."

### FIFTH FLOOR 🅜　　25　25　24　$71
*Hotel Palomar, 12 Fourth St. (Market St.), 415-348-1555*
■ The Hotel Palomar's "elegant", "abstract modern" "oasis"
is on its second life with new chef Laurent Gras (of NYC's
Peacock Alley), but his "top-notch" menu "keeps this place
on the top shelf", with "thought-provoking" New French
specialties; sommelier Rajat Parr's "encyclopedic" wine
list remains, as does the "attentive" (if a tad "cold") service;
just "bring the gold card", because at these "prodigious
prices", "you're paying for the four floors beneath you"; P.S.
the "full menu is available at the bar", "sans reservations."

### F.I.G.S. 🅢🅜　　–　–　–　M
(fka Rocca's Seafood Grill)
*2080 Van Ness Ave. (Pacific Ave.), 415-567-7606*
Veteran restaurateur Sam Duval (Izzy's Steakhouse) has
transformed his old-timey seafood grill on Van Ness into
this casual Mediterranean cafe serving food from France,
Italy, Greece and Spain (FIGS, get it?); nothing on the bill of
fare, which includes 20 types of tapas, is above $15, and
the 150-seat interior has been remodeled to reflect the
festive cultures of those sunny climes.

### Fior d'Italia 🅛🅢🅜　　16　15　18　$37
*601 Union St. (Stockton St.), 415-986-1886*
◪ This Northern Italian has been "one of the cornerstones
of North Beach" since 1886; there's no denying the "waiters
have plenty of personality" (ok, they're "brusque"), and
"interesting photographs" line the walls, but cuisine-wise,
while "some call it traditional", others opine "boring's
more like it", insisting "this place exists purely for the
tourists' and history's sake."

### Firecracker 🅜　　21　17　18　$26
*1007½ Valencia St. (21st St.), 415-642-3470*
◪ The "name amply warns diners about the hot dishes"
served at this "sexy", "hip Chinese" "crowded" with yuppies
in the Latino Mission; "the atmosphere is a step above the
usual" ("beaded chandeliers" and lots of "red velvet"), as is
the "healthy", fiery fare ("your favorite dishes, only better");
however, you'd better "make reservations in advance" or
withstand an "unreasonable wait."

### Firefly ⑤Ⓜ
24 | 21 | 20 | $37

*4288 24th St. (Douglass St.), 415-821-7652*

■ "Tucked away" in Noe Valley, this "shining" star serves "fabulous" Eclectic "comfort foods from all corners of the globe" "in an un-self-consciously hip setting"; chef/co-owner Brad Levy "can always be counted on to have a fresh and inventive menu" (with the "light, flavorful pot stickers" the sole staple), and "the staff couldn't be nicer or friendlier"; simply put, it's "quixotic" but never too exotic.

### First Crush ●⑤Ⓜ
17 | 14 | 18 | $34

*101 Cyril Magnin St. (Ellis St.), 415-982-7874*

◪ Its location in Downtown's "Hotel Central", "close to several theaters", makes this voluminous vino bar/eatery "worth visiting" for its "massive" number of "hard-to-find California vintages at the best prices"; the "weird layout" offers two levels of dining, but despite numerous New American entrées, imbibers insist you "stick with the wine and appetizers"; P.S. the Food score may not reflect a recent chef change.

### FlatIron Grill ⑤Ⓜ
– | – | – | M

*1440 Lincoln Ave. (bet. Fair Way & Washington St.), Calistoga, 707-942-1220*

Brought to you by the folks behind Brannan's Grill, this "reasonably priced" Calistoga newcomer's already "a hit with locals" who fill the "beautiful" booths; oil paintings of grazing cows bedeck the walls, and meat dishes of all stripes abound on the American menu, from the namesake steak to dry-rubbed babyback ribs and roast chicken.

### Flea St. Café Ⓛ⑤
21 | 17 | 20 | $40

*3607 Alameda de las Pulgas (Avy Ave.), Menlo Park, 650-854-1226*

◪ Owner Jesse Cool's "out-of-the-way oasis" in Menlo Park is where "aging, successful hippies have their special meals"; although good "if you want to avoid meat", the kitchen serves "sophisticated, organic" Cal–New American fare "that anyone can eat"; some sniff the "down-home decor" feels "like your grandmother's house", but a new martini bar may well rejuvenate the joint, as might other renovations come fall.

### FLEUR DE LYS Ⓜ
27 | 26 | 26 | $71

*777 Sutter St. (bet. Jones & Taylor Sts.), 415-673-7779*

■ "If chef-owner Hubert Keller had passed around the hat to help rebuild" his fire-damaged "old-world, *très romantique*" "SF institution", "the city's diners might have gladly obliged"; all are "anxiously awaiting the reopening", slated as this *Survey* goes to press, to once again "splurge" on the "lavish", "pricey" New French and Vegetarian prix fixes (plus a new build-your-own tasting menu) under a "dreamy", "canopied ceiling" while being pampered by "impeccable", if slightly "snooty, service."

### Flint's Barbecue L S M⇄   21  3  9  $14
*6637 Bancroft Ave. (Havens Ct.), Oakland, 510-568-2941*
*3114 San Pablo Ave. (31st St.), Oakland, 510-595-0524*
*6609 Shattuck Ave. (66th Ave.), Oakland, 510-652-9605*
■ "Thank God" this legendary (since 1961) chainlet of "authentic barbecue" shacks "reopened" say slaves to its "extra-smoky tender ribs"; although iconoclasts insist it's "inconsistent", most maintain the "finger-lickin'" fare and "tasty sauce" (mild, medium and "masochist"-ic) are "still messy, wonderful" and among the "best in America"; "good thing it's takeout" however, since there's serious "apathy from the folks behind the counter."

### Florio S M   20  20  20  $38
*1915 Fillmore St. (bet. Bush & Pine Sts.), 415-775-4300*
■ When "you get sick of nouvelle cuisine and *le petit* this and that", head to this "fabulous little bistro" on Upper Fillmore serving "divine" "steak (or chicken) frites" for two and other rustic French-Italian classics; "it feels like Paris" thanks to its "big-city buzz", bustling "wood-paneled" bar and "crowded" quarters that ensure you'll "rub elbows with Pac Heights movers and shakers."

### Flying Fish Grill S M   24  20  24  $35
*Carmel Plaza, Mission St. (bet. Ocean & 7th Aves.), Carmel,*
*831-625-1962*
■ "Exceptional presentations" of "inventive" Cal-Asian cuisine (tending toward Japanese) keep supporters swimming to this seafooder "tucked away in the Carmel Plaza"; punctuated by paper mâché "flying fish hanging around", the "decor is intimate", even "romantic", and made even sweeter by "incredible personal service."

### Fly Trap L S M   19  17  19  $36
*606 Folsom St. (2nd St.), 415-243-0580*
■ "To relive Old SF, come to this" "unpretentious" 1898 "throwback to the days when waiters wore ties instead of jeans", Traditional American "classics" such as celery Victor were considered happening, not "historical", and "sensational bartenders" ensured crowds; it suffers from "a poor location", but boosters believe the "new hotels" in SoMa will help "this trap attract more flies."

### Fog City Diner L S M   19  19  17  $30
*1300 Battery St. (The Embarcadero), 415-982-2000*
■ You're more apt to "sit behind Chris Isaak" than a truck driver at this "luxe" "facsimile of a '30s diner just off the Embarcadero," serving "small plates" of "comfort food" "gone wild" (e.g. tuna Sloppy Joes and moo shu pork burritos); even if it "doesn't quite live up to its Visa commercial reputation" – you'll need "a platinum-card budget" – its "terrific bar", "cheerful staff" and "sense of humor" ensure a steady "flow of tourists" and natives.

**Fook Yuen** L S M 23 11 13 $25

*195 El Camino Real (Millbrae Ave.), Millbrae, 650-692-8600*

Although it's "conveniently located near SFO", eating at this "fabulous" Chinese is "like a Hong Kong experience", from "the good variety of dim sum and then some" and the "live fish tanks from which you can choose" entrées to the "brusque" "staff that speaks little English" ("makes dining here a guessing game"); "just overlook the decor" and the weekend crowds.

**Foothill Cafe** S 24 14 18 $37

*J&P Shopping Ctr., 2766 Old Sonoma Rd. (Foothill Blvd.), Napa, 707-252-6178*

Only in the wine country would folks refer to a "much-loved" hangout as "your typical neighborhood strip-mall gourmet restaurant"; "don't let the location deter you" from chowing down on "finger-licking ribs" and "wonderful" Cal fare; even if it is a "great-kept secret" among insiders, it's still mighty "loud and crowded" with Napans who know a "good value."

**Foreign Cinema** S 18 24 16 $39

*2534 Mission St. (bet. 21st & 22nd Sts.), 415-648-7600*

"You haven't really dined until you've had" lavender-cured pork chops "with an art-house film playing over your shoulder" at this Mission "oasis" that "continues to define hip"; it offers an "outdoor courtyard" for moviegoers (and Sunday brunchers) and an "industrial chic" dining room for everyone else sampling the "tasty" Med-inspired French menu; however, "heat lamps do nothing to dispel the chill" of the air or the "flat-out rude service."

**Fork** – – – E

*198 Sir Francis Drake Blvd. (bet. Bank St. & Tunstead Ave.), San Anselmo, 415-453-9898*

Though it's named after cutlery, the real hook at this San Anselmo newcomer is the dishes – a Cal-French variety from chef Scott Howard (ex Rose Pistola); waiters in crisp smocks preside over the chic dining room featuring local artwork and an open kitchen.

**42 Degrees** 21 22 18 $41

*235 16th St. (3rd St.), 415-777-5559*

"Still the ultimate in decor" declare the design-inclined about the "cool, stark" "garage-esque" setting of this "fun, hip" "hideaway" where "the young and beautiful" "can't get enough" of the "imaginative" "Mediterranean cuisine", "great views of the Bay from upstairs" and "easy [and free] parking"; however, the seasonal "live jazz occasionally threatens to drown out the conversation", and you'll need a compass to find it "hidden in the warehouse district" near Potrero Hill.

### Fountain Court ⏻ⓈⓂ    18 | 12 | 13 | $21
*354 Clement St. (bet. 4th & 5th Aves.), 415-668-1100*

◪ When you're "tired of gravy-laden Cantonese" cooking, let yourself be "shanghaied" to this Inner Richmonder where Sinophiles sink their teeth into "Shanghai specialties [that] you don't often see in the U.S."; however, a Service score slide reinforces grumbles about "not very much guidance" from the staff.

### Fournou's Ovens ⏻ⓈⓂ    20 | 21 | 22 | $52
*Renaissance Stanford Court Hotel, 905 California St. (Powell St.), 415-989-1910*

◪ "It may be old, but it's an old favorite" declare devotees of this "dignified" denizen "in the Renaissance Stanford Court Hotel"; for the full experience "sit by the [vast brick] ovens" and watch the "marvelous meats" on the Cal-Med menu "prepared to order" and proffered by a "first-class" staff; though antagonists admit it "wouldn't take much to make it a top destination", "for now" it's just "stuffy and dull."

### Frantoio ⓈⓂ    22 | 23 | 21 | $40
*152 Shoreline Hwy./Hwy. 1 (west of Hwy. 101), Mill Valley, 415-289-5777*

■ Although it "sits in the least posh location in Marin", this "inventive" Northern Italian is also "one of the best in Marin" thanks in part to a "big" "beautiful room" overlooking the glassed-in working olive press for which it's named ("great idea to display it"); "outstanding pizzas, pastas and grilled meats" and a "quirky" but "knowledgeable staff" make you forget it's next to the Mill Valley Holiday Inn.

### Frascati ⓈⓂ    25 | 21 | 25 | $39
*1901 Hyde St. (Green St.), 415-928-1406*

■ A "new chef" and "recent remodeling", including the addition of a wine bar, "have revitalized this old Russian Hill standby" (and its ratings) that's always "full of locals who love" the "mind-blowing" Med menu, "mega-romantic" atmosphere and "amazing service"; go "when you're tired of the big Downtown resto scene", but regulars beg "please don't tell your friends – we want it for ourselves."

### FRENCH LAUNDRY ⏻ⓈⓂ    29 | 26 | 28 | $113
*6640 Washington St. (Creek St.), Yountville, 707-944-2380*

■ "Gaining a table has become a badge of courage" at Yountville's New American–French "epicurean cathedral" – but "everything you've heard is true": "Thomas Keller should have his hands bronzed" for the "culinary pyrotechnics" that produce his "ethereal", "humorous" tasting menus (both meat and veggie) in a "sublime setting"; even with "seamless service", you must "plan on three hours", and expect "obscene prices", but it's an "experience" that every foodie "should indulge in" "before he dies."

### FRESH CREAM 🆂Ⓜ | 26 | 25 | 25 | $59 |
*Heritage Harbor, 99 Pacific St. (bet. Artillery & Scott Sts.),
Monterey, 831-375-9798*
■ A "peaceful oasis from the surrounding tourist clamor",
this twentysomething veteran is still the cream in many
a commentator's coffee; it's "hard to beat" for its "so-
romantic", "setting over Monterey Bay", "wonderful
service" and "artfully presented" "fine French cuisine"
that, while "not groundbreaking", "oozes flavor."

### FRINGALE ⓁⓂ | 25 | 18 | 21 | $44 |
*570 Fourth St. (bet. Brannan & Bryant Sts.), 415-543-0573*
☑ "Close your eyes and smell the Galoises (virtually", of
course) at this "authentic French bistro" "in the middle of a
nowhere" stretch of SoMa; "it's tough to get a table, for good
reason" – namely, the "marvelous Basque menu"; *oui*,
"the tables are stacked like LEGOs", the "French waiters"
"are aloof" and "prices have crept" higher, "but the food
makes up for it" all.

### Fritz Fries Ⓛ🆂Ⓜ | 18 | 16 | 13 | $14 |
*Woolin Bldg., 900 North Point St. (Bay St.), 415-928-1475*
*579 Hayes St. (Laguna St.), 415-864-7654*
☑ At these "casual cafes", "nothing beats a crêpe and
cappuccino while lounging in the window seat" and
listening to "pulsating DJ beats" or "sitting on the back
patio sipping Belgian beer and munching" "fabulous fries
from a paper cone" ("make sure you try a variety of dipping
sauces"); but while either Hayes Valley or Ghirardelli Square
is "a great place to hang out", "the staff is too worried
about looking hip" "to help."

### Fuki Sushi Ⓛ🆂Ⓜ | 20 | 17 | 17 | $32 |
*4119 El Camino Real (bet. Arastradero & San Antonio Rds.),
Palo Alto, 650-494-9383*
☑ "As good as any I've had outside Japan" sigh "sushi
connoisseurs" about the eats at this "dependable" Palo
Alto address; the "broad" menu covers all the bases,
"from bento boxes" to shabu-shabu making it "great for a
[group of] friends or a business occasion"; however, the
disappointed are dismayed by "slow, slow, slow service"
and "prices straight from Tokyo."

### Gabriella Café Ⓛ🆂Ⓜ | ▽ 24 | 20 | 24 | $28 |
*910 Cedar St. (bet. Church & Locust Sts.), Santa Cruz,
831-457-1677*
■ Santa Cruzans hail "chef Jim Denevan as a visionary" for
"so much attention to detail, so much emphasis on local
organic produce" and so much "attentive service" at
this "small and cozy" Cal–Northern Italian institution; it's
"perfect for a peaceful" meal, but if you crave a quick bite,
"go to their fantastic sandwich and wine shop [located]
down one block."

### Galette 🄻🅂🄼                    18 │ 13 │ 13 │ $21

*2043 Fillmore St. (bet. California & Pine Sts.), 415-928-1300*
◪ It feels like "a piece of Brittany" at this "local crêperie" serving "delicious sweet and savory *galettes*" (as the Bretons call them) that pair well with the native hard cider on tap; but while it's "handy when shopping on Upper Fillmore", pessimists posit "it's not as good as sister Chez Nous" and "you can fly to France faster than the service here."

### GARDEN COURT 🄻🅂🄼            18 │ 29 │ 20 │ $49

*Palace Hotel, 2 New Montgomery St. (Market St.), 415-546-5010*
◪ "You might get a crick in the neck looking up at the huge stained-glass roof that dates from the 1906 earthquake era" at this "dramatic", "garden-like venue" "in the Palace Hotel" – "the grandest dining room on the West Coast" and the *SF Survey*'s No. 1 for Decor; not surprising, the "fantastic setting" "beats the Cal food", but "when you have a special occasion, there's no better place" for "amazing Sunday brunches", Saturday afternoon teas and "the most gorgeous Christmas and Thanksgiving buffets imaginable."

### Garibaldis on Presidio 🄻🅂🄼      22 │ 21 │ 20 │ $38

*347 Presidio Ave. (Sacramento St.), 415-563-8841*
### Garibaldis on College 🄻🅂🄼
*5356 College Ave. (Manila Ave.), Oakland, 510-595-4000*
■ Prized in Presidio Heights and "treasured in Oakland" this pair of "crowded", "jet-engine loud" "local haunts" "hits the mark with the total package": "consistently" "terrific Cal-Med" food, a "swank" setting and "gracious hospitality"; as "great places for observing the well-coiffed", both boast an "active bar scene, which either adds or detracts to the atmosphere, depending on your point of view."

### Gary Chu 🄻🅂                    23 │ 19 │ 21 │ $26

*611 Fifth St. (bet. D & Mendocino Sts.), Santa Rosa, 707-526-5840*
◪ "Santa Rosa isn't known for its Chinese food", but this eatery's eponymous restaurateur-about-town (he also owns Osake) woks up "Asian fare with a twist and zest" in an "upscale" yet "friendly" setting; but while it's the "best in the county", critical cosmopolites carp "it would be considered second-tier by SF standards."

### GARY DANKO 🅂🄼                  29 │ 26 │ 28 │ $81

*800 North Point St. (Hyde St.), 415-749-2060*
■ "If God was a chef he would cook" at this Wharf "winner", but even in His absence, Gary Danko's eatery is "almost flawless in all respects", from his "drop-dead superb" New American–New French "build-your-own tasting menu" (the winner by a hair of SF's No. 1 for Food slot) to the "perfectly orchestrated staff" and "Armani"-esque dining room; "you walk in a mere mortal but leave transformed" by "three hours of pure fantasy", so "sell the car, pawn the TV, do whatever you have to do to eat here."

### GAYLE'S BAKERY & ROSTICCERIA L S M

26 | 13 | 18 | $17

*504 Bay Ave. (Capitola Ave.), Capitola, 831-462-1200*
■ "You can get fat really fast" in this deli/cafe known for its "fabulous baked goods" and "exceptional" ("if rather pricey") "light food items"; while "there are a few tables", most Capitola-area locals eschew the "take-a-number service" and "minimal decor" and "get Gayle's to go."

### Gaylord India L S M

18 | 14 | 16 | $30

*1 Embarcadero Ctr. (bet. Battery & Sacramento Sts.), 415-397-7775*
*Ghirardelli Sq., 900 North Point St. (bet. Larkin & Polk Sts.), 415-771-8822*
*1706 El Camino Real (Encinal Ave.), Menlo Park, 650-326-8761*
◪ They're "not the cheapest" in the city, but a "formal atmosphere" and "decent" dishes make this trio of "white-tablecloth" Indians "fine" for "not-too-adventurous" types; however, pickier palates "can't help feeling" the "wimpy" "flavors have been dumbed-down for the California market" and suggest "you can do far better elsewhere for a lot less."

### General's Daughter, The L S M

19 | 24 | 20 | $40

*400 W. Spain St. (4th St.), Sonoma, 707-938-4004*
◪ "The general himself [Vallejo, that is] would enjoy the experience" afforded at his daughter's "historic" "Victorian home", converted into a "charming" spot for "special-occasion" evenings or sunshiny "brunches alfresco"; the "rustic Californian cuisine" is "mostly good", but "not good enough for the price" attack antagonists; still, "Sonoma locals love this place", and visitors can enjoy boutique "wines that you [often] cannot buy outside the area."

### Gervais Restaurant Francais L

▽ 27 | 19 | 25 | $42

*14560 Big Basin Way (bet. 4th & 5th Sts.), Saratoga, 408-867-7017*
■ After pampering San Jose gentry for more than 25 years, this "classic French eatery" has taken up residence in the "former Le Mouton Noir" location, a 145-year-old Victorian building; but while it's "new to Saratoga", longtime chef Felix Medina continues to create textbook renditions of "good" old favorites such as coquilles St. Jacques and "great soufflés for dessert."

### Geyserville Smokehouse, The L S M

▽ 21 | 18 | 19 | $22

*21021 Geyserville Ave. (Hwy. 128), Geyserville, 707-857-4600*
■ Smoking some of the "best ribs and brisket in Sonoma County", this year-old "midpriced" "true locals'" BBQ "joint" in sleepy Geyserville is a "sorely needed" cure for an area overrun with "haughty" wine-country establishments; "despite the restaurant's newness, the fabulously restored antique building" decorated with Old West bric-a-brac "offers wonderful character and atmosphere."

### Ginger Island ⬛L⬛S⬛M　　17 | 17 | 16 | $27
*1820 Fourth St. (bet. Cedar St. & Hearst Ave.), Berkeley,
510-644-0444*

◪ "Paradise" for ginger junkies, this "quirky" Berkeley New
American serves an "amazing" menu highlighted by made-
to-order ale and namesake fries that "are worth every
penny", and while there's "no Mary Ann", the "fun", "airy"
dining room ("love the retractable roof") has "plenty of
charisma"; yet, foes feel the cuisine's "novelty wears off
fast", and "dense service" displeases some irate islanders.

### Giorgio's Pizza ⬛L⬛S⬛M　　21 | 9 | 16 | $17
*151 Clement St. (bet. 2nd & 3rd Aves.), 415-668-1266*

◼ "NYC it's not", but this Inner Richmonder's "tantalizing
thin-crust pizzas" "with real toppings, not some chichi
California rendition", come "pretty darn close" pronounce
pie-zanos, who also praise the "no-fuss Italian-American
'50s favorites"; "mellow" service and "cheesy", "classic
pizzeria decor" help make it "a haven for families with
kids" (which explains why the "noise level is *fortissimo*").

### Gira Polli ⬛S⬛M　　20 | 12 | 16 | $22
*590 E. Blithedale Ave. (Camino Alto), Mill Valley, 415-383-6040
659 Union St. (bet. Columbus Ave. & Powell St.), 415-434-4472*

◼ While it's true that this "bargain" poultry pair in Mill
Valley and North Beach revolves around the "wonderful
rosemary-scented" "rotisserie chickens" (served with
"perfect side dishes"), it serves Italian dishes as well;
cronies crow over the "welcoming service", but there's
"little ambiance to speak of", so most bird buyers "risk a
ticket to double park and pick it up" "to go."

### girl & the fig, the ⬛L⬛S⬛M　　21 | 19 | 20 | $40
*110 W. Spain St. (1st St.), Sonoma, 707-938-3634*

◼ Owner Sondra Bernstein "knows what she's doing" at
her "whimsical gourmand fantasy" on the Sonoma square,
where "innovative" yet "solid Country French" dishes and
fancy "flights of wine" from an "eclectic list" are served in
a "cozy" dining room graced with "eye-catching art" or on
an "inviting patio"; "friendly" service and a delightfully
"low snobbery appeal" help make it a "popular spot with
locals and tourists alike."

### girl & the gaucho, the ⬛S⬛M　　▽ 23 | 18 | 20 | $39
*13690 Arnold Dr. (O'Donnell Ln.), Glen Ellen, 707-938-2130*

◼ A gaggle of gauchos goes gaga over the "small plates
with big flavors" and Southern Hemisphere wine flights at
this slice of South America "in the Glen Ellen countryside"
where you can have "something fabulous" that "won't
break your bank"; although a few fashionistas fume owner
"Sondra [Bernstein] has gone to one too many garage
sales", most feel the "fun", funky decor (with a "velvet
bullfighter on the wall") "works."

## Glen Ellen Inn Restaurant ⑤Ⓜ  ▽ 22 | 22 | 21 | $44
*13670 Arnold Dr. (Warm Springs Rd.), Glen Ellen, 707-996-6409*
■ "Fine dining and romance" await at this "charming" Glen Ellen Californian where "civilized evenings" can last "overnight" in the luxury creekside cottages; "wonderful" (not "overly fussy") Golden State fare (including dayboat-scallop BLTs and "homemade ice cream") and "great local wines" are served in a "lovely setting" (especially "outdoors in the summer") by a "superb" staff; N.B. now serving lunch Friday–Tuesday.

## Globe ●ⓁⓈⓂ  21 | 17 | 19 | $39
*290 Pacific Ave. (bet. Battery & Front Sts.), 415-391-4132*
☑ "Where all the chefs in SF eat", this "friendly", nocturnal New American Downtowner is the "darling" of city toques as well as transplanted New Yorkers and the après-theater crowd for its "serious", "satisfying" fare "in the land of the 5:30 dinner"; while hipsters hail the "groovy", "industrial" setting, wet blankets warn that the "closely packed" room gets "damn noisy" and the seating downstairs should be "avoided at all costs."

## Godzila Sushi ⑤Ⓜ  20 | 7 | 12 | $24
*1800 Divisadero St. (Bush St.), 415-931-1773*
☑ "Monster portions" of "smashing, consistently great" raw fin fare at Lilliputian prices excuse the "long waits" and "awful service" at this "kitschy" Pacific Heights "hole-in-the-wall" groupies grin; "overrated and undersized" grouse giant-killers, who sneer the rubber-suited leviathan (whose image is "all over" the room) "could make better sushi."

## Golden Turtle ⑤  21 | 18 | 20 | $30
*2211 Van Ness Ave. (bet. Broadway & Vallejo St.), 415-441-4419*
■ "Authentic", "subtle and achingly fresh" Vietnamese specialties ("roasted crab is a winner") glitter at this "hidden" Van Ness veteran, while the "fabulous" wood paneling and "helpful, attentive" service "add to the lovely experience"; it's a bit "expensive", but fans are willing to shell out extra because the menu contains "so many things you can't say no to."

## Gordon Biersch ⓁⓈⓂ  13 | 14 | 14 | $26
*2 Harrison St. (The Embarcadero), 415-243-8246*
*640 Emerson St. (bet. Forest & Hamilton Sts.), Palo Alto, 650-323-7723*
*33 E. San Fernando St. (bet. S. 1st & 2nd Sts.), San Jose, 408-294-6785*
☑ "The beer's the thing" at this chain of "microbreweries/ meat markets" where a "rowdy" crowd of "reformed frat boys and sorority gals" ("yuppie hell" despair disparagers) quaffs the house beverage "after work"; cynics may slight the American "standard beer-hall" menu as a "sort of palatable" "supporting cast" to the suds, but defenders

insist the kitchen "has its moments", especially with "the burgers and garlic fries."

### Gordon's **L S**                         ▽ 22 | 16 | 15 | $25

*6770 Washington St. (Madison St.), Yountville, 707-944-8246*
■ Early-birds scramble for "big, yummy breakfasts" and "local vintners" "gather around the long center table for lunch and conversation" at Sally Gordon's Yountville American; most of the week it's a counter-service affair offering "incredibly reasonable" morning and midday fare, but on Fridays, "excellent" "special" dinners (including an "amazing selection" of Napa wines at wholesale prices) are served in a "completely transformed" room.

### Gordon's House of Fine Eats **L S**  19 | 20 | 19 | $36

*500 Florida St. (Mariposa St.), 415-861-8900*
■ Diehards declare Drysdale's New American in the Mission's "multimedia ghost town" just "fine", thanks to a "cleverly" "diverse" menu of "hearty, unaffected" comfort food served in a "high-tech", "urban" setting; "live tunes" and a "fabulous" "bar scene" reflect its original "venture capital–sucking" clientele, but now that many "of the customers are gone", concerned cronies wonder whether it'll "survive the dot-bomb fallout."

### Grand Cafe **L S M**                    21 | 26 | 20 | $42

*Hotel Monaco, 501 Geary St. (Taylor St.), 415-292-0101*
■ A "dramatic" dining room with "fabulous booths" and a "soaring ceiling" sets the stage for the Hotel Monaco's behemoth of a brasserie that's a "solid performer" "before or after theater" dining; not to be overlooked are the "glorious, yet simple" Cal–New French fare and "amiable" service; N.B. the recent arrival of chef Paul Arenstam (ex Belon) may outdate the Food score.

### Grandeho's Kamekyo **L S M**             23 | 15 | 20 | $28

*943 Cole St. (bet. Carl St. & Parnassus Ave.), 415-759-8428*
*2721 Hyde St. (bet. Beach & North Point Sts.), 415-673-6828*
■ "Heavenly tasting" sushi rolled out by "hilarious" chefs reels in finatics to this "comfortable" Japanese duo in Cole Valley and the Wharf; "the brutal wait" "can seem longer than a flight to Japan", but pros promise that your patience will be rewarded by the "excellent" (though "expensive") raw fin fare; a hint from insiders: "sit at the bar" and "ask the chef to go for it."

### Grasing's Coastal Cuisine **L S M**   ▽ 25 | 20 | 21 | $44

*Sixth & Mission Sts. (opp. fire station), Carmel, 831-624-6562*
■ "Not your father's Carmel restaurant", "culinary genius" Kurt Grasing's Californian "wows" a "well-heeled" crowd with its "innovative" cooking highlighted by "sublime pairings of sauces and seafood" and complemented by a "well-priced wine list"; "a subdued splendor" fills the

room, and while a few grouse over service glitches, loyalists
laud the chef-owner as a "great friend."

### Grasshopper **L** **S**          22 | 18 | 18 | $30

*6317 College Ave. (Claremont Ave.), Oakland, 510-595-3559*
◪ Taking an ever-"so-hot" theme to the max, this Oakland
tapas try offers an "interesting" array of "artful, tasty"
"Asian-inspired small plates" and "helpful" service in a
"high-ceilinged", "modern" setting; wallet-watchers whine
that the "appetizer-size portions" "make it expensive to fill
up" and a no-reservations policy makes others jumpy –
although fans insist the "sake list alone is worth the wait."

### Graziano's Ristorante **S**⊘     ∇ 24 | 21 | 21 | $35

*170 Petaluma Blvd. N. (Washington St.), Petaluma, 707-762-5997*
■ "Wonderful" chef-owner Graziano Perozzi "knows how
to cook" "delicious, classic Italian" dishes in the "open
kitchen" of his popular ristorante housed in Petaluma's
historic Wickersham Building; the "congenial atmosphere"
extends to "waiters who remember loyal patrons" and
while the room "may be a little loud for most", *amici* say
*grazie*, "it's nice to have an upbeat place in this sleepy
town", even if it is a bit "pricey."

### Great China **S** **M**          22 | 8 | 15 | $16

*2115 Kittredge St. (Shattuck Ave.), Berkeley, 510-843-7996*
◪ "Berkeley's little secret" is this "hole-in-the-wall" "near
the Downtown movie theaters" serving "spectacular",
"authentic" Chinese fare that aficionados attest is the "best
in the East Bay" at prices that are a "bargain hunter's
delight"; the "dive" digs are "always crowded" in spite
of the "hurried" service from a staff that isn't shy about
"letting you know if you're eating too slowly."

### Great Eastern ◑ **L** **S** **M**          24 | 14 | 16 | $27

*649 Jackson St. (bet. Grant Ave. & Kearny St.), 415-986-2500*
■ Boosters tout this sprawling Sino seafooder in Chinatown
as "the best place" for "fresh" fin fare and "authentic
cuisine" without "traveling to China", and though the
enormous menu includes "conventional" "Americanized
dishes", aficionados "don't even think of ordering sweet-
and-sour pork" when there's live abalone, frogs and crabs
in tanks; regulars report that it's "improved under new
ownership", with "much friendlier" service than before.

### Greens **L** **S** **M**          23 | 24 | 20 | $35

*Ft. Mason Ctr., Bldg. A (Buchanan St.), 415-771-6222*
◪ A "trillion-dollar view" of "the sun setting behind the
Marina" is the backdrop for this "Vegetarian nirvana"
where a diverse crowd of non-carnivores and meat-eaters
converges for "flavorful", "Cordon Bleu–level" cooking
that's a far cry from "rabbit food", e.g. "not light on calories
or your wallet"; a few gripe about the staff of "Zen Buddhists

with attitude", but others praise the "attentive" service; N.B. a prix fixe is served exclusively on Saturday nights.

### Green Valley Cafe █
∇ 21 | 12 | 19 | $25

*1310 Main St. (Hunt Ave.), St. Helena, 707-963-7088*
■ St. Helenans "hesitate to give away the secret" of this "terrific", "family-owned" Northern Italian specialist "favored by locals" for more than 10 years, serving "freshly prepared", "simple", "*delicioso*" pastas, soups and other hearty grub in a "casual", "friendly" atmosphere that's rare for an area "full of attitude."

### Guaymas █ S M
18 | 21 | 16 | $31

*5 Main St. (Tiburon Blvd.), Tiburon, 415-435-6300*
◪ A "beautiful panoramic view of the SF skyline", "high-end", "sophisticated" Mexican cuisine ("if you go there for a burrito or tacos, you'll be disappointed") and "the best margaritas this side of Cancun" all make amigos ask "what's not to love" about this address located "only a few feet from the Tiburon ferry"; antagonists answer: "uneven", "overpriced" fare, a "deafeningly loud" atmosphere and too many "service gaffes" for comfort.

### Guernica ▊
∇ 17 | 15 | 19 | $34

*2009 Bridgeway (Spring St.), Sausalito, 415-332-1512*
■ For 28 years this Sausalito sleeper has been basking in the popularity of its "well-prepared" French Basque staples ("wonderful paella", shrimp with a garlic Basquaise sauce), complemented by "superb service and hospitality"; while it may be no Picasso, amigos assure us that it will be a "pleasant surprise" to those who "don't expect too much."

### Hamano Sushi █ S M
22 | 13 | 15 | $31

*1332 Castro St. (24th St.), 415-826-0825*
◪ Sushi savants are split over this Noe Valley Japanese "institution" – maguro-maniacs rave over the "biggest, freshest slabs" of "succulent" fin fare and credit the new management with "much-improved service", while cold fish regard the "overpriced", "medium ok" eats as something of a raw deal; all agree, however, that the counter is preferable to the "uninspired" dining room.

### HANA JAPANESE █ ▊
26 | 14 | 19 | $38

*Doubletree Plaza, 101 Golf Course Dr. (Roberts Lake Rd.), Rohnert Park, 707-586-0270*
■ "*Kampai!*" cheer champions of this flower "in the middle of a strip mall" near Santa Rosa serving some of the "best Japanese fare north of the Golden Gate", including specials such as the *unagi*-and-foie-gras *nigiri* that "rivals any fancy restaurant in SF", as well as an "extensive sake list"; chef-owner Ken Tominaga is "truly dedicated to delighting customers", so cognoscenti counsel "just put yourself in his hands and be prepared to smile."

### Happy Cafe Restaurant ⑤Ⓜ⌀ _–_ | _–_ | _–_ | _I_

*250 S. B St. (bet. 2nd & 3rd Aves.), San Mateo, 650-340-7138*
"Don't judge a book by its cover" diehards declare, or else
you might miss the "best *siu long bao* (little dragon buns)",
"great fried noodle dishes" and other "excellent" "Chinese
comfort food" served up at this San Mateo "hole-in-the-
wall" with "no decor" and "only a few tables."

### Harbor Village Ⓛ⑤Ⓜ 21 | 17 | 15 | $31

*4 Embarcadero Ctr. (Sacramento St.), 415-781-8833*
◪ This "businessman's Chinese" "on the Embarcadero
waterfront" is also a good "place to take the parents" for
some of the "best dim sum in SF" or splurge with a large
group on an elaborate Hong Kong–style, 10-course banquet
meal in one of the private rooms; despite the "upscale"
atmosphere, however, detractors take a dim view of the
"unhappy service" that leaves some uncertain whether
they "have a waiter."

### Hard Rock Cafe Ⓛ⑤Ⓜ 11 | 18 | 12 | $24

*1699 Van Ness Ave. (Sacramento St.), 415-885-1699*
◪ "Always entertaining" "if you're really into music", this
Van Ness sample from the rock 'n' roll "cookie cutter" is
just more of the "same old" sigh cynics who sneer that
the "best things are the shirts and the hats" and eschew
the American eats (save maybe the "pig sandwich" and
milkshakes); "why bother, when you're in SF?" mystified
locals ask the tourists who flock here; N.B. at press time it
was scheduled to move to Pier 39 in August.

### Harris' ⑤Ⓜ 23 | 19 | 23 | $49

*2100 Van Ness Ave. (bet. Broadway & Pacific Ave.),*
*415-673-1888*
◪ Offering "spiritual healing through beef" since 1984,
this Downtowner is the "real 'Cow Palace' in SF", serving
"mouthwatering" 21-day dry-aged beef and "bone-dry,
killer martinis" in a "traditional suit-and-tie" setting right
"down to the last cliché", from the "dark wood" to the "old-
fashioned red leather booths"; bashers, however, have a
bone to pick with the "overpriced", "mundane" fare and the
"old-boys'" scene that's getting "worn around the edges."

### HAWTHORNE LANE Ⓛ⑤Ⓜ 24 | 24 | 21 | $53

*22 Hawthorne St. (bet. Folsom & Howard Sts.),*
*415-777-9779*
◪ SoMa's "luxurious" "stalwart" "continues to deliver"
"excellent" Asian-Californian specialties complemented by
an addictive "bread basket" and "dreamy desserts" in "one
of the most beautiful" spaces in town; twentysomethings
find the "stuffy" atmosphere more hospitable to "suits" and
conventioneers, though, and while the staff glides through
the room as "stealthily as cats", it's dogged by some
complaints about "chip-on-the-shoulder" "attitudes."

### Hayes & Vine Wine Bar ●⑤Ⓜ   14 | 20 | 17 | $28
*377 Hayes St. (bet. Franklin & Gough Sts.), 415-626-5301*
■ A "playful, exotic wine list" and "terrific cheese and charcuterie plates" make this Hayes Valley wine bar a "popular hangout for the younger variety of culture vulture" hoping to "take off with one of their flights" "before the symphony or opera"; foodies warn "don't go with a big appetite", for "they just have snacks", but with 900 primo vinos to choose from (and help from a "knowledgeable staff"), "who needs to eat?"

### Hayes Street Grill Ⓛ⑤Ⓜ   22 | 16 | 21 | $38
*320 Hayes St. (bet. Franklin & Gough Sts.), 415-863-5545*
■ "Like the Energizer Bunny", this 24-year-old American grill "just keeps on going and going" by churning out "impeccable, fresh fish" "prepared any way you like" with "your choice of sauces" and "the best frites"; the "classic", somewhat "tame" dining room is "the kind of place to take mom" and gets booked up well in advance on performance nights, but "they do an excellent job getting ticket-holders in and out on time."

### Helmand, The ⑤Ⓜ   24 | 17 | 20 | $30
*430 Broadway (bet. Kearny & Montgomery Sts.), 415-362-0641*
■ Allies of this "excellent", "fairly priced" Afghan "trapped between strip joints" in North Beach don't patronize it just because it's owned by "the brother of Afghanistan's new president" but rather to "explore with their palates" the "tender morsels of lamb" and "unreal pumpkin dishes" laced with "delicious spices and herbs from the ancient spice route" that are served by a "charming staff."

### Herbivore Ⓛ⑤Ⓜ   19 | 15 | 15 | $17
*531 Divisadero St. (bet. Fell & Hayes Sts.), 415-885-7133*
*983 Valencia St. (21st St.), 415-826-5657*
◪ "Animal-friendly" advocates insist "there's nothing bland or boring" about the International menu at these "Vegetarian havens" in the Western Addition and the Mission (though "there's nothing great" either, carnivores carp), and it's "cheap, cheap, cheap"; however, even Beckett fans find no humor in "service that's like *Waiting for Godot.*"

### Higashi West Ⓛ Ⓜ   23 | 20 | 18 | $36
*632-636 Emerson St. (bet. Forest & Hamilton Aves.), Palo Alto, 650-323-9378*
■ "The ultimate East meets Silicon Valley" is how surveyors describe this "oh-so-smooth" Japanese in Palo Alto where "you might run into Oracle's Larry Ellison dining with Steve Jobs" on the "fresh" "creative fusion sushi", *sashimi* and other "unusual Cal-Asian" creations in the "funky, yet Zen" room (with "its waterfall-backed bar" and bamboo poles); a few purists wonder how "authentic" the fare is, but no one doubts the "Tokyo prices."

### Home 🅂🅼  18 | 17 | 15 | $25 |
(fka Johnfrank)
*2100 Market St. (Church St.), 415-503-0333*
⚠ Owner John Hurly has reinvented his Upper Market Street establishment to "fit the shrinking wallets of SF's dining public" with a new menu of "American comfort food" "gone gourmet" and "white wainscoted decor that would make Martha proud"; the beautiful gay crowd still "packs" the place, especially in the heated outdoor bar, but as a dip in Food and Service scores suggests, half the portions at half the price means half "the charm."

### Hong Kong Flower Lounge 🅻🅂  21 | 14 | 13 | $27 |
*51 Millbrae Ave. (El Camino Real), Millbrae, 650-692-6666* 🅼
*560 Waverley St. (bet. Hamilton & University Aves.), Palo Alto, 650-326-3830*
⚠ "Fantastic dim sum", "fresh seafood" ("you can watch them swimming") and "Hong Kong–style" banquets are the highlights of this Sino duo that wins praise for bringing "real Chinese to the suburbs", albeit in "bare basic" digs with "rude" service; the Sunday line for dumplings "has more people than seats", so you know "this must be the place" (though partisans of the Millbrae flagship dismiss the Palo Alto branch as "no carts, no fun").

### Hotei 🅻🅂🅼  20 | 15 | 17 | $18 |
*1290 Ninth Ave. (Irving St.), 415-753-6045*
■ Surveyors just love "slurping" heaping piles of "yummy noodles for mere pennies" at this Inner Sunset Japanese, the "low-key" sibling of the "more expensive Ebisu across the street", decked out with a "stuffed panda perched unrealistically on a bamboo tree" and a Zen fountain; the "not-so-secret tip" is that you can now get the "mothership's sushi" "without waiting in its dreadful line", so use your noodle – "what's not to like?"

### House 🅼  25 | 17 | 19 | $34 |
*1230 Grant Ave. (bet. Columbus Ave. & Vallejo St.), 415-986-8612* 🅻
*1269 Ninth Ave. (bet. Irving St. & Lincoln Way), 415-682-3898* 🅂
⚠ "If heaven serves fish", it would be Larry Tse's "sea bass with miso sauce" and other "absolutely stunning" dishes "cooked just right" at his Asian-Eclectic duo in North Beach and the Sunset; while the "austere", "high-decibel" dining rooms are "not quite as cozy as my home", "faithful patrons" are "willing to suffer tinnitus" for fin fare they'd gladly "have paid much more for in many other restaurants."

### House of Nanking 🅻🅂🅼  21 | 3 | 10 | $17 |
*919 Kearny St. (bet. Columbus Ave. & Jackson St.), 415-421-1429*
⚠ "Line up", "shut up and just order what the owner" "commands" – for "he's usually right" – and then get out

"as fast as you can" is the routine at this "famous Chinatown hole-in-the-wall" that's "so crowded your fork can end up in your neighbor's plate"; still, the never-ending "line of tourists and fans" proves that even its harshest critics can't touch this "institution."

### House of Prime Rib 🆂🅼    | 24 | 18 | 22 | $39 |
*1906 Van Ness Ave. (Washington St.), 415-885-4605*
☑ At this "old-time", "all-you-can-eat" beef palace (circa 1949) "your only choices will be how you want your prime rib" and whether your potato is "mashed or baked", while "waitresses from another era" "spin salads tableside"; the "funky" "throwback" setting ("think King Arthur's court") is as "loud as a bus station"; still, adamant admirers insist "there's no better rib, at any price" and "wouldn't change a thing" about it.

### Hunan 🅛🅼    | 20 | 7 | 14 | $19 |
*1016 Bryant St. (8th St.), 415-861-5808*
*110 Natoma St. (bet. New Montgomery & 2nd Sts.),*
*415-546-4999*
*674 Sacramento St. (bet. Kearny & Montgomery Sts.),*
*415-788-2234*
*924 Sansome St. (Broadway), 415-956-7727* 🆂
☑ "Call your spice – carefully" at Henry Chung's veteran quartet of "Hunanalicious" "lusty Chinese" "greasy spoons" because the kitchen really "knows how to cook" "big portions of fiery fare" that'll "defeat your worst cold"; they're served in "minimalist (all right, industrial) surroundings" "with zero atmosphere", but it's "worth it for the scallion pancakes and smoked [in-house] ham dishes."

### Hunan Home's Restaurant 🅛🆂🅼    | 23 | 10 | 18 | $19 |
*622 Jackson St. (bet. Grant Ave. & Kearny St.), 415-982-2844*
*4880 El Camino Real (Showers Dr.), Los Altos, 650-965-8888*
■ Located in "the heart of SF's Chinatown" (with a branch in Los Altos), this Hunan haunt with "funky decor" lures locals and "out-of-town guests" alike with its "somewhat Americanized but excellent" Chinese fare (including "great dumplings" and "the best sweet-and-sour soup"); leisurely diners, however, may suffer jet lag from the "extremely speedy (almost too quick) service."

### Hyde Street Bistro 🆂    | 21 | 18 | 20 | $34 |
*1521 Hyde St. (bet. Jackson & Pacific Sts.), 415-292-4415*
■ At this "small", "cozy, welcoming Russian Hill bistro", "located right on the cable car line", the "consistently" "fantastic" "rustic" menu will "transport you to France's countryside"; toss in a "friendly chef who often spends time at your table" (who knew "the French could be so gracious"?) and a three-course prix fixe for $22 that's "the best deal in town", and you'll see why *amis* call it the "jewel in the Hyde Street restaurant crown."

### Iberia **L S M**　　　　19 | 20 | 15 | $43

*1026 Alma St. (bet. Oak Grove & Ravenswood Aves.),
Menlo Park, 650-325-8981*

◪ When Palo Alto pueblos crave "real Spanish cuisine
beyond paella" as well as "tasty tapas", they come to this
"posh" place boasting a "romantic" "European" setting
complete with fireplace and patio; the "lackadaisical
service", though, leaves some foes wondering "how the
staff occupies itself."

### I Fratelli **S M**　　　　18 | 18 | 19 | $30

*1896 Hyde St. (Green St.), 415-474-8240*
*388 Main St. (bet. 1st & 2nd Sts.), Los Altos, 650-941-9636* **L**

◪ "Ride the cable car" and "spend a romantic evening"
"drinking Chianti" and tucking into "to-die-for bruschetta"
and "handmade pastas" at this "charming", "dependable"
trattoria atop Russian Hill (with branches in Los Altos and
Guatemala City); after 23 years it's "still the prototypical
neighborhood" joint "where everyone knows you and
welcomes you back", which may explain the "long waits";
to some less kindred locals, however, it "smells too much
like a chain."

### Il Davide **L S**　　　　20 | 17 | 18 | $33

*901 A St. (bet. 3rd & 4th Sts.), San Rafael, 415-454-8080*

◪ This "warm and atmospheric" "local favorite" generates
"as much buzz as you can get" in San Rafael thanks to
"rustic homestyle Italian" cooking that "ranges from good to
very good" (the tapenade and Caesar salad are "reasons
alone to come") and a "sociable, sophisticated" "scene";
although its location is "great for pre-movie dinners",
cushion in extra time, as "service can be very slow."

### IL FORNAIO **L S M**　　　18 | 20 | 17 | $34

*Levi's Plaza, 1265 Battery St. (bet. Greenwich & Union Sts.),
415-986-0100*
*327 Lorton Ave. (bet. Burlingame Ave. & California Dr.),
Burlingame, 650-375-8000*
*The Pine Inn, Ocean Ave. (Monte Verde St.), Carmel,
831-622-5100*
*Corte Madera Town Ctr., 223 Corte Madera Town Ctr.
(Madera Blvd.), Corte Madera, 415-927-4400*
*520 Cowper St. (bet. Hamilton & University Aves.), Palo Alto,
650-853-3888*
*Hyatt Sainte Claire, 302 S. Market St. (San Carlos St.), San Jose,
408-271-3366*
*1430 Mt. Diablo Blvd. (bet. Broadway & Main St.), Walnut Creek,
925-296-0100*

◪ Striving to break loose from the "chain, chain, chain"
stigma with "dependable", "rustic" Northern Italian fare,
including wood-fired-oven–baked pizzas, pastas and
breads that "really shine", these "classy", "high-energy",
"tried-and-true" outposts of a western U.S. group also

offer "monthly dinner specials" that keep the experience from becoming "tired" and "pleasant patios" that are at once "kid-friendly" and "where deals get done" over "power breakfasts"; "uneven service" is the weakest link.

### Incanto S M — — — M
*1550 Church St. (Duncan St.), 415-641-4500*
The name is Italian for 'enchantment', and this tony Tuscan newcomer on the edge of Noe Valley is hoping to provide just that with barrel-vaulted ceilings, marble floors and mahogany-paneled walls; chef Paul Buscemi (ex the late Square One) has crafted a small yet vibrant rustic menu complemented by Florence-born sommelier Claudio Villani's *piccolo enoteca* (wine bar), which features more than 20 vinos by the glass.

### Indian Oven S M 24 16 18 $25
*233 Fillmore St. (bet. Haight & Waller Sts.), 415-626-1628*
◪ There's a reason why this Lower Haight tandoori house is always "bustling with an edgy crowd" "spilling into the streets to get a table" – "fantastic food at a reasonable price", including "outstanding vindaloos", "amazing fish tikka" and "numerous varieties of breads" that you smother in the "brilliantly spiced entrées"; fanatics swear it's "well worth" the waits, "cramped", "noisy" room and "eat-and-run" service.

### Indigo S 20 20 20 $38
*687 McAllister St. (bet. Franklin & Gough Sts.), 415-673-9353*
■ Although it's a "dark horse" for the Civic Center "pre-performance" "rush", ticket-holders for "Herbst Theater harangues" "always get that mood indigo" when dining at this "über-funky" New American with a "creative menu", a "fantastic wine list" and "(gasp) friendly service" in a "chic", "eye-catching dining room" (hint: "if you wear blue, you'll seem invisible"); P.S. "after 8 PM" the three-course prix fixe offers "all-you-can-drink wines by the glass."

### Infusion Bar & Restaurant L M 16 15 15 $29
*555 Second St. (bet. Brannan & Bryant Sts.), 415-543-2282*
◪ "Post–Giants game" groupies and South Beach beauties decamp at this hidden "happy-hour" haunt for an "infusion of vodka" and "cool cocktails" from "its namesake in glass jars that sit high on the shelves, infused with a myriad of fruits, roots and peppers"; though the kitchen gives a game effort with its American cuisine, the "friendly bartenders'" concoctions remain the "best thing about this place."

### Insalata's Restaurant L S M 22 20 19 $39
*120 Sir Francis Drake Blvd. (Barber Ave.), San Anselmo, 415-457-7700*
■ Heidi 'Insalata' Krahling's "consistently creative" Med outpost provides "big-city quality" fare and "SF ambiance"

to "little San Anselmo"; although the service may "not be as peppy as the food", dishes that are "different and delicious without getting too eclectic" and a "sophisticated" setting make it easy to see why it "remains a favorite" for the "older local crowd" of Marin.

### Isa  25 | 18 | 20 | $37

*3324 Steiner St. (bet. Chestnut & Lombard Sts.), 415-567-9588*

■ "French dim sum, tapas or whatever you want to call it", it's all the same to fans who flock to this "husband-and-wife–run" "little gem in the Marina" for "small plates" of chef/co-owner Luke Sung's "superb" contemporary Gallic fare, served in a "stylish" (albeit "cramped") slip of a room that opens onto a spacious heated patio; "great service" means that "the food is always served at the appropriate time and temperature", and grateful groupies whisper that it "could charge more", but "it doesn't."

### Italian Colors L S M  18 | 17 | 20 | $29

*2220 Mountain Blvd. (bet. Park Blvd. & Snake Rd.), Oakland, 510-482-8094*

■ A "consistently satisfying" "neighborhood haunt" with a "great family atmosphere", this Cal-Italian "is a good bet in what is otherwise a dining void" in Oakland's swanky enclave of Montclair; while a few skeptics shrug that the fare is "good, but not great", with such "friendly service" and a "convenient location", defenders want to know "who's complaining?"; P.S. a "serenading guitarist warms up the room" Thursday–Saturday.

### It's Tops Coffee Shop ◗ L S M  14 | 15 | 13 | $14

*1801 Market St. (bet. Guerrero & Valencia Sts.), 415-431-6395*

◪ "Great balls of fire!"– this "kitschy", Upper Market "1950s greasy spoon" has been in the same family "since it opened way back when" Harry Truman was president, offering a complete diner experience, from the basic "burgers-and-pancakes" menu to the booths to the "friendly waitresses" in retro garb; it's also a "late-night haunt for clubbers and flubbers" – but mainly "because everyplace else is closed" sneer cynics.

### Izzy's Steak & Chop House S M  19 | 16 | 18 | $37

*3345 Steiner St. (bet. Chestnut & Lombard Sts.), 415-563-0487*
*55 Tamal Vista Blvd. (Madera Blvd.), Corte Madera, 415-924-3366*

◪ "Honest", "old-time" fillets and chops "without the attitude (or high prices)" lasso loyal carnivores into this pair where prime rib and "the best bargain steaks" are the bill of fare and come with "Izzy's potatoes and creamed spinach" included; "there's no extra foo-foo in the decor department", but it's also much "more fun and laid-back than your standard steakhouse"; however, the "average" meat just "doesn't cut it" with fussy flesh-eaters.

### Jackson Fillmore Trattoria ⑤Ⓜ    21   13   15   $32
*2506 Fillmore St. (Jackson St.), 415-346-5288*
### Cucina Jackson Fillmore ⑤
*337 San Anselmo Ave. (Tunstead Ave.), San Anselmo,*
*415-454-2942*
◪ Jack Krietzman's "fun", "hole-in-the-wall" trattoria in
Upper Fillmore has earned "cult status" thanks to diehards
who "can endure the waits", the "noisy", "claustrophobic"
setting where waiting diners "stand over your table" and
"grumpy", "pushy" service for Italian fare ("stick-to-your-
ribs pastas", "delicious complimentary bruschetta") that
"beats North Beach any night"; N.B. the San Anselmo
branch delivers the same fare in a less frenetic setting.

### Jade Villa Ⓛ⑤Ⓜ    18   9   11   $19
*800 Broadway (8th St.), Oakland, 510-839-1688*
◪ Oakland's dim sum darling is always "crowded on
Sundays" with "local Chinese" citizens and "big families"
who come for the "vast variety" of "first-rate" dumplings
rolled around on carts; the decor is "nonexistent" and the
service is "atrocious" ("go with someone who speaks"
Cantonese), but defenders overlook these glitches for fare
they insist is "more authentic" than that of other stalwarts.

### JARDINIÈRE ⑤Ⓜ    26   27   24   $58
*300 Grove St. (Franklin St.), 415-861-5555*
■ This luminous Hayes Valley supper club "continues to
burn bright" thanks to Traci Des Jardins' "amazing" Cal-
French cuisine that "glides over the palate" and Pat Kuleto's
"glamorous" "upside-down-champagne-glass" decor,
along with "well-informed" service; "ask for a table on the
balcony rail" for a "dramatic view overlooking" "one of
SF's swankiest bars"; it's pretty "pricey", "but the memory
will be with you long after the credit card bill is paid."

### Jay's Cheese Steak Ⓛ⑤Ⓜ⊄    21   12   17   $9
*553 Divisadero St. (bet. Fell & Hayes Sts.), 415-771-5104*
*3285 21st St. (Valencia St.), 415-285-5200*
■ "Where else can you get an awesome-tasting seitan
'cheese steak'?" challenge champions of this duo, voted
Best Bang for the Buck, that also serves the real meaty
deal (though "not very authentic" by "Philly" standards –
"what, no Velveeta?") as well as garlic fries that make
spud-niks "drool just thinking about them"; both the
Mission and Western Addition houses are open late enough
for "filling, quick" pre-pub repasts.

### Jeanty at Jack's ◗Ⓛ⑤Ⓜ    ▽ 25   24   23   $48
*615 Sacramento St. (Montgomery St.), 415-693-0941*
■ "Only Philippe Jeanty [Bistro Jeanty] could slip into
a classic SF restaurant [the historic Jack's] and make it
seem as if he'd always been there" swoon early-birds who
come to roost at his new Downtown big-city brasserie with

wine-country *savoir faire*; the New French menu includes a variety of seafood entrees, as well as the "unbelievable" tomato soup in puff pastry, prompting city slickers to rejoice "now we don't have to drive to Napa for his wonderful food."

### Jianna ⑤ⓜ | 25 | 22 | 22 | $41 |
*1548 Stockton St. (bet. Green & Union Sts.), 415-398-0442*
◼ A "hidden gem among North Beach's macaroni and pizza haunts", this "sexy" "sleeper" is "a refreshing change of pace" with its "affordable", "kick-ass" New American menu (chef Marc Valiani "cooked for the snowboarders at the Winter Olympics, and they won the gold, silver and bronze"); the "cozy, lovely, candlelit surroundings" and professional service "will put anyone in the mood."

### Jimmy Bean's ⓛⓈⓜ | 22 | 13 | 14 | $14 |
*1290 Sixth St. (Gilman St.), Berkeley, 510-528-3435*
◲ Early-risers and those capable of "sleeping well past brunch" come for the "best breakfast wrapped in a tortilla" and "silver-dollar pancakes" (and of course, lattes) "served all day" at this "little" walk-up-service cafe "operated by the Lalime's people"; the Californian menu is "totally granola, totally Berkeley", but "you can find some red meat hidden between the organic stuff"; "tight seating" and the "usual crowds at lunch" are the only drawbacks.

### Jimtown Store ⓛⓈⓜ | 20 | 16 | 13 | $15 |
*6706 Hwy. 128 (1 mi. east of Russian River), Healdsburg, 707-433-1212*
◼ This "kitschy" old general store/deli "is not to be missed" when winery-hopping in Alexander Valley; most travelers "stop in for a snack" or "takeout" from their array of "creative sandwiches and addictive spreads", although there are "outdoor tables", which are "especially fun" in "good weather"; toss in "nice wines by the glass, fabulous retro merchandising" and "views of vineyards" and "what else could you want in a country store?"; N.B. no dinners.

### JoAnn's Cafe ⓛⓈⓜ⊘ | ▽ 22 | 9 | 17 | $15 |
*1131 El Camino Real (Westborough Blvd.), South San Francisco, 650-872-2810*
◲ South SF's "all-star breakfast joint" cranks out "inspired alternatives for the most important meal of the day", but "in a city not famous for its cuisine", this "little cafe" also serves "reasonably priced, delicious" "American lunches" (and now dinners Thursday–Saturday); the setting leaves much to be desired, but it's "overshadowed" by the grub and "friendly service."

### Jocco's ⓛⓜ | 24 | 15 | 21 | $38 |
*236 Central Plaza (bet. 2nd & 3rd Sts.), Los Altos, 650-948-6809*
◲ Los Altos loyalists laud chef-owner Jamie 'Jocco' Carpenter, whose "innovative" New American cooking

offers epicurean hope to a "restaurant backwater"; with its "wonderful" fare, "accommodating" service and "changing art exhibitions", it's the kind of place where you'd like to have private, "romantic conversations" with someone special, but unfortunately it's so "noisy and crowded" that you "feel like you're eating with the next table."

### Joe's Taco Lounge & Salsaria ᴸSᴹ
20 | 15 | 15 | $17 |

*382 Miller Ave. (Montford Ave.), Mill Valley, 415-383-8164*

☑ Although it looks low-key, this "fun, local taqueria" in Mill Valley whips up "an interesting American spin on old Mexican [and Yucatan] favorites", such as grilled-fish tacos, "modeled after those of a roadside taco stand in Baja", and corn cakes with "tons of hot sauces to choose from"; despite "no service" and "frequent waits for a table", it's "still a great place for famished hikers leaving Mount Tam."

### John Ash & Co. ᴸSᴹ
24 | 25 | 23 | $49 |

*Vintners Inn, 4330 Barnes Rd. (River Rd.), Santa Rosa, 707-527-7687*

■ This Santa Rosa stalwart feels like a "little find off a back road in Provence", thanks in part to the "killer setting" overlooking "the vineyards that probably grew the grapes for that glass of wine"; the kitchen "continues to offer some of the best California wine-country cuisine", complemented by "impeccable service"; while the warren-like dining rooms are "a bit more formal" than other spots in the Valley, it's "a good place to impress someone" – just be sure to "dust off your credit card."

### John Bentley's ᴸ
24 | 18 | 24 | $50 |

*2991 Woodside Rd. (bet. Cañada & Whiskey Hill Rds.), Woodside, 650-851-4988*

☑ "The setting may be an old firehouse, but there's a constant fire in the kitchen" at this chic Woodside spot where hands-on chef-owner John Bentley sizzles with his "meticulously prepared", "fresh, seasonal" New American fare; adding fuel to the flames are the "intimate, cozy" environs with a "cute log-cabin feel" and "attentive service" that make it an ideal site for a "romantic tryst", although some warn that the "cramped seating" makes it tough to enjoy a "quiet meal" in private.

### John's Grill ᴸSᴹ
∇ 20 | 20 | 17 | $34 |

*63 Ellis St. (bet. Powell & Stockton Sts.), 415-986-0069*

☑ In 1908, long before steakhouses were all the rage, this quintessential grill located Downtown was serving old-time fare like oysters Rockefeller and crab Louis to the likes of Dashiell Hammett ("if you haven't heard of Sam Spade, then you're not old enough to eat here"); these days, cynics sneer that tourists visit for the "*Maltese Falcon*" memorabilia rather than the "disappointing" fare, but diehards stick to their guns and insist "you gotta love SF to understand it."

### Jojo   22 | 17 | 21 | $37
*3859 Piedmont Ave. (bet. Monte Vista & Rio Vista Aves.), Oakland, 510-985-3003*

■ A "dining mecca on Oakland's Piedmont Avenue", this "postage stamp–size" bistro scores big with "wonderful" Country French dishes, a "brief but well-thought-out wine list" and "smooth, attentive service" that excuse the "tight quarters"; speaking of room, make sure you save enough for Mary Jo Thoresen's "scrumptious desserts."

### Jordan's L S M   ▽ 19 | 21 | 24 | $49
*Claremont Resort & Spa, 41 Tunnel Rd. (Claremont Ave.), Berkeley, 510-549-8510*

■ "Breathtaking views" of the Bay, "solicitous" service and a scene that's "quiet enough to hold a conversation but busy enough to be interesting" make the Claremont's Pacific Rim "gem" a "great place to take your grandma" or parents for an "elegant breakfast buffet"; but critics kvetch that at other times, the fare can be "inconsistent."

### Joubert's L S   ▽ 18 | 15 | 25 | $26
*4115 Judah St. (46th Ave.), 415-753-5448*

■ "Established vegetarians looking for something new" ride off into the Sunset, where this South African specialist showcases "tasty" regional meatless dishes and a "very good" all–Cape Dutch wine list, served in an "elegant" setting by a "friendly" staff; although a few caution that it's "not the place to take visiting relatives from the Midwest", aficionados assure us that the "far-out" fare "grows on you."

### Juan's Place L S M   17 | 9 | 16 | $15
*941 Carleton St. (9th St.), Berkeley, 510-845-6904*

■ "Humongous portions" of "authentic" Mexican eats "may make weight-watchers faint", but that's precisely why "UCal students" and budget "birthday" diners go "out of their way" to this "family-owned" Berkeley "dive" decked out with Mexicali curios; throw in a pitcher of margaritas and a basket of chips with "addictive salsa" (but "don't fill up on" 'em) and you've got the makings of a "rollicking evening."

### Juban L S M   19 | 17 | 16 | $29
*Japan Ctr., 1581 Webster St. (bet. Geary Blvd. & Post St.), 415-776-5822*
*1204 Broadway (bet. California Dr. & El Camino Real), Burlingame, 650-347-2300*
*712 Santa Cruz Ave. (El Camino Real), Menlo Park, 650-473-6458*

■ This trio of "attractive" Japanese *yakiniku* houses offers "exquisitely fresh" "meats and seafood" that you sear on "tabletop hibachi" ("you have only yourself to blame if your food is overcooked"), along with "great *kimchi* and pickled veggies" on the side; "the thrill" of the grill makes it fun for "older kids", but some find it a bit "pricey", "considering that you have to do you own cooking."

### Julia Ⓜ　　　– | – | – | M

*2101 Sutter St. (Steiner St.), 415-441-2101*
Comfort-food cravers rejoice over the return of chef Julia McClaskey, who wowed 'em with her American eats at Dine and Universal Cafe and now has her own home in Pacific Heights (in Laghi's old digs); she's serving her signature seared chicken livers, as well as new classics like hazelnut-crusted sea bass, in a quiet room whimsically bedecked with columns topped with dried palm fronds, cushy banquettes and black-and-white-striped chairs.

### Julia's Kitchen Ⓛ Ⓢ Ⓜ　　　25 | 15 | 21 | $44

*COPIA, 500 First St. (Soscol Ave.), Napa, 707-265-5700*
■ Living up to Julia Child's name is a tall order, but chef Mark Dommen rises to the challenge, creating "deftly balanced", "refined Cal–New French" dishes (utilizing organic produce) in the "open kitchen" at this newcomer in Napa's COPIA center; an all-American wine list, tendered by an "excellent staff", complements the cuisine, served in an "austere", "modern" room; N.B. the museum entrance fee is waived for visitors to both the restaurant and the take-out Market Cafe.

### JULIUS' CASTLE Ⓢ Ⓜ　　　18 | 27 | 18 | $55

*1541 Montgomery St. (Union St.), 415-392-2222*
▣ "Out-of-towners" and locals find the "breathtaking views" at this "enchanted" "out-of-the-way" North Beach French-Italian retreat "worth the trip alone", but the 600-deep wine list and "gracious" service also help to make it a "perfect" "romantic rendezvous"; while most can't resist the "cheesy" "pageantry", it's just another castle in the sky to cynics, who yawn at the "old-fashioned" fare and advise sticking to "cocktails in the cozy bar."

### JZ Cool Ⓛ Ⓢ Ⓜ　　　21 | 12 | 15 | $17

*827 Santa Cruz Ave. (bet. Crane St. & University Dr.), Menlo Park, 650-325-3665*
■ "What takeout (or eat-in) should be" declare devotees of Menlo Park's "all-organic", "hip-deli" leg of Jesse Cool's triad (Flea St. Cafe, Cool Cafe), which keeps improving, as a leap in the Food score will attest; the "incredible" selection of "seasonal salads and sandwiches" promises "a lunch break worth leaving the office for", consumed at long communal tables à la "summer camp"; N.B. now serving dinner until 8:30 PM Tuesday–Saturday.

### KABUTO SUSHI Ⓢ　　　26 | 11 | 17 | $32

*5116 Geary Blvd. (15th Ave.), 415-752-5652*
■ "Mesmerizing" chef-owner Sachio Kojima is "without peer", and "his skill with the knife is as sharp as ever",

which is why "admirers come from all over" (including the city's "top chefs") to this "unassuming" Richmonder for "impeccably fresh", "melt-in-your-mouth" "bounties of the sea"; regulars recommend sitting at "one of the prized seats at the bar" and "letting him take care of you" – or "better yet, go elsewhere, the wait is long enough as is!"

### K&L Bistro L S    ▽ 24 | 19 | 22 | $37

*119 S. Main St. (Bodega Hwy./Hwy. 12), Sebastopol, 707-823-6614*
■ Chefs-spouses Karin and Lucas Martin's (ex SF's Hayes Street Grill) "more-than-wonderful addition to the local food scene" brings "a touch of France to Sebastopol"; in the open kitchen of their "charming", "intimate" bistro, they whip up "outstanding" boudin blanc sausages, addictive frites and other Gallic goodies on a daily changing menu.

### Kan Zaman ◗ L S M    17 | 19 | 16 | $21

*1793 Haight St. (bet. Cole & Shrader Sts.), 415-751-9656*
■ "Where else but Haight Street" can you "recline on comfy cushions" to dine on "tasty Middle Eastern mezes" and drink "cheap wine" while "watching belly dancers", then "pucker up" to a "flavored [tobacco] hookah pipe" ponder pros who proclaim that you can't find a more "festive ambiance" for a "date" or a "birthday party" than this "throwback to the *Arabian Nights*."

### Kate's Kitchen L S M ⊅    21 | 10 | 14 | $15

*471 Haight St. (bet. Fillmore & Webster Sts.), 415-626-3984*
◪ "Big honkin'" breakfasts ("portions fit for a starving bike messenger") are the come-on at this "all-American" dive where "young and old, rich and poor alike" wait up to an hour on weekends for Southern-inspired goodies such as "hushpuppies with Pooh butter"; less alluring are the "pierced and tattooed servers" and "funky" ambiance, but they're par for the Lower Haight neighborhood.

### Katia's Russian Tea Room L S    19 | 13 | 18 | $27

*600 Fifth Ave. (Balboa St.), 415-668-9292*
■ "In a city full of Russian immigrants", Katia Troosh's Inner Richmonder is "as good as it gets" for "hearty fare like mother used to make", including blinis, borscht and beef stroganoff, and it's "cheaper" than "flying to Moscow"; "warm", welcoming waiters and a "live accordion player" add to the ambiance of the "cozy" "storefront"; N.B. tea parties can be pre-arranged for large groups.

### Kelly's Mission Rock L S M    11 | 17 | 11 | $20

*817 China Basin St. (Mariposa St.), 415-626-5355*
◪ This China Basin American "has all the potential a waterside establishment could ever want" – "a wonderful deck to take in the sun", "terrific views of the Bay (albeit the industrial part)" and "an interior bathed in sunlight with big, garage-style windows"; yet, it's far better appreciated

for its "daytime parties" and late-night "raves" than for "oh, the food" ("who eats here?").

### Kenwood L S   24 | 21 | 22 | $41

*9900 Sonoma Hwy./Hwy. 12 (Warm Springs Rd.), Kenwood, 707-833-6326*

■ "What a find on Highway 12!" gush "wine-country travelers" who stumble upon this "roadside retreat" in Kenwood where chef-owner Max Schacher's "well-crafted and -presented" "fine French-American" dishes are served in a charming setting graced with "vibrant paintings" and a delightful patio "nestled among the vineyards"; "professional, unintrusive service" is another reason it's a "wonderful alternative to all the trendy places" in Sonoma.

### Khan Toke Thai House S M   21 | 23 | 20 | $27

*5937 Geary Blvd. (bet. 23rd & 24th Aves.), 415-668-6654*

■ "You can really impress" a guest at this Thai "palace" in the "hinterlands of the Richmond", where the "Buddhist-temple, carved-wood decor" and "cushiony" "sunken tables" "complement the delicate, spicy" cuisine; just "remember to wear nice socks" or get a pedicure 'cause "you gotta take your shoes off" "to gain entry."

### Kingfish L S M   21 | 23 | 18 | $35

*201 S. B St. (2nd Ave.), San Mateo, 650-343-1226*

◪ Three levels offer "a choice of quiet to noisy dining" at this "trendy" Big Easy catch that's becoming a big fish in the small pond of San Mateo; the New Orleans food and raw bar "will put a smile on your face" and the "club atmosphere" a groove in your step, even if the service isn't quite as "lively"; the management also runs A Tavola and Mistral, so it may well thrive in a spot that's defeated others.

### King of Thai L S M ⊅   20 | 5 | 14 | $11

*346 Clement St. (bet 4th & 5th Aves.), 415-831-9953 ◗*
*639 Clement St. (bet. 7th & 8th Aves.), 415-752-5198 ◗*
*3199 Clement St. (bet. 32nd & 33rd Aves.), 415-831-1301*
*420 Geary St. (bet. Mason & Taylor Sts.), 415-346-3121 ◗*
*156 Powell St. (O'Farrell St.), 415-397-2199 ◗*
*1541 Taraval St. (26th Ave.), 415-682-9958 ◗*

◪ "Bringing Bangkok to your palate" and lots of bang to your wallet, this empire of cheapo Thai joints "popping up all over the city" is winning loyal subjects with its "brilliant" *tom yum kai* soup, "heaping plates of noodles", et cetera, et cetera; of course, the decor and service are as "scarce" as the portions are "abundant", but knights of the late-night note "what do you expect from this price range?"

### Kirala L S M   25 | 16 | 16 | $31

*2100 Ward St. (Shattuck Ave.), Berkeley, 510-549-3486*

◪ "Sushi so fresh it practically jumps off the plate" and a smokin' good robata bar grilling up an unusual "assortment of skewered dishes" have boosters bellowing "*banzai*" to what they deem is the "best Japanese" in Berkeley ("and there are so many to choose from"); "show up early or suffer the consequences", however – namely an "excruciating one-hour wait" for a table that's only slightly "mitigated by a helpful sake bar"; unfortunately, it may take "even longer for your food to arrive."

## KOI PALACE 🇱🇸Ⓜ    26 | 19 | 15 | $31
*365 Gellert Blvd. (bet. Hickey & Serramonte Blvds.), Daly City, 650-992-9000*
☑ You can count on this Daly City Chinese for rolling carts "loaded" with "fantabulous" dim sum "delicacies" that "go far beyond the standard" dumpling fare and the "freshest seafood west of Hong Kong" from a "huge tank" bubbling with "you name it, they've got it – live!"; unfortunately, you can also expect "hellacious waits" in a foyer that gets as "crowded as a train station" "on weekends" ("call ahead for a number") and "frustrating" service.

## KOKKARI ESTIATORIO 🇱Ⓜ    24 | 26 | 22 | $46
*200 Jackson St. (Front St.), 415-981-0983*
■ "You want to smash dishes in delight" after dining on the "divine" delicacies "straight from Mount Olympus" ("lamb chops and whole fish are standouts") at this "classy" Downtown Greek (a sibling of Palo Alto's Evvia) whose "stunning" "super-cozy" taverna decor is as warming as a shot of ouzo, particularly "in the front room by the fireplace"; spartan types express "guilt over paying more than $10 for moussaka", but the "well-heeled", "expense-account crowd" simply shouts '*opa!*'

## Koryo Wooden    24 | 6 | 10 | $21
## Charcoal BBQ ❶🇱🇸Ⓜ
*4390 Telegraph Ave. (Shattuck Ave.), Oakland, 510-652-6007*
☑ "Don't wear anything too nice" or else "expect to take your clothes to the dry cleaners" after dining at this "smoky" "grill-it-yourself" hole-in-the-wall in Oakland where you'll find some of the "best Korean BBQ in the East Bay"; the decor recalls a "1950s cafeteria" and "service is marginal", other than having "hot coals brought to your table", but that doesn't stop Seoul-mates from confabbing "there for a midnight snack."

## Kuleto's 🇱🇸Ⓜ    20 | 18 | 18 | $37
*Villa Florence Hotel, 221 Powell St. (bet. Geary & O'Farrell Sts.), 415-397-7720*
## Kuleto's Trattoria 🇱🇸Ⓜ
*1095 Rollins Rd. (Broadway), Burlingame, 650-342-4922*
☑ Although there's "nothing too unusual" about this Northern Italian duo, "everything overall seems to work well", since they're perpetually packed "with a zillion tourists" "young and old, having a good time" in Pat Kuleto's

"designer" settings; even so, they seem almost as coveted for their locations ("convenient" to Union Square "shopping and theaters" and SFO airport in Burlingame) as for their "mainstream" fare, whose rating may not reflect the advent of executive chef Sharyl Seim (ex Mustards Grill).

### Kyo-Ya 🄻　　24　19　24　$52
*Palace Hotel, 2 New Montgomery St. (Market St.), 415-546-5090*
■ "Sushi nirvana doesn't come cheap" at this high-end Japanese in the Palace Hotel; "awesome" raw fin fare, a "wonderful" seven-course *kaiseki*, a "great range of sake", "a beautiful room" and "polite" service all attract an "expense-account" crowd made up predominantly of traveling salarymen from Japan, which is a "good sign" for foodies, but perhaps not couples ("don't bring a date here").

### La Cumbre Taqueria 🄻🅂🄼　　21　8　15　$10
*515 Valencia St. (bet. 16th & 17th Sts.), 415-863-8205 ♥*
*28 N. B St. (bet. 1st & Tilton Aves.), San Mateo, 650-344-8989*
■ A "whole lotta great burrito for minimal pocketbook impact" (the *carne asada* "melts in your mouth") and a staff that has "quick service down to a science" are a "combination that keeps Mission residents [and San Mateans] coming back" to these taquerias; as long as you "don't go for the ambiance", "you won't be disappointed."

### La Felce 🄻🅂🄼　　▽ 20　14　20　$29
*1570 Stockton St. (Union St.), 415-392-8321*
■ There's "nothing fancy" or "Hollywood" about this "old-time" paesano in North Beach that still serves a "full dinner" ("soup, antipasti, pasta and huge entrée") "at a great price"; the "down-at-the-heels" digs are "not for those inclined to upscale dining", but it's the kind of place with "something for everyone" on the "set menu" and service that makes you feel like "family."

### LA FOLIE 🄼　　27　22　26　$73
*2316 Polk St. (bet. Green & Union Sts.), 415-776-5577*
■ "Take someone for a romantic date if you definitely want another" counsel cognoscenti at Roland Passot's Polk Streeter showcasing his "flawless" New French dishes that are "works of art both in presentation and taste" ("patrons have been observed photographing their meals") with museum-quality "prices to match"; the "playful" decor of the main dining room festooned with marionettes creates "a decidedly un-Gallic atmosphere (i.e. warm, relaxed)" that encourages some amorous *amis* "to pursue a *folie à deux.*"

### La Forêt 🅂　　25　26　26　$57
*21747 Bertram Rd. (Almaden Rd.), San Jose, 408-997-3458*
▣ "Hidden in the boonies" of San Jose, this converted historic boarding house with a "beautiful" "creekside setting" pampers patrons with "excellent" (if "heavy")

French cuisine highlighted by "creative sauces" that, together with "great service", create such a romantic ambiance that devotees "defy you not to kiss on the way in or out or over the soufflé"; gripes about the "overpriced" menu dampen the ardor of many, however.

### La Ginestra **S**    ▽ 22 | 14 | 19 | $26
*127 Throckmorton Ave. (Miller Ave.), Mill Valley, 415-388-0224*
■ Since 1964, this Southern Italian "institution" has been "packed with local families" "who chat on the street while they wait" to get a table for "great brick-oven pizzas", homemade ravioli and other "old-fashioned home cooking"; although nostalgists lament a recent redo and miss the former "down-and-dirty" digs, it remains "a nice escape from other uppity Mill Valley restaurants."

### Lalime's **S M**    24 | 19 | 23 | $41
*1329 Gilman St. (bet. Neilson St. & Peralta Ave.), Berkeley, 510-527-9838*
■ The famed prix fixe menus are offered only twice a month, but this "very Berkeley" "institution" where "natural ingredients and old hippies abound" soldiers on with its "winning formula" of "imaginative", "delicious" and "ever-changing" Cal-Med cuisine, "attentive" service and "gracious decor"; it's one of those "quiet", unpretentious places "that restores your faith in nice restaurants."

### La Luna **L S**    ▽ 19 | 19 | 20 | $30
*3126 24th St. (bet. Folsom & Shotwell Sts.), 415-282-7110*
■ At this Mission District Nuevo Latino, sunny yellow walls and blue canvas drapery are matched by equally "bright" renditions of traditional favorites (empanadas, *carne asada*, paella, Caribbean coconut rice), accompanied by a modest list of South American wines and sangria, all at very affordable prices; a "super-friendly staff" adds allure.

### La Méditerranée **L S M**    19 | 14 | 16 | $19
*2210 Fillmore St. (Sacramento St.), 415-921-2956*
*288 Noe St. (bet. Market & 16th Sts.), 415-431-7210*
*2936 College Ave. (Ashby Ave.), Berkeley, 510-540-7773*
◪ A "standby that's still standing", this Mediterranean–Middle Eastern trio wins applause for its "tasty" dishes that are some of the "best culinary deals" around; the setting that's "not too fancy without being slobby" and "friendly" service put enthusiasts at ease, and for those who feel "cramped" in the "smaller-than-a-shoebox" space, the takeout is "great for potlucks."

### L'Amie Donia    24 | 19 | 22 | $45
*530 Bryant St. (bet. Hamilton & University Aves.), Palo Alto, 650-323-7614*
■ "There's not a gram of phoniness anywhere" at Donia Bijan's "cute little" bistro ("little being the key word") in

Palo Alto with "authentic French country fare" and a "loud, cramped" "no-nonsense setting" that "feels like Paris"; "counter seating" is an easy way to slip in without a reservation, and it also offers "the extra entertainment of watching the [open] kitchen in action."

### La Mooné Ⓜ︎     ▽ 24 | 24 | 21 | $29

*4072 18th St. (bet. Castro & Hartford Sts.), 415-355-1999*

■ This snug Asian–New French walk-up "hidden" on the second floor of a Castro Victorian has found its niche among gay weekend scenesters; seated at "blue-hued", illuminated low-slung "hibachi tables", diners choose from an array of "excellent and unique" small and large plates (the Hawaiian-style ahi poke is "surely worth traveling for") while tippling "tropical [sake-infused] cocktails."

### La Note Ⓛ︎Ⓢ︎Ⓜ︎     21 | 20 | 15 | $21

*2377 Shattuck Ave. (bet. Channing Way & Durant Ave.), Berkeley, 510-843-1535*

◩ "Fabulous breakfasts and lunches" "with a French accent" (*pain perdu* with lavender honey, salade niçoise) sing at this "Provençal bistro" full of "pastel colors, warm sunshine and alluring smells of the garden", "instantly" "transporting" fans from "Downtown Berkeley to the south of France"; by contrast, naysayers note the "less satisfying" dinners, "excruciating waits" and "ditzy service."

### Lapis Restaurant Ⓛ︎Ⓜ︎     21 | 25 | 19 | $47

*Pier 33, The Embarcadero (Bay St.), 415-982-0203*

◪ Pros promise "you won't be blue" at this waterfront "sleeper" in the Embarcadero, unlike the "cool" hued, "NY-style" space where "interesting, delicious" Med dishes and a "strong wine list" are served by a "knowledgeable" staff; still, a few feel the fare "pales in comparison" to the view that's "one of the best in the city" and "breathtaking" decor that's "so intimate" it might make you "fall in love with your companion if you're not dating already."

### Lark Creek Ⓛ︎Ⓢ︎Ⓜ︎     21 | 19 | 20 | $37

*50 E. Third Ave. (bet. El Camino Real & San Mateo Dr.), San Mateo, 650-344-9444*
*1360 Locust St. (Mt. Diablo Blvd.), Walnut Creek, 925-256-1234*

◪ In San Mateo and Walnut Creek, these suburban spin-offs of Bradley Ogden's Larkspur icon "stand above other chains" and offer a slice of "Americana" with "fancy yet familiar" traditional eats served in "polished" settings by a "friendly" staff; but critics cluck that they're "not up to par with the original" and are a tad "too casual for the prices."

### LARK CREEK INN, THE Ⓛ︎Ⓢ︎Ⓜ︎     25 | 24 | 23 | $47

*234 Magnolia Ave. (Madrone Ave.), Larkspur, 415-924-7766*

■ For frantic San Franciscans, Bradley Ogden's "classic" Larkspur "country getaway 20 minutes from the city" is "just what the doctor ordered": there's his "extremely well-executed" "high-end" (and high-priced) American comfort fare, "a soothing", "serene setting" complete with a garden patio next to a creek (perfect for a dreamy "summer night") and "polite", "personal" service; for many it's the "best in dining in Marin" "for lunch", "anniversary dinners or any other event."

### La Rondalla ●L S⊘　　　11 | 13 | 12 | $17
*901 Valencia St. (20th St.), 415-647-7474*
☑ This "kitschy" Mission Mexican beckons "boisterous crowds" "who heed the call of margaritas" (rueful regulars warn that one "will knock you over", "two, and you're psychedelic"); although the eats are merely "passable" and the service can be "grumpy", when you want "twinkling Christmas lights year-round" and "live mariachi music", it "can't be beat."

### LaSalette S　　　▽ 29 | 18 | 24 | $35
*18625 Sonoma Hwy. (Siesta Way), Sonoma, 707-938-1927*
■ The "best of Portugal" awaits at chef-owner Manuel Azevedo's "cozy" cottage off Highway 12 in Sonoma, serving his "lovingly prepared", "fantastic" dishes and "interesting Portuguese wines" recommended by the "attentive" staff "to complement the food, not to please the wine salesman"; N.B. monthly Fado Nights feature live traditional folk music and a set menu.

### Las Camelias L S M　　　20 | 15 | 16 | $22
*912 Lincoln Ave. (bet. 3rd & 4th Sts.), San Rafael, 415-453-5850*
■ "Tequila-marinated game hen" on the "huge" menu is your first clue that this San Rafaelite is "not your run-of-the-mill taqueria"; its "consistently good" "gourmet approach", "fast" service and "festive" setting (adorned with "superb artwork") are why amigos anoint it one of "the best overall Mexican eating experiences in Marin County."

### La Scene Café & Bar　　　▽ 20 | 18 | 21 | $40
*Warwick Regis, 490 Geary St. (Taylor St.), 415-292-6430*
■ While this "under-appreciated and under-patronized" "theater row" Downtowner is hardly a 'see-and-be-scene' spot, season subscribers count on its "well-trained staff" to deliver "intriguing" Mediterranean dishes in a "civilized" "clubby NY atmosphere" and "still get you to the show on time"; thrifty types bank on pre-curtain prix fixes "that won't empty your wallet."

### La Taqueria L M　　　24 | 7 | 13 | $11
*2889 Mission St. (25th St.), 415-285-7117 S*
*15 S. First St. (Santa Clara Ave.), San Jose, 408-287-1542 ⊘*
☑ Whether "you need a burrito to buffer your stomach prior to a night of drinking" or you're an out-of-work dot-commer "budgeting your own capital", this "longtime

taqueria" is "*mas mejor*" "of all the taco joints in the Mission" (with a "*numero uno*" *hermano* in San Jose); there's "no rice, no black beans" (and no decor, for that matter), but "there are reasons for the lines."

### LA TOQUE S     27 | 25 | 26 | VE
*1140 Rutherford Rd. (Hwy. 29), Rutherford, 707-963-9770*

■ "These people know what they're doing, in the kitchen, at the table, in the cellar" at Ken Frank's "romantic", refined Rutherford affair exclaim enthusiasts enraptured by "absolutely dazzling" "multiple-course prix fixe menus" of "fantastic" French fare enhanced by "creative combinations and terrific sauces" and "inspired wine pairings" suggested by the "exceptional" staff; so "why sit on hold for French Laundry" when it's "so much easier to get into" this spot, "one of the must-stops in the Napa Valley"?

### Lauren's ⊄     ∇ 20 | 13 | 21 | $27
*14211 Hwy. 128 (across from fairgrounds), Boonville, 707-895-3869*

■ For a "real Mendocino County experience" or a break "on your way" as you drive through Anderson Valley, cognoscenti recommend this "marvelously down-home", "Boonville funky" spot for its American-International "homestyle cooking" that's "better than your mother's" and "friendly", "casual" atmosphere; chances are you'll find it packed with "locals (including [owner] Lauren Keating)" "enjoying themselves."

### La Vie L S M     20 | 11 | 17 | $23
*5830 Geary Blvd. (bet. 22nd & 23rd Aves.), 415-668-8080*

☑ Insiders hint "you can always get a table" at this low-key Vietnamese that's "one of the better-kept secrets" in Richmond, offering "upscale fare without pretensions or high cost" (including "crabs to die for" and "flaming beef and prawns") and "friendly" service; by comparison, "the atmosphere" fizzles, but it's a "sacrifice" Saigon suppers are happy to make.

### Le Bistrot S M     20 | 19 | 19 | $41
*1177 California St. (Jones St.), 415-474-2000*

■ "Formal, fancy and filled with socialites", this "sleeper" "hidden in a large high-rise" is "a real high on Nob Hill" thanks to its "fabulous" French bistro "favorites" with an "odd" sushi segue that "somehow works" ("this is SF", after all); the classic Gallic decor and hostess would make "you feel like you're in Paris" but for the "view of Grace Cathedral"; N.B. the building offers parking.

### Le Central Bistro L M     19 | 16 | 19 | $39
*453 Bush St. (bet. Grant Ave. & Kearny St.), 415-391-2233*

☑ "Where all the Downtown power brokers eat", this "Bastille block" bistro is a "place to be seen" and offers "a bit of Paris, SF style", with "unstuffy, real French" fare served by "experienced" waiters; claustrophobes clamor that the tables are "too close together", but insiders point out that the "cozy seating arrangements" are good for "eavesdropping" on notable regulars like Mayor Brown.

### Le Charm French Bistro L S M — 21 | 16 | 19 | $33
*315 Fifth St. (bet. Folsom & Harrison Sts.), 415-546-6128*
■ "One of the best deals in town" report value hunters "charmed" by this "petite", "quaint" Fifth Street bistro's "delicious, no-nonsense" Gallic dishes and its "fabulous" "bang-for-your-buck" prix fixe (you're likely to "spend more on the wine than the food"); "friendly, attentive" service adds allure, and "if weather permits", "ask for a table outside" in the "magical" garden where "you'll think you're in the south of France and not south of Market."

### Le Cheval L S M — 21 | 15 | 15 | $22
*1007 Clay St. (10th St.), Oakland, 510-763-8495*
◨ Insiders insist this Oakland venture sets "the Vietnamese standard in East Bay", but "the problem is that everyone knows it", so "go early" or "expect to wait and wait"; the "tasty" regional dishes offer "great value", but phos find the "loud", "spiffed-up warehouse" setting and "hurried" staff that "rushes you out" are horses of a different color.

### Le Colonial S M — 20 | 25 | 18 | $44
*20 Cosmo Pl. (bet. Post & Sutter Sts.), 415-931-3600*
◨ It's fun to pretend "you're in a Bogie-Bacall movie" at this Downtowner with a "colonial French-Indochina plantation" theme that feels like old "Saigon without the heat" ("you expect to see rice paddies out the window"); however, "you'll be talking about the room" and the "too-cool-for-school" upstairs bar more than the upscale Vietnamese fare that's "big on taste but oh-so-small on portions" or the "questionable" service from a staff "with issues."

### Ledford House S — 22 | 22 | 23 | $45
*3000 Shoreline Hwy./Hwy. 1 (Spring Grove Rd.), Albion, 707-937-0282*
■ "Wonderful" service, a "splendid setting" "overlooking the blue Pacific" ("get there before sundown") and an "artfully prepared" "North Coast meets the south of France" menu have made this Cal-Med one of the "Mendocino coast's favorites" "for a romantic dinner" since 1987; there's "live jazz every night", and on Sundays "a three-course 'supper club special' that's a terrific value."

### LEFT BANK L S M — 20 | 20 | 17 | $36
*507 Magnolia Ave. (Ward St.), Larkspur, 415-927-3331*
*635 Santa Cruz Ave. (Doyle St.), Menlo Park, 650-473-6543*
*60 Crescent Dr. (Contra Costa Blvd.), Pleasant Hill, 925-288-1222*
◨ From the "glamorous", "bustling" bar and "vintage French posters adorning the walls" to the "loud", cramped quarters,

owner Roland Passot's casual triad are "the closest thing to" a "Parisian bistro that one is likely to find" in the suburbs – although the "fine cuisine Grandmère" is "prepared for a California palate", and "local suits and dot-commers" "fill the seats"; "so it's not La Folie" (Passot's primary place), and even fans concede "uneven service", but still "it's head and shoulders above most."

### Le Krewe S   12 | 15 | 18 | $25

*995 Valencia St. (21st St.), 415-643-0995*

☑ "N' Awlins, here we come" crow the cheering krewe at this "lively" Mission joint that takes you to the "bayou when you walk in the door", with New Orleans–Californian fusion fare that's doled out (along with "Jell-O shots, if you stay long enough") by a "friendly" staff (plus chef-owner David Tsang, who'll "be your best friend by the end of the evening"); yet, ragin' Cajuns are "insulted" by the "bland", "ersatz" Big Easy eats and snort "y'all go back home now."

### LE PAPILLON L S M   26 | 24 | 25 | $60

*410 Saratoga Ave. (Kiely Blvd.), San Jose, 408-296-3730*

■ This "superlative" San Jose "butterfly" is "cocooned in a uninspiring nest of streets", but it emerges on the strength of chef Scott Cooper's "original" and "sublime" New French tasting menus, an "excellent wine cellar", a "charming", "subdued" interior and an "enthusiastic" (if sometimes "mixed-up") staff that takes you "gently under its wings"; be prepared to "hold the pinkie high", for it's Sand Hill dining at "Beverly Hills prices."

### Le Petit Robert L S M   19 | 16 | 17 | $32

*2300 Polk St. (Green St.), 415-922-8100*

☑ Pascal Rigo (whose empire includes Chez Nous and Galette) continues his Gallic sprawl with this "charming" yet "lively" new corner bistro on Polk named for the French dictionary; the menu features affordable classics such as "wonderful onion soup" and a passel of "small plates to share"; while the "atmosphere is charming", you might "need a hearing aid" afterward, and the "friendly" staff can be "forgetful" at times.

### LE POISSON JAPONAIS S M   27 | 16 | 20 | $51

*642 Ramona St. (bet. Forest & Hamilton Aves.), Palo Alto, 650-330-1147*

☑ In a town "ruled by computer nerds", you gotta give Wolfgang Puck protégés Kenji Seki (with "his wild suits") and chef Naoki Uchiyama credit for their effort "at making Palo Alto hip"; they succeed fairly well at this "nouvelle Japanese" that brings "artful and inventive" exotic fish dishes (including "miso-glazed sea bass that's out of this world") and "an extensive sake list to wash it down with"; however, for "Internet-bubble prices", many expect more than "miniscule portions" and a "narrow, noisy layout."

### Le Soleil **L** **S** **M**     19 | 10 | 15 | $22
*133 Clement St. (bet. 2nd & 3rd Aves.), 415-668-4848*

■ "Be prepared to be blown away by fab Vietnamese food at bargain prices" smile soleil-worshipers about their "favorite place on all of Clement Street"; despite an "atmosphere-less", "fluorescent-lit" interior ("bring your sunglasses"), the "fresh creative fare" is just the ticket when "you don't want to wait for a table" at "the bigger-name" places but want something way "better than the grease-pot" pho joints.

### Le Zinc **L** **S** **M**     ▽ 12 | 16 | 11 | $35
*4063 24th St. (bet. Castro & Noe Sts.), 415-647-9400*

◪ From the antique zinc bar to the red leather banquettes, this continuously serving Noe Valley nouveau comer seems a *très* authentic "French bistro"/wine bar – as it should, given that the husband and wife behind it were restaurateurs in France; advocates find the fare "amazing", but enemies argue there are "a few kinks to work out": "reliving Paris [here] means surly waiters" and "unexceptional food."

### Lhasa Moon **L** **S**     ▽ 15 | 14 | 19 | $22
*2420 Lombard St. (bet. Divisadero & Scott Sts.), 415-674-9898*

■ Consuming "warm butter tea", "various kinds of momos" (dumplings) and other "traditional Tibetan food" while being "watched over by a photo of the Dalai Lama" is guaranteed to make you "feel like you've made a trek" to Lhasa when you've only migrated to the Marina; "it's a great introduction to an exotic cuisine", though – some wistfully say – "not as weird as I thought it was gonna be."

### Liberty Cafe & Bakery **L** **S**     23 | 18 | 21 | $28
*410 Cortland Ave. (bet. Bennington & Wool Sts.), 415-695-8777*

■ "A glass of wine, a chicken pot pie and thou" is all fans of this "homey-but-hip" "postage stamp of a place" could ever wish for – though in truth "everything made with dough" on the New American menu exemplifies "tummy-warming comfort food at its best"; however, this "cozy neighborhood place" "has a reputation outside of Bernal Heights" and it takes "no rezzies", so "expect to wait" (though a "friendly" staff and the wine bar/bakery in the "cottage out back make that fairly pleasant").

### Lion & Compass **L** **M**     19 | 18 | 19 | $40
*1023 N. Fair Oaks Ave. (Weddell Dr.), Sunnyvale, 408-745-1260*

■ "An oasis of fine dining" in Sunnyvale, this 20-year-old "Silicon Valley icon" with an "open tropical flair" may be "less crowded than in its heyday", but it's "still earning its reputation" as "*the* power-broker restaurant" whose "solid" New American meals are "good for makin' high-tech deals" – just ask "the good ol' boys" who hang here to "see and be seen" at lunch or at the bar.

### Lisa Hemenway's Bistro ▣Ⓜ  22 | 19 | 23 | $37
*Town & Country Shopping Ctr., 1612 Terrace Way (Town & Country Dr.), Santa Rosa, 707-526-5111*
▣ Run by a "locally famous chef with some unique ideas", this Asian–New French gets "an uneven dining report card" from Santa Rosa patrons: friends find "everything here is letter-perfect", from "the quote painted on the beams" to its "well-executed menu" to the "staff that makes strangers feel as welcome as regulars", but tough graders say the food is "just not as creative or consistent" "as it once was."

### Little Joe's ▣Ⓢ  18 | 11 | 16 | $20
*523 Broadway (bet. Columbus Ave. & Kearny St.), 415-433-4343* Ⓜ
*2642 Ocean Ave. (bet. Junipero Serra Blvd. & 19th Ave.), 415-564-8200*
■ This North Beach "old-timer" "on the verge of the red-light district" (and its younger Sunset sibling) continues its third decade of delivering "solid old-fashioned Italian food and plenty of it" at a "reasonable price" in an "unpretentious" setting "complete with red-checked vinyl tablecloths"; although it definitely "falls into the dive category", it remains a "favorite" among average Joes who love to "watch the cooking action while sitting at the counter."

### Little River Inn ⓈⓂ  21 | 21 | 22 | $35
*Little River Inn, 7901 Shoreline Hwy./Hwy. 1 (Little River Airport Rd.), Little River, 707-937-5942*
■ After a day of golf or tooling around Mendocino village, head to this "romantic" resort where "chef Silver Canul's Mexican roots add a touch of innovation and spice" to the Californian menu served in the "lovely dining room that overlooks an immaculate garden"; weekend "brunches are just as wonderful", though some prefer "pulling up a stool" at the Ole's Whale Watch bar, which has a "less pricey menu" and a "beautiful view of the surf."

### Little Shin Shin ▣ⓈⓂ  17 | 8 | 16 | $19
*4258 Piedmont Ave. (bet. Linda Rd. & Pleasant Valley Ave.), Oakland, 510-658-9799*
▣ "A strong local following" fawns this is the "best Chinese in the East Bay" ("life would be incomplete without Shin Shin special prawns"), but sophisticates shun the hype, saying it's "solid but not outstanding" ("prices are higher than average and the serving sizes are smaller – welcome to Piedmont Avenue"); either way, "be prepared to wait", as it's "where the families go after the kids' soccer games" and the usually "attentive" "service can get harried."

### Liverpool Lil's ◑▣ⓈⓂ  15 | 17 | 18 | $25
*2942 Lyon St. (bet. Greenwich & Lombard Sts.), 415-921-6664*
■ "The neighborhood regulars" who frequent this "cozy" Cow Hollow "English-style pub" "probably want it kept a

secret", but "people from across the city" already know of its "great distraction of a decor" (historical "pictures on every square inch of the walls"); "it's better for drinking than eating" – "it's a pub, for God's sake" – but it'll do if you "stick to the simple stuff" (burgers and such).

### LoCoCo's Restaurant & Pizzeria S  21 | 11 | 19 | $20
*1400 Shattuck Ave. (Rose St.), Berkeley, 510-843-3745* L
*4270 Piedmont Ave. (Echo Ave.), Oakland, 510-652-6222*
■ Though "really small", these East Bay veterans "pack a big kick" in the "this-is-terrific department"; while "they're known for their killer" pies (the anchovy, artichoke heart and green onion "special is a monument to pizza"), the other "nothing-fancy", "filling" "Southern Italian dishes" also get a nod; however, "in-the-know regulars" "hate to see it in the *Survey* – it will just make the lines longer."

### L'Olivier L M  20 | 18 | 21 | $42
*465 Davis Ct. (Jackson St.), 415-981-7824*
◪ Although it's been around since 1978, this "homely French's" "hidden" location "close to the Embarcadero Center" makes it "still a relatively undiscovered gem"; it's "a step back in time" to days of "quiet and relaxing" atmosphere, "gracious service" and "consistently" "honest food" (plus "awesome soufflés"); admittedly, "the old decor needs some updating", but "it's nice to be able to get into such a decent place at a moment's notice."

### Lorca S  – | – | – | E
*3200 24th St. (S. Van Ness Ave.), 415-550-7510*
Named for an icon of the Spanish Civil War, this "mellow" newcomer is "what you would expect to find in Madrid or San Sebastian", not "a developing area of the Mission"; "the intimate back dining room" offers "excellent contemporary Spanish cuisine" (e.g. oxtail croquettes rather than "your typical tired paella"), while the "front bar" serves "tasty tapas" and "loud" "live music" on weekends.

### L'Osteria del Forno L S M  22 | 13 | 17 | $23
*519 Columbus Ave. (bet. Green & Union Sts.), 415-982-1124*
■ In "authentic osteria" fashion, "everything comes from the oven (*al forno*)" at this "nook" "right on Columbus Avenue"; the "inexpensive" Italian menu is equally *minuscolo* ("the specials double the [number of] offerings"), but the thin-crust pizza and milk-braised roast pork "can be off-the-charts good"; just expect a wait, as "there are only 10 tables and one overwhelmed waitress"; N.B. open all day.

### Lotus Cuisine of India L S M  20 | 16 | 19 | $26
*704 Fourth St. (bet. Lincoln & Tamalpais Aves.), San Rafael, 415-456-5808*
■ "Great breads from the tandoori, excellent curries" and other "yummy" eats meted out by an "anxious-to-please"

"Indian staff" all curry favor with clients who declare this San Rafael dal house naanpareil "in the North Bay"; while budget bingers favor the "$7.45 buffet lunch" for the "great value", romantic reviewers prefer "dinner time, when they open the [retractable] roof and you're dining with the stars."

### Lovejoy's Tea Room L S　　　20　22　21　$20
*1351 Church St. (Clipper St.), 415-648-5895*

■ Chicks craving a cuppa and "guys who are in touch with their feminine side" love this "fabulous English tearoom" in Noe Valley "that recalls your wacky old auntie's parlor, with fringed lampshades and charmingly mismatched china"; a "friendly staff makes it a nice alternative to the pretentious Nob Hill" places, so if you like your "dainty finger sandwiches" with a spot "of funkiness", "then it will be your cup of tea."

### Lucy's Restaurant, Bar & Bakery L S M　　　▽ 18　18　15　$24
*6948 Sebastopol Ave. (bet. Main St. & Petaluma Ave.), Sebastopol, 707-829-9713*

◪ It boasts a "new location", new chef and newly added bar, but this Sebastopol standby is still the same Cal-Med hippie hangout, serving "breads baked on the premises" and "excellent pizzas topped with wonderfully fresh ingredients from the [organic] garden"; however, some snipe "they're still getting used to" all the changes ("service is a little shaky, and timing in the kitchen is off").

### Luna Park L S M　　　21　16　17　$28
*694 Valencia St. (18th St.), 415-553-8584*

◪ "Prepare to scream" at this splitting-at-the-seams "hip spot" "within walking distance of Mission bars", not only because the French-Italian (among other cuisines) "comfort food" is "amazing" and "doesn't require a fat checkbook" but also because the "out-of-hand" bar scene necessitates "a megaphone to whisper to your companions"; "even with reservations", the waits are amusement-park length, but after "blue-ribbon tuna poke" and "make-your-own s'mores", "how can you not like this place?"

### MacCallum House S M　　　23　23　23　$38
*MacCallum House Inn, 45020 Albion St. (Lansing St.), Mendocino, 707-937-5763*

■ Both "hungers and moods are wonderfully satisfied" at "the 'MacHouse'", a historic "seaside home" turned B&B in Mendocino village; "chef-owner Alan Kantor is nuts about choosing the penultimate purveyor" for his "stunningly good" "North Coast cuisine", served by a "very friendly staff"; while "you can dine in the old Victorian rooms and gaze at the Bay or the garden", "locals belly up to the bar" where they "lie on a humpback sofa and have their lovers feed them succulent" yet "cheaper" fare.

### Maddalena's & Café Fino **L M**    20 | 19 | 22 | $40
*544 Emerson St. (bet. Hamilton & University Aves.), Palo Alto,*
*650-326-6082*
■ For "an old-time romantic night out" on the town, Palo
Altans go either to Fred Maddalena's namesake "traditional,
elegant" Continental-Italian establishment or to the affiliated
1920s-like "NY-style supper club" that hosts nightly
cabaret shows next door; the restaurant's been a Peninsula
bastion for "gourmet" dining nearly that long, thanks to the
"charming maitre d'" who, "upon request, will cater to every
need, including private rooms and private entrances"; "great
entertainment" gives the cafe a "livelier atmosphere."

### Madrona Manor **S M**    25 | 25 | 24 | $55
*Madrona Manor Wine Country Inn, 1001 Westside Rd.*
*(W. Dry Creek Rd.), Healdsburg, 707-433-4231*
■ The most "manorly" of experiences can be had at this
1881 "grand Victorian" mansion outside Healdsburg: from
chef Jesse Malgren's (ex Stars) "exquisite" Cal-French fare
(employing ingredients plucked from the grounds' garden) to
the "exceptional" staff working a series of "homely elegant"
candlelit rooms, everything is "impeccable across the
board"; P.S. "if possible, stay overnight at the beautiful inn."

### Maharani **L S M**    ▽ 19 | 18 | 15 | $27
*1122 Post St. (bet. Polk St. & Van Ness Ave.), 415-775-1988*
◨ "Super-hot" curries "are the standouts" at this Polk Street
palace offering a bit of Bangalore by the Bay; perhaps you
can get "better Indian elsewhere for a fraction of the price",
but modern-day maharanis and maharajas moan "once
you are spoiled by eating like royalty in the pink room,
you'll never go elsewhere" – this is by "far one of the most
romantic restaurants" around ("just ask my wife, I proposed
to her there").

### Maki **L S**    24 | 16 | 21 | $33
*Japan Ctr., 1825 Post St. (Webster St.), 415-921-5215*
◨ Although the "place is puny" ("reservations are a must"),
this "secluded" Japan Center spot begets a big score for
its "dainty flavors that show you Japanese food doesn't
start and end with sushi"; but while the *wappa-meshi*
(wood bowls of meat or vegetables and steamed rice) is
"unique", it's "somewhat expensive for what you get" sniff
skeptics feeling squeezed by the "cramped quarters."

### Mama's on
### Washington Square **L S ⇆**    22 | 15 | 14 | $18
*1701 Stockton St. (Filbert St.), 415-362-6421*
■ "Tourists and early-morning yuppies with their papers"
wait around Washington Square Park to get into this
"campy", "cafeteria-style" coffee shop that whips up
what worshipers consider the "best" "gut-busting"
American "breakfasts and brunches in town" ("specialty

breads made into French toast", "massive omelets");
while "it's not cheap", most would happily "stand in line all
day to eat" here – though, alas, mama only serves till 3 PM.

### Mama's Royal Cafe ⚫🅂🅜✄　　20　13　14　$15
*4012 Broadway (40th St.), Oakland, 510-547-7600*
▧ Sure, "the front of this" "funky" Oakland "old-fashioned
diner" "looks like a fire drill", what with all the "crowds of
hipsters" waiting "an hour" for a seat; "the tattooed and
pierced staff serves up a lot of attitude with your food", but
the "great breakfast dishes of all kinds" (from "the best
eggs Benedict" to "the tasty tofu scramble") are "really so
much better in every way than my mama's" (and so is the
really "good coffee").

### Mandalay ⚫🅂🅜　　▽ 21　13　16　$20
*4348 California St. (6th Ave.), 415-386-3895*
■ The "excellent Burmese food" "tastes like one is in
Rangoon" instead of Inner Richmond at this large "no-
frills" "favorite" that also offers "Chinese and other Asian"
fare; a burst of Bengalese bric-a-brac punctuates the
otherwise stark room, but for those who find the ambiance
"a bit [too] funky", "takeout is better."

### Mandarin, The ⚫🅂🅜　　19　21　19　$35
*Ghirardelli Sq., 900 North Point St. (bet. Larkin & Polk Sts.),*
*415-673-8812*
▧ Boasting "sumptuous" "*Flower Drum Song* decor" and a
"magnificent" view of the Bay, this "upscale Chinese"
perched on its throne above Ghirardelli Square is "a good
place" to take visitors, but given that the "acceptable"
fare commands "prices only fit for tourists", some suggest
that this "once-great" ("those *Playboy* awards for cuisine
are now sagging") Mandarin suffers from a case of the
emperor's new clothes.

### Mangiafuoco 🅂　　22　19　20　$30
*1001 Guerrero St. (22nd St.), 415-206-9881*
■ Missionites take their main squeeze to this "intimate
(read: cramped)", "quirky" Northern Italian where "the
aromas from the [open] kitchen bombard your senses and
the adorable waiters" – who act "just off the boat from
Rome" – "will keep your date on his best behavior"; the
cuisine includes "sublime pastas" and "special sauces"
"that you won't find on every menu in North Beach."

### Manka's Inverness Lodge 🅂🅜　▽ 23　26　19　$59
*30 Callendar Way (Argyle St.), Inverness, 415-669-1034*
▧ "Ralph Lauren meets Chez Panisse" at this "cozy",
"eccentric" 1917 hunting lodge ("watch for the world's
hugest dog to wander through at dinnertime"); from the
Sonoma greens to the Tomales Bay oysters, nothing on the
"passionately prepared" prix fixe comes from more than

30 minutes away, and "many items are cooked in an open fireplace"; although "it's a little too gamey" "for the PETA crowd" and "service is sometimes spacey", it's a "perfect getaway" "near Point Reyes National Seashore."

### Manora's Thai Cuisine L S M　　23 | 14 | 17 | $22
*1600 Folsom St. (12th St.), 415-861-6224*
■ "For the best of Thailand" "without buying a plane ticket to Bangkok", "native San Franciscans" depend on this SoMa "favorite" where the kitchen "excels at dishes that can be hit-or-miss at many" a competitor; "other perks include [easy] parking and no wait (ever)", prompting "sentimental" surveyors to sigh "I grew up eating Manora's and will probably bring my kids as well."

### Manzanita S　　23 | 18 | 21 | $43
*336 Healdsburg Ave. (North St.), Healdsburg, 707-433-8111*
◪ At this Healdsburg haven, stacks of Manzanita timber tip you off that the "best items" on the "constantly changing and clever Med menu" are from the "wood-fired oven" that dominates the room ("the flatbread in particular inspires severe cravings"); the addition of a "world-class savvy wine list" ("one of the few in Sonoma that has great European" vintages) causes most to call this freshman a "wonderful find", but frigid types fuss that the "decor's too cold" and everything else is "overhyped" and "overrated."

### Marché　　▽ 26 | 24 | 25 | $56
*898 Santa Cruz Ave. (University Dr.), Menlo Park, 650-324-9092*
■ Co-owner Howard Bulka takes up the toque at this "new kid on the block" that groupies gush is "the greatest thing to hit Menlo Park since sliced bread"; as the name implies, the "superb", slightly "limited" New French "menu changes daily" based on the bounty of the local markets, and it's dished up by an "inviting staff" in a "serene, sophisticated" dining room; while "the windows looking into the kitchen are entertainment for foodies who love to watch", a private chef's table is also available "for groups of six or more."

### Marché aux Fleurs L　　▽ 24 | 17 | 23 | $45
*23 Ross Common (off Lagunitas Rd.), Ross, 415-925-9200*
■ For "a little Provence in little Ross", fans march over to this "delightful" "hideaway" known for its "spectacular New French food" meted out by "servers who know your name" and an "affordable wine list focusing on family vineyards" that "you'll never be able to find again"; perhaps "portions are relatively" *petit,* but all is forgiven "sitting out on the wonderful patio" "perfectly placed under the trees."

### Marica S M　　– | – | – | M
*5301 College Ave. (Bryant Ave.), Oakland, 510-985-8388*
Longtime East Bay favorite son Christopher Cheung has re-emerged at this Oakland newcomer named for a Greek

water nymph; the kitchen specializes in fresh seafood, such as blackened tuna or the signature twice-cooked lobster, prepared with the chef's unique New French–Asian sensibility, while his wife oversees the friendly service in the diminutive blue-and-yellow dining room.

### Marin Joe's ◑ L S M
18 | 10 | 18 | $28

*1585 Casa Buena Dr. (south of Tamalpais Dr.), Corte Madera, 415-924-2081*

◪ "One of the last of the original Joes", an "old-style heavy Italian" chain also known for broiled "huge hamburgers" (go figure), this "Marin favorite" exists "in a time warp", "since it opened" back in 1954; while it offers a "good food-value ratio", neither the leather-boothed interior nor the Decor score has improved with age ("feels like an upgraded Denny's"); still, night-owls note that "if it weren't for" its late service, "we'd all have to go to bed at 9 in this county."

### Marinus S M
▽ 29 | 24 | 27 | $59

*Bernardus Lodge, 415 Carmel Valley Rd. (Laureles Grade Rd.), Carmel, 831-658-3500*

■ For an epicurean evening that "can't be beat", this lodge locale is "a must for serious foodies" "when visiting the Carmel area"; "what could be better" than Cal Stamenov's "stunning" "Californian cuisine, New French style" coupled with an "impressive and intimidating wine list" (1,400 varietals deep) and "detailed service" ("all we had to do was think about something and our server appeared with it"); "for a treat, ask to sit in front of the [12-ft.-wide limestone] fireplace" that dominates the "elegant dining room."

### Mario's Bohemian Cigar Store Cafe L S M ⇗
19 | 14 | 14 | $15

*566 Columbus Ave. (Union St.), 415-362-0536*

◪ "Hey, man", this "quintessential SF cafe" is the place to "spend a few unpressured hours" and remember what it felt "like when North Beach was all poets"; the "authentic old-world" Northern Italian eats ("ethereal meatball focaccia sandwiches") "will make you drool and feel cool, especially if you nab the corner table along Washington Square Park", but "service can switch from friendly to feisty depending on the hour."

### Marnee Thai L S M
24 | 14 | 14 | $21

*2225 Irving St. (bet. 23rd & 24th Aves.), 415-665-9500*

◪ What spurs Sunset citizens to suggest that this Siamese is "the best Thai in the city" is "partly the amazing food" and partly the "stand-up routine by owner Marnee"; while there's no quibbling over the dishes "from her home village", "she'll either read your fortune or irritate you throughout the meal"; in either event, expect to "stand in line on the sidewalk" for a while and then have a "cramped", "hurried" experience once in.

### Martini House ▯▯▯ | 24 | 26 | 22 | $51 |
*1245 Spring St. (bet. Hwy. 29/Main & Oak Sts.), St. Helena, 707-963-2233*

■ Co-owner "Pat Kuleto does it again" at this "converted Craftsman house"; boasting a "cozy river-rock fireplace", "the downstairs bar is *the* happening scene in St. Helena", but the entire "rustic" setting is "an appropriate showcase" for executive chef Todd Humphries (ex Campton Place), who presents "thoughtful", "inventive" New American dishes of locally foraged ingredients; they're accompanied by "an awesome wine list" featuring both international vintages and regional heavy-hitters.

### MASA'S | 28 | 26 | 27 | $83 |
*Hotel Vintage Court, 648 Bush St. (bet. Powell & Stockton Sts.), 415-989-7154*

■ With "Ron Siegal at the stoves", there's "never a wrong bite or a wrong move" at this Downtown special-occasion "classic"; his "beyond-fabulous" New French tasting menus are "the pinnacle of SF dining", "with a mind-blowing wine list to complement"; the "first-class service" is almost as "impeccable", while the redone decor, "a mix of clean lines and warm tones", is merely "the city's most elegant"; sure, the scary tabs are for those "without pocket problems", but you can't put a price on "consummate greatness."

### Mas Sake ▯ | 13 | 13 | 13 | $31 |
*2030 Lombard St. (bet. Fillmore & Webster Sts.), 415-440-1505 ▯*
*260 S. California Ave. (Birch St.), Palo Alto, 650-321-6447*

▰ This "hoppin'" "Marina pick-up scene" ("made famous by Don Johnson's indiscretions") and its new Palo Alto sibling lure "raucous twentysomethings" with "bizarre creations" such as "'freestyle rolls' – tortillas cut like sushi rolls at sushi prices", lethal "sake bomb" libations and "all-you-can-eat" raw-fish happy hours; but negatives just say "no mas", arguing the Japanese-Mexican fare "is like the clientele – shallow and loose" and asking "if you're not there for the waitresses in their midriffs, then why go?"

### Massawa ▯▯ | ▽ 21 | 9 | 15 | $15 |
*1538 Haight St. (bet. Ashbury & Clayton Sts.), 415-621-4129*

▰ "You eat with your hands and leave with a full, full belly" at this "low-key" wallet-friendly Haight Street spot, named for an "Eritrean port city"; the *injera* bread to sop up "hot and spicy" meat stews is "really delicious", but the "plain decor" could use an "injection" of pizzazz; the "service is as sweet as the fresh guava juice", but it's "slow", so you "can't be in a hurry."

### Ma Tante Sumi ▯▯ | 25 | 20 | 23 | $38 |
*4243 18th St. (bet. Castro & Diamond Sts.), 415-626-7864*

■ "While everyone wonders why this" "tranquil", "refined and romantic" place "isn't well known" outside the Castro, they're "glad, as it allows them to get in the door"; chef Brenda Buenviaje's (top toque at the late Oritalia) "exciting combinations of Cal-Franco-Asian fusion" "are every bit as good as" the usual "city-foodie" spots "at a fraction of the price"; plus, a staff that is "pleasant without hovering" makes it feel "more like having dinner at a friend's house than eating out."

### MatrixFillmore ●🅂Ⓜ ∇ 16 | 24 | 14 | $33

*3138 Fillmore St. (Greenwich St.), 415-563-4180*

■ PlumpJack restaurateurs have transformed this former Cow Hollow hippie hangout into an "LA wanna-be"-like cocktail lounge for the "Triangle scene" with "cool" *Wallpaper*\* decor – overstuffed Louis XVI couches, a Jenga-like cement fireplace and giant plasma TVs; while it's "more of a liquid (drinking) routine" "than a real dining establishment", executive chef James Ormsby has created just enough "excellent New American appetizers" to keep the mojitos from going to your head.

### Matterhorn Swiss Restaurant 🅂 20 | 18 | 18 | $35

*2323 Van Ness Ave. (bet. Green & Vallejo Sts.), 415-885-6116*

■ At this little "wedge of the Alps" on Van Ness, "the only thing missing is the yodeler"; all else is here: the "Swiss chalet decor", "waitresses in [traditional] attire" and "fun with fondue"; although it's a romantic spot "for two", "the more the merrier, since you can experiment with meat, cheese and various dessert" variations; although a few fume it's "too much work on my part for the price", most deem it "the place" to "stuff your face."

### Maurice Restaurant & Lounge 🅂 − | − | − | M

*312 Divisadero St. (bet. Oak & Page Sts.), 415-431-0712*

With comfy couches and a small, hip bar area, caterer-cum-restaurateur Maurice Mogannam has created a "cheap and cheerful" "welcome addition" to the Lower Haight; the kitchen serves up "consistently good" "homey" American eats with a dash of eastern Med (falafel-encrusted chicken with hummus gravy shares the menu with good ol' meatloaf), and nothing is priced over $15.

### MAX'S 🅛Ⓜ 15 | 13 | 14 | $22

*1 California St. (Market St.), 415-781-6297*
*555 California St., Concourse Level (bet. Kearny & Montgomery Sts.), 415-788-6297*
*Union Sq., 398 Geary St. (Mason St.), 415-646-8600* 🅂
*311 Third St. (Folsom St.), 415-546-6297* 🅂
*601 Van Ness Ave. (Golden Gate Ave.), 415-771-7301* 🅂
*1250 Old Bayshore Hwy. (Broadway), Burlingame, 650-342-6297* 🅂
*60 Madera Blvd. (Hwy. 101), Corte Madera, 415-924-6297* 🅂

(continued)

(continued)
**MAX'S**
*Oakland City Ctr., 500 12th St. (bet. Broadway & Clay Sts.),*
*Oakland, 510-451-6297*
*Stanford Shopping Ctr., 711 Stanford Shopping Ctr. (Sand Hill Rd.),*
*Palo Alto, 650-323-6297* **S**
*1001 El Camino Real (James Ave.), Redwood City,*
*650-365-6297* **S**
☑ When you want "NYC-style" "comfort food", these
"dependable haute delis" are the "closest thing to [Jewish]
in the Bay Area"; service and decor vary at each outpost, but
"you can rely" on the "same old shtick" for all: "ridiculously
huge" servings – e.g. "macaroons that look like one of
Madonna's old bras" – "guaranteed to expand the waistline"
but not "bust your budget"; still, the maxed-out moan
"quantity trumps quality" – "who needs such portions?"

**Max's Diamond**      –| –| –| **M** |
**Bar & Grill** **L** **S** **M**
*128 King St. (bet. 2nd & 3rd Sts.), 415-896-6297*
Everything's oversized at the fast-growing Max's chain,
and this latest link, a sprawling 400-seater with four floors
located just a fly ball away from Pac Bell Park, is no different;
owner Dennis Berkowitz has packed the American menu
with the usual suspects – huge deli sandwiches and kosher-
style noshes – but has also added a mess of barbecue and
dry-aged steaks; N.B. opens at 10 AM on game days.

**Maya** **L** **S** **M**     ▽ 18| 19| 15| $26|
*101 E. Napa St. (1st St. E.), Sonoma, 707-935-3500*
■ This "upscale Mexican" located in a 150-year-old stone
building "close to the Sonoma square" offers Yucatan-style
dinners that "make good use of spices and fruit"; however,
what really gets surveyors to shout are the offerings made
at the Temple of Tequila bar, including the "yum-yum"
house lemonade and the "best fresh-squeezed", "hand-
shaken margaritas" "in town."

**Maya** **L** **S** **M**     22| 20| 19| $40|
*303 Second St. (Harrison St.), 415-543-2928*
☑ "*Ay caramba!*" cry amigos of this "upmarket" place
south of Market – "this is what Mexican food must taste
like in heaven"; for most, the combination of south-of-the-
border fare "taken to a new level" ("do not come here
expecting burritos"), "tequila galore" and "hammered silver
water pitchers" adds up to an "elegant, refined" experience
(albeit "service could use some oomph"); but peso-pinchers
"can't get over paying so much for guac and chips."

**Mayflower** **L** **S** **M**     22| 11| 14| $24|
*6255 Geary Blvd. (27th Ave.), 415-387-8338*
■ "Great dim sum" ("heaven in a noodle wrapper") and
"fine" "fresh seafood (just look at the tanks)" are "the real

deal in Chinese food" at this "crowded" Richmond behemoth "where tourists are few" but "families are numerous"; "service is far from perfect" (you gotta work around the "language barrier"), and although "the live geoducks at the entrance may intrigue and gross out at the same time", at least they provide distraction while you wait for a table on "crowded weekends."

### Maykedah ▯▯▯                          23 | 18 | 20 | $30

*470 Green St. (bet. Grant Ave. & Kearny St.), 415-362-8286*
■ "One of the only and best Persian restaurants in the city", this North Beach kebab house is perennially "popular" with "adventurous" diners eager to celebrate "a meat festival with huge skewers of lamb, beef and chicken" ("we can't believe how much we can eat when we're here"); oddly, "the decor is Euro '80s swank, but somehow it fits the place"; P.S. "parking is hellacious", so the valet is much valued.

### McCormick & Kuleto's ▯▯▯              18 | 22 | 19 | $38

*Ghirardelli Sq., 900 North Point St. (bet. Larkin & Polk Sts.), 415-929-1730*
▨ Offering a "stadium-style seating arrangement" that ensures "incredible views of the Bay" and Alcatraz, this chain link "has tourist destination written all over it" (expect a "constant flash [from cameras] trying to recreate the postcard" panorama); the "reliable seafood" is "a cut above" other Fisherman's Wharf spots, fans find; still, snipers suggest you go at lunch or "at sunset", because once "it's dark", it "is less than remarkable."

### mc² ▯▯                                19 | 22 | 18 | $46

*470 Pacific Ave. (bet. Montgomery & Sansome Sts.), 415-956-0666*
▨ With decor that "feels more like an art gallery than a restaurant", this "modernist" Downtowner has a "new chef" (Todd Davies), but it still hasn't made any quantum leaps; while the old "yupscale [fusion] cuisine" has been jettisoned for a more "earthy" Californian–New French focus and admirers applaud "great wines, with glasses charged by the ounce", irritated experimenters say the service and "price-value ratio" need to return to the drawing board.

### Meadowood Grill ▯▯▯                   21 | 22 | 23 | $44

*Meadowood Resort, 900 Meadowood Ln. (Howell Mountain Rd., off Silverado Trail), St. Helena, 707-963-3646*
▨ "Located in the plush Meadowood Resort", this Californian's "view from the terrace" "overlooking the croquet field", paired with "professional service", "puts you in such a state that they could serve cold hot dogs and it would be a great meal"; happily, the "food is much better than that", and though some sniff "it's not quite worth the dollar", the wine list (strong on Napa Valley bottlings) helps ensure a "relaxing atmosphere."

## Mecca ⑤Ⓜ | 18 | 22 | 17 | $41 |

*2029 Market St. (bet. Dolores & 14th Sts.), 415-621-7000*
■ This "noisy", "swanky" supper club on Upper Market offers "a bit of New York in SF" with a live DJ and an illuminated bar that's ground zero for "people-watching" and "foofy drinks"; it's a "great scene (even if you are straight)", and there's "yummy" New American fare (with Asian accents) and service "as yummy as the food" "to go along with it"; P.S. if you're so inclined, "make sure to catch the drag shows on Sunday night."

## Meetinghouse, The ⑤Ⓜ | 24 | 21 | 23 | $43 |

*1701 Octavia St. (Bush St.), 415-922-6733*
☑ You'll "feel like you're in New England", not Pacific Heights, at this snug "storefront" thanks to its "fabulous" modern yet "quintessential American home cooking" that stars "orgasmic" "just-made biscuits" (available to go), as well as a "simple Quaker setting" and a "congenial staff"; "the only drawback is there's no bar or waiting area" during "interminable waits"; still, it's "so good they should call it the Eatinghouse."

## Mei Long ⓁⓈⓂ | 21 | 17 | 19 | $31 |

*867 E. El Camino Real (bet. Bernardo Ave. & Hwy. 85), Mountain View, 650-961-4030*
☑ "Don't mention too loudly what a wonderful place this is" whisper wowed fans of this "upscale" Mountain View Mandarin "hidden in a strip mall", adding the combination of "high-quality dishes" and "interesting wine-by-the-glass pairings" "beautifully presented" by a "polite staff" "is a cut above your typical Chinese"; however, the less impressed lament that pricey portions and "slow service" are "not quite as good as the raves would indicate."

## Mel Hollen's
## Bar & Fine Dining ⓁⓈⓂ | – | – | – | M |

*673 Union St. (Powell St.), 415-434-2900*
Former Dallas restaurateur Mel Hollen (of that town's Mel Hollen's and Jaxx Cafe) and Dallas Cowboys "former quarterback great" Craig Morton have teamed to open this North Beach venue; the 100-seat space is bedecked with "tons of sports memorabilia", including mementos of Mickey Mantle, a Hollen buddy; the menu is straight-up Traditional American – hand-carved hot turkey sandwiches for lunch, "large, quality steaks" and chops at dinner.

## Mel's Drive-In ◑ⓁⓈⓂ | 11 | 14 | 13 | $16 |

*3355 Geary Blvd. (bet. Beaumont & Parker Aves.), 415-387-2255*
*2165 Lombard St. (Steiner St.), 415-921-2867*
*801 Mission St. (4th St.), 415-227-4477*
*Richelieu Hotel, 1050 Van Ness Ave. (Geary St.), 415-292-6357*
☑ "*Happy Days*" are here again at this string of diners with "flashback soda fountains", jukeboxes and "kids' meals in

cardboard" "'57 Chevys"; it's "overrun with tourists" by day
and "the after-hours drinking crowd at 2 AM", however
while the "purely forgettable food" (stick to the "regular
ole burgers" and "thick, real ice cream milkshakes") will
"take you back to 1950", it'll run you "2003 prices."

### Memphis Minnie's BBQ Joint L S      20 12 14 $16

*576 Haight St. (Fillmore St.), 415-864-7675*

✓ For 'cue cravers, this "trippy" Lower Haight Street "joint"
smokes up the "closest thing to Texas BBQ they've had in
a long time"; they don't care so much for the "trailer-trash
kitsch interior", but they're pigs in heaven when it comes to
the "tasty" "pulled-pork sandwiches", "melt-in-your-mouth
ribs" and soulful sides (don't forget to "eat your greens").

### Mendo Bistro S M      21 17 19 $29

*301 N. Main St. (Redwood St.), Fort Bragg, 707-964-4974*

■ Chef-owner Nicolas Petty may don a "jester cap", "but
he's dead serious about his" "sophisticated" Med–New
American cooking that's "better than most at a fraction of
the price"; the interactive menu lets you "pick your main
course, its preparation and sauce" (do start with his "award-
winning crab cakes" though); despite its location "in the
Old Company Store", the food, along with the "dedicated,
loyal staff", makes it worth the drive to Fort Bragg.

### Merenda L S      25 19 24 $42

*1809 Union St. (bet. Laguna & Octavia Sts.), 415-346-7373*

■ "Everyone feels like family" at this "fabulous addition to
Cow Hollow"; despite "tight quarters", the "red-walled"
room is quiet, and the "friendly staff is knowledgeable
without being stuffy", but it's chef/co-owner Keith Luce's
(ex PlumpJack) "terrific Northern Italian–Southern French"
"dishes that are the star of the show"; unlike most prix fixe–
only menus, you get to choose the "number of courses", so
it can be "easy on your wallet"; P.S. the "great takeout" deli
counter has now moved around the corner.

### Mescolanza S M      ▽ 20 15 17 $28

*2221 Clement St. (bet. 23rd & 24th Aves.), 415-668-2221*

✓ "This quaint little spot makes you feel like you're dining
in the heart of Italy" (or at least North Beach), but instead
it's "hidden in Little Asia"; it's "bustling on the weekends"
thanks to the "excellent thin-crust pizza", "always-fresh
pasta" and "inviting feel", all of which outweigh the "pretty
tacky decor" and "the wait without a waiting area."

### Mezza Luna L S M      22 17 21 $31

*459 Prospect Way (Capistrano Rd.), Princeton by the Sea,
650-728-8108*

✓ For a taste of the Amalfi Coast on the California Coast,
Luna-tics lunge for this "fun Italian find" in the sleepy fishing

town of Princeton by the Sea, known for its "authentic fare" ("so good" the Food rating has risen) and "generally friendly staff"; although the "noisy", "spartan interior" could use "some sprucing up", day-trippers appreciate the chance to "relax and remember they're out of the city."

### Mezze **L S** ▽ | 19 | 19 | 18 | $29 |
*3407 Lakeshore Ave. (bet. Hwy. 580 & Mandana Blvd.), Oakland, 510-663-2500*

◪ Some suburban sophisticates smile over this "SF-style" sophomore near Lake Merritt that "serves a creative Mediterranean menu"; while many make a full dinner out of the "great meze platter", others praise the place as a "hidden brunch" spot with live music but "no waiting"; still, critics carp "it's been long enough that the 'new restaurant kinks' should be gone by now", and they're not.

### Michelangelo Restaurant Caffe **S M**⇄ | 17 | 15 | 16 | $23 |
*579 Columbus Ave. (Union St.), 415-986-4058*

◪ "Kitschy" and "sardine can"–cramped, this "garliceria" "is a favorite North Beach locale for out-of-towners" and couples on a "cheap date"; from the "family-style seating" to the "meant-to-be-shared" servings of "homestyle Italian fare" to the "huge hunk of Parmesan" and "community bowl of free Gummi Bears" "at the end", "communal" is the watchword here, a "gimmick" that "delights some and puts off others – so you be the judge."

### Mifune **L S M** | 18 | 10 | 13 | $16 |
*Japan Ctr., 1737 Post St. (bet. Buchanan & Webster Sts.), 415-922-0337*

■ "At peak dining hours there's always a line out the door" – "but it moves very fast" – "for huge", "heartwarming" bowls of "fresh and tender" homemade udon and soba (served "hot or cold") at this "dirt-cheap" noodle shop in Japantown; despite the "get in, get out" "perfunctory service" and exposed-"pipe atmosphere", it's "comforting on a cold rainy day or after a movie" at the Kabuki Theater; P.S. go ahead, "it's ok to slurp" (everyone else in the "crowded dining room" does).

### Mikayla at the Casa Madrona **S M** | 23 | 26 | 20 | $46 |
*Casa Madrona Hotel, 801 Bridgeway (San Carlos Ave.), Sausalito, 415-331-5888*

■ Tourists insist "no trip to the Bay Area is complete without a visit" to this "picturesque" Sausalito stalwart with double-take–inspiring "panoramic views" from the dining room (maximized by open picture windows and a retractable roof); the "good, solid Cal-Med cuisine" is worthy of "a second look" as well (particularly the "superb spread" for Sunday brunch).

### Millennium ⓢⓜ　　22　19　22　$35

*Abigail Hotel, 246 McAllister St. (bet. Hyde & Larkin Sts.),
415-487-9800*

■ Chef Eric Tucker's "Vegan Valhalla" pushes the envelope
of what you think food "without animal products" can taste
like (and cost); while it's not everyone's cup of organic tea,
the "innovative, eclectic cuisine" is "appreciated by veg-
heads and carnivores alike", as is the "impeccable service";
surprisingly, even the "funky basement location" (where you
might see Civic Center–goers, "a dreadlocked hippie and
Woody Harrelson all waiting for tables") is deemed "cozy."

### Minako ⓢⓜ　　－　－　－　I

*2154 Mission St. (bet. 17th & 18th Sts.), 415-864-1888*
This homey, seven-table Japanese in the Mission offers a
refreshing contrast to SF's slicker, Tokyo-style sushi joints;
owner Minako hosts the dining room while her mom uses
organic ingredients to prepare comforting country-style fare
that ranges from traditional tempuras to a modern Asian
take on seviche; there are several vegan options too.

### Miramonte　　19　19　19　$38
### Restaurant & Café ⓛⓢⓜ

*1327 Railroad Ave. (bet. Adams & Hunt Sts.), St. Helena,
707-963-1200*

◪ "If you like foods of the Americas" (anything from fish
tostadas to duck burgers) then "you'll love" owner Cindy
Pawlcyn's (Mustards Grill) yearling that whips up "a
creative mix of fare" along with "exotic cocktails" and
"Mexican wines from Baja" in a "bright", "contemporary"
(some say "stark") interior; but while amigos appreciate
this "refreshing change" in the all-"too-touristy mecca" of
St. Helena, enemigos find it "disappointingly" "inconsistent"
considering its pedigree.

### Mirepoix　　－　－　－　E

*275 Windsor River Rd. (Bell Rd.), Windsor, 707-838-0162*
In Mariposa's old place, this New French–New American
newcomer seems "definitely worth a trip" to Windsor say
early-birds who've found it; such "imaginative" specialties
as arctic char with mushrooms, served in a room with
floor-to-ceiling windows or on the seasonal patio, make
for a most "enjoyable" experience.

### Miss Millie's ⓢ　　20　17　14　$25

*4123 24th St. (bet. Castro & Diamond Sts.), 415-285-5598*
◪ Good golly, Miss Millie, your fan club would "wait all
morning for those yummy lemon-ricotta pancakes" and
other "amazing" Sunday brunch items served in a "cute"
"unpretentious setting"; in-the-know Noe Valleyites also
go for the dinners featuring New American "down-home
cookin' with a twist"; still, a sizable minority would give
this a miss, muttering the "food has sass, but the staff is

crass" – as a lowered Service score confirms – and musing are "high prices" for "comfort food" not "a paradox"?

### Mistral L S M  20 19 16 $37
*370-6 Bridge Pkwy. (Marine World Pkwy.), Redwood Shores, 650-802-9222*
◪ This "oasis" "right on the Redwood Shores waterfront" is a "favorite of locals and business folks in the surrounding areas" ("you might spot Oracle CEO Larry Ellison here at lunch"); "the bread that comes out of the oak-fired oven" "is the No. 1 reason to go", but the "good" Cal-Med menu makes an honorable second (unfortunately, "the service always finds new ways of falling short"); the "inside gets noisy" and "crowded around happy hour", so romantics prefer "sitting outside" for an "elegant" dinner.

### Mixx Restaurant L M  22 19 22 $37
*Historic Railroad Sq., 135 Fourth St. (Davis St.), Santa Rosa, 707-573-1344*
◪ This Santa Rosa stalwart "in Railroad Square" "used to be Sonoma County's hot spot" and its "beautiful", "roomy" "old-fashioned bar" *the* "meeting place to wine and dine" (thanks to a "nice vino list featuring local producers"); while many feel the Californian "food is still good", especially if you "trust the staff's recommendations", trendoids mixx things up by dissing the "rude service" and declaring the place "is played out."

### Model Bakery L S  ▽ 24 15 17 $12
*1357 Main St. (bet. Adams & Spring Sts.), St. Helena, 707-963-8192*
■ This St. Helena bakery sporting a "vintage interior" bakes up "the yummiest way to start off the day in Napa Valley" – namely "disgustingly good pastries and coffees" to be consumed at communal tables; locals are equally sweet on the "super soups" and wood-fired, oven-baked pizzas that round out the day's offerings; N.B. closes at 6 PM.

### Moishe's Pippic L M⊅  ▽ 15 5 15 $12
*425A Hayes St. (bet. Gough & Octavia Sts.), 415-431-2440*
◪ In a tiny room crammed with civic paraphernalia, Hayes Valley's Chicago-style "Jewish deli" comes "oh-so-close to the real" thing, offering "the best corned beef sandwich west of" Illinois and "the only Chi-town hot dog in the city" (topped with "amazing relish"); but critics kvetch it's close but no cigar, and the nerve of charging "ballpark prices for ballpark dogs!"

### Moki's Sushi & Pacific Grill S M  – – – M
*830 Cortland Ave. (Gates St.), 415-970-9336*
Moki's knows maki is the consensus at this "funky Bernal Heights" "hangout" featuring "fantastic" fin fare ("the Ecstasy Roll, tempura'd to a crisp shell while the fish inside

is still raw, lives up to its name") and other Pacific Rim options ("coconut fried tofu", anyone?); while "the service can be slow" and "the space is a little crowded", neighbors insist "the food makes up for any other deficiencies."

### MoMo's L S M     15 | 17 | 14 | $33
*760 Second St. (The Embarcadero), 415-227-8660*

◪ There are plenty of "bridge-and-tunnel" sports fans who ask "why not" come to this "fancy watering hole" "across from Pac Bell Park" for drinks, "yummy appetizers" and "great people-watching" "before or after a Giants game"; but the belligerent boo the New American fare is "more so-so than MoMo", the "service is as slow as the pace of a baseball game" (as signaled by a drop in the score) and "the prices hit harder than Barry Bonds."

### Montrio S M     23 | 22 | 20 | $37
*414 Calle Principal (Franklin St.), Monterey, 831-648-8880*

■ Named for the town, plus the trio of cooking influences on the "fabulous" Eclectic menu (Italy, France and America), this "lighthearted" bistro offers a "hip", "high-energy" alternative to the more staid choices "in the heart of Monterey"; it boasts another holy trinity: a wonderfully "wacky" setting (a historic firehouse), an "extensive wine list" and "service that's always willing to help out", so what's not to like?

### Moose's L S M     22 | 21 | 21 | $42
*1652 Stockton St. (bet. Filbert & Union Sts.), 415-989-7800*

■ "Gracious proprietor" "Ed Moose runs a great supper club in the heart of North Beach", "the kind of place to take out-of-towners" "to see what SF is all about"; "you can watch sports" or eyeball the "hoity-toities" inhaling martinis while listening to "live piano jazz" (hey, "you might even see Mayor Brown"); "once you get past the bar scene", "you'll find flavorful, well-prepared" (but "pricey") American fare in a dining room that's especially nice "when the sun streams through the windows from the park."

### Moosse Cafe L S M     22 | 16 | 18 | $33
*Blue Heron Inn, 390 Kasten St. (Albion St.), Mendocino, 707-937-4323*

◪ "In an area with a lot of good food", this Mendocino Californian "set in a redone Victorian [house] with a tiny inn upstairs" and a stunning "garden with ocean view" outside "stands out for its coziness, creativity and deliciousness"; the space is "unfortunately small" and "scrunched" "for such large flavors", "however the staff is lovely."

### Morton's of Chicago S M     23 | 19 | 21 | $55
*400 Post St. (bet. Mason & Powell Sts.), 415-986-5830*

◪ Fat cats "hankering for red meat" "head Downtown" to this "SF branch" of the "high-end" "Chicago-based steak chain" boasting a "clubby" "dark wood–type atmosphere" (made even darker by "no windows") to get a little bit fatter; while the "obscenely large portions" are "not for the faint of stomach" and most would prefer the staff "skip" the "shtick"-like "theatrical presentation", those seeking prime-rib paradise purr it's "heaven."

### Mo's Burgers Ⓛ Ⓜ 20 10 15 $14
*Yerba Buena Gardens, 772 Folsom St. (bet. 3rd & 4th Sts.), 415-957-3779*
### Mo's Grill Ⓛ Ⓢ Ⓜ
*1322 Grant Ave. (bet. Green & Vallejo Sts.), 415-788-3779*
■ Regulars who've had Mo than enough meals here know this "classic diner" duo offers "better burgers than the steaks at most restaurants", plus "awesome shakes" and "great fries"; just be warned, there's "no ambiance" – unless you count the Yerba Buena garden view in SoMa and "the flaming [patties] in the window" at North Beach; P.S. the latter also serves "greasy-spoon breakfasts."

### Moss Beach Distillery Ⓛ Ⓢ Ⓜ 14 18 15 $31
*140 Beach Way (Ocean Blvd.), Moss Beach, 650-728-5595*
◩ For coastal day-trippers, this "low-key" (reputedly haunted) Moss Beach landmark "is worth the drive", thanks to its "incredible views" of "the blue-water ocean" and enough "ghost stories to occupy even a dubious guest"; while some stick to sunset cocktails and snacks on the downstairs "deck while snuggling with a sweetie under the blankets that they provide", others enjoy the well-priced "traditional surf 'n' turf" fare, with a side order of "breathtaking" views from the "beachside setting."

### Mustards Grill Ⓛ Ⓢ Ⓜ 23 18 20 $39
*7399 St. Helena Hwy./Hwy. 29 (Yountville Rd.), Napa, 707-944-2424*
■ Cindy Pawlcyn's "wine-country roadhouse" "broke new ground when it opened" in 1983, and today it still cuts the mustard; her "innovative twists on" New American fare with Asian influences coupled with "knowledgeable servers" (especially "helpful" with the "huge wine list") "make for a fun escapade"; since it lacks Napa's usual "atmospheric prices", it's perennially packed, but you can always have "a quick bite at the bar among local winemakers" ("we sat next to the Mondavis").

### Nan Yang Rockridge Ⓛ Ⓢ 21 14 18 $25
*6048 College Ave. (Claremont Ave.), Oakland, 510-655-3298*
◩ This Rockridge veteran is *the* place in the East Bay for "wonderful Burmese food" (ok, so it's also the only place); the "friendly, knowledgeable staff" will help you navigate the menu, but insiders assure you can't go wrong with anything ("the garlic noodles are to die for, everything else is merely excellent"); however, the "sterile decor" makes many consider it "great for carry-out nights."

### Napa Valley Grille 🅛🅢🅜   19 | 18 | 19 | $37

*Washington Sq., 6795 Washington St. (Madison St.), Yountville, 707-944-8686*

◪ This Yountville chain link has staked a claim with "filling portions" of Californian fare and "easygoing" ambiance that's a "pleasant, less-expensive alternative to the high-priced" Napa eateries; however, while the "all-day menu" and "nice patio" offer a good "bet for lunch", foes find "staff changes in the back of the house" "have made the food inconsistent" (as reflected by a drop in the score) and ask "why waste a night [here] with so many better alternatives."

### Napa Valley Wine Train 🅛🅢🅜   16 | 22 | 19 | $60

*1275 McKinstry St. (bet. 1st St. & Soscol Ave.), Napa, 800-427-4124*

◪ Even "though it's touristy", train buffs say this three-hour excursion on a historic locomotive "through the Napa Valley" is "a wonderful way to spend the afternoon" with "visiting relatives" in tow (especially recommended: "the fun wine-tasting car"); however, some feel taken for a ride by the "standard" Californian cuisine and "premium prices", cracking "clickety-clack, won't go back"; P.S. if you don't want to "bother with their food", there's now a package that includes lunch at the Domaine Chandon winery.

### Navio 🅛🅢🅜   ▽ 19 | 24 | 16 | $54

*Ritz-Carlton Hotel, 1 Miramonte Point Rd. (Hwy. 1), Half Moon Bay, 650-712-7000*

◪ This "stunning" seafooder sequestered in the swanky Ritz-Carlton resort serves up "romance à la carte" (the "great ocean views will sweep you away") along with its "good food"; however, surveyors suggest it "still needs to work the bugs out": while it's long on ambiance, it comes up short on portions (dubbed "not worth" the ritzy prices "they're asking") folks also "wish they could get the service up to drive-thru levels"); N.B. a post-*Survey* chef change many outdate the Food rating.

### Neecha Thai Cuisine 🅛🅢🅜   21 | 13 | 17 | $21

*2100 Sutter St. (Steiner St.), 415-922-9419*

■ While there's plenty of mock meat on the menu (nearly half the options are vegetarian), nobody's mocking the "very good and original food" served at this Pacific Heights Siamese; true, it "looks modest", but it's also "without an attitude or much of a line" and, given the expensive area, a "great value" – "a Thai to stick with", in short.

### Nepenthe 🅛🅢🅜   15 | 24 | 16 | $31

*Hwy. 1 (¼ mi. south of Ventana Inn & Spa), Big Sur, 831-667-2345*

◪ Looking out over the "breathtaking Big Sur coastline" ("it's not uncommon to see the spouts of whales swimming in the ocean"), it's hard to imagine how "Rita Hayworth never took Orson Welles up on his offer of owning" this 1949 cliffside getaway, now "a favorite stopping ground" for day-trippers doing the drive down Highway 1; sure the American bill of fare (hamburgers, etc.) is "priced at twice its worth", but "with a view like this, the food doesn't matter."

### Night Monkey ●ⓈⓂ   _ | _ | _ | M
*2223 Union St. (bet. Fillmore & Steiner Sts.), 415-775-1130*
This new Cow Hollow eatery, run by kitchen vets of Foreign Cinema and Greens, serves up organically inclined, Cal-inspired blue-plate specials such as humanely raised steak with buttermilk smashed potatoes and grilled duck-breast salad with figs; nocturnal noshers can monkey around with the small and large plates until the wee hours, since the kitchen serves late.

### 955 Ukiah ⓈⓂ   22 | 18 | 20 | $36
*955 Ukiah St. (Lansing St.), Mendocino, 707-937-1955*
◪ Arty advocates adore the atelier-like interior "filled with paintings" of this homespun "establishment in Mendocino Village", which specializes in "wonderfully" "innovative" New American–New French fare plucked from "local specialty produce"; dissenters dismiss it as an "overgrown natural-foods cafe", but scores side with supporters who say this "charming" "obscure venue" is well "worth the path placed before you" to reach it.

### Nizza La Bella ⚫ⓈⓂ   19 | 18 | 18 | $29
*825-827 San Pablo Ave. (Solano Ave.), Albany, 510-526-2552*
◪ "You'd swear you were in some chic brasserie in some Mediterranean port" instead of a "rather bleak [stretch of] San Pablo Avenue" at this "snazzy Southern French" bistro, what with its "distinct niçoise flavors", "great zinc bar" and "cozy" atmosphere; "unfortunately, the service can vary from excellent to rude."

### Nob Hill Café ⚫ⓈⓂ   20 | 16 | 18 | $27
*1152 Taylor St. (bet. Clay & Sacramento Sts.), 415-776-6500*
■ "Quaint" and "hospitable", this "cozy eatery" drums up such "long lines that it makes you wonder 'is the whole neighborhood eating here tonight?'"; in fact, most Nob Hillers do "enjoy a lovely bowl of Italian pasta or one of the pizzas" on a fairly regular basis, and the management eschews reservations, "so be prepared to wait"; N.B. for the ultimate people-watching op, the Brown sisters (aka The Twins) dine here every Tuesday.

### Nola ⚫ⓈⓂ   17 | 19 | 15 | $28
*535 Ramona St. (bet. Hamilton & University Aves.), Palo Alto, 650-328-2722*
◪ "New Orleans meets Palo Alto" at this "gaudy" Big Easy eatery that's "one of the few places with any atmosphere in the area"; while the "spicy" Southwestern–ragin' Cajun cuisine is "decent", the service is as "slow" as a river

boat; but no matter, as "you come here" for the "uninhibited atmosphere" and bar that's "packed shoulder-to-shoulder" with "the I'm-single-but-I-don't-want-to-drive-to-SF crowd."

### Norikonoko L S M
– – – I

*2556 Telegraph Ave. (bet. Blake & Parker Sts.), Berkeley, 510-548-1274*

"If you're tired of eating the same Japanese food" (or simply tired of waiting in line for it), this "quaint little shop run by a husband-and-wife outfit" "is a good place to go" in Berkeley for its "authentic homestyle fare" (bento boxes "just like mom made"); just be warned: there's "no sushi", no tempura and "nothing [remotely] fancy" about the decor.

### North Beach Pizza L M
16 8 12 $15

*1499 Grant Ave. (Union St.), 415-433-2444 ◗ S*
*1310 Grant St. (Vallejo St.), 415-433-2444 S*
*1649 Haight St. (Belvedere St.), 415-751-2300 ◗ S*
*715 Harrison St. (3rd St.), 415-371-0930 ◗*
*4787 Mission St. (bet. Persia & Russia Aves.), 415-586-1400 S*
*Pier 39 (bet. Grant & Stockton Sts., off The Embarcadero), 415-433-0400 S*
*800 Stanyan St. (Haight St.), 415-751-2300 ◗ S*
*3054 Taraval St. (41st Ave.), 415-242-9100 S*
*1598 University Ave. (California St.), Berkeley, 510-849-9800 ◗ S*

☑ This Bay Area chain of "old-fashioned pizza joints" specializes in "great big, fat" pies with "any topping you can think of"; though the persnickety purport to be "puzzled by its popularity" ("inevitably soggy" 'cause "it has too much on it"), the more positive proclaim it's "all a pizzeria needs to be" – they "sell slices to go" and "deliver way late."

### North Beach Restaurant ◗ L S M
19 18 20 $33

*1512 Stockton St. (bet. Green & Union Sts.), 415-392-1700*

■ Although this "venerable North Beach Italian" "has been around forever" (or at least since 1970), "whatever's missing in innovation is more than compensated for in consistency"; the "traditional no-frills food" is a "notch above most" (as is the "ample wine cellar"), "but what keeps you coming back" are "old-style" (and plain "old") "waiters in tuxedos" who "turn a meal into an event" (as a boosted Service score suggests).

### O Chamé L M
24 22 19 $27

*1830 Fourth St. (Hearst Ave.), Berkeley, 510-841-8783*

☑ There's something about this "Zen-like" refuge, away from the "maddening crowds of Fourth Street", that makes people feel like they are sitting "zazen" – and are "in love" with chef David Vardy's "wonderfully fresh Japanese food with a twist"; some grumble the name, which means "precious little thing", reflects the "small portions and high prices", but this "peaceful place" pleases most.

### Olema Inn **L S**   ▽ 17 | 19 | 16 | $36

*10000 Sir Francis Drake Blvd. (Hwy. 1), Olema,*
*415-663-9559*

■ This 123-year-old hostelry "with beautiful gardens" "is a romantic stop while driving up the coast" or "after a nice hike at Point Reyes" ("at the end of the evening, simply stroll upstairs and spend the weekend"); fans report the SF couple who took it over a few years back have "greatly expanded the wine list" and added "a touch of European elegance" to the "seasonal" New American cuisine (tip: "look for local seafood on the menu").

### Olive Bar & Restaurant ● **S M**   — | — | — | ı

*743 Larkin St. (O'Farrell St.), 415-776-9814*

Olives – in myriad martinis and other potent cocktails – are the stars of this sleek, art-filled hipster bar situated in the grungy heart of the Tenderloin, but Eclectic tapas-size savories such as pizza and fried calamari (at equally petit prices) are offered to keep all that gin and vodka from going to your head.

### Oliveto Cafe & Restaurant **L S M**   24 | 21 | 21 | $45

*5655 College Ave. (Shafter Ave.), Oakland, 510-547-5356*

◪ If you ever "imagined what life would be like at a Tuscan villa", you can envision the allure of this Oakland "culinary institution" where "only the signage isn't homemade"; since portions are "intensely flavored but small", regulars recommend you do as "the Italians do" "and share" a full three courses; although some are put off by the "too-elegant" atmosphere and the "knowledgeable" staff's occasional "arrogance", most award the place "a Ph.D."; P.S. the downstairs cafe is "more informal."

### Omei **L S M**   ▽ 24 | 15 | 14 | $23

*2316 Mission St. (King St.), Santa Cruz, 831-425-8458*

◪ This "most popular Santa Cruzian eatery" scores high with the "university crowd", which appreciates the "unbelievably tasty" offerings that "deviate substantially from the cookie-cutter fare you find at most Chinese places" in the area; Sinophiles "go for the food, not the decor" or the servers that "treat you like an unwanted houseguest."

### Ondine **S M**   21 | 25 | 19 | $51

*558 Bridgeway (Princess Ave.), Sausalito, 415-331-1133*

◪ Only in Sausalito would surveyors complain about the "absolutely breathtaking [sight] of the Bay Bridge and the SF skyline" ("makes it difficult to focus on the food or the company"); seriously though, the panorama is this "pier-top" spot's strong point – it certainly "beats the food" on the "good" though "painfully" pricey, seafood-oriented Med menu; a slip in the score confirms the service may be a tad too "unobtrusive" ("is the staff worried about blocking the view?").

### One Market **L M**                        22 | 20 | 20 | $48 |
*1 Market St. (Steuart St.), 415-777-5577*
☑ Co-owner Bradley Ogden's monument to born-in-the-USA cuisine ("very Californian ingredients" and an "awesome" all-American wine list) has changed a mere Embarcadero "power-lunch staple" into something more "memorable" – thanks largely to chef Adrian Hoffman, who "serves serious food to sophisticated palates"; nonetheless, the non-"expense-account set" claims the "cavernous" room and sometimes "stiff" service make them "feel cold."

### Original Joe's **◑ L S M**                17 | 13 | 17 | $26 |
*144 Taylor St. (bet. Eddy & Turk Sts.), 415-775-4877*
*301 S. First St. (San Carlos St.), San Jose, 408-292-7030*
☑ Travel through the "time tunnel" to this Tenderloin "institution" "from the [FDR] administration" that's venerated as much for its "quirky" "tuxedo-clad waiters" as it is for its "big portions" of "passable" "Italian-American food"; however, modernists moan the "dimly lit" decor "could use a dusting" and demand "how much of this pedestrian fare do you really want to eat" anyway; P.S. although the "San Jose landmark" is owned by a different family, it serves the same ole, same ole.

### Osake **L M**                        ▽ 24 | 18 | 20 | $39 |
*2446 Patio Ct. (Farmer's Ln.), Santa Rosa, 707-542-8282*
■ "Sitting at the sushi bar" at this Santa Rosa Cal-Japanese is "like walking into *Cheers,* with fish instead of beer" being proffered; indeed chef-owner Gary Chu "knows everyone's" name, and everyone seems to adore his "very eclectic menu", which features both "nice new-wave rolls" and cooked seafood; "the huge fish tank at the entrance is beautiful", even if "it's a bit unnerving looking at the live version of what's on my plate."

### Osteria **L M**                        20 | 15 | 18 | $30 |
*247 Hamilton Ave. (Ramona St.), Palo Alto, 650-328-5700*
☑ While it's "not chic or cutting-edge", Palo Alto's "unpretentious Northern Italian classic" draws "long lines" (even with reservations) for its "amazing" "fresh pastas"; the "rushed", heavily accented "career waiters" either detract or "add to the ambiance" (depending on how sensitive you are), but most concede the "reasonable bill at the end" "makes the cramped seating tolerable."

### Oswald's **S**                        ▽ 27 | 18 | 25 | $42 |
*1547 Pacific Ave. (Cedar St.), Santa Cruz, 831-423-7427*
■ This "sweet", "cozy spot" that's short on space but long "on European ambiance" is constantly full of "repeat customers" enjoying a "romantic, intimate dinner"; the combo of "first-rate", farmer's-market-fresh Californian fare and "very good service" (a rarity in this college town) makes it "unquestionably the best in Santa Cruz county."

## Ozumo L S M                    23 | 26 | 19 | $46

*161 Steuart St. (bet. Howard & Mission Sts.), 415-882-1333*

■ Owner and baseball phenom Jeremy James "hits a home run" with his "high-end" Japanese on the Embarcadero whose "minimalist yet beautiful" setting is a fitting stage for the equally innovative fare; a veritable three-ring circus, it boasts a "fresh, fresh, fresh" "sushi bar", an "exceptional robata" grill and a sake lounge with lots of fun cocktails, all at very "Tokyo prices"; already, the "trendy people" declare it threatens to "dethrone" other Asian hipsters.

## Pacific L S M                    25 | 19 | 22 | $46

*Pan Pacific Hotel, 500 Post St. (Mason St.), 415-929-2087*

■ "Hidden in the shadows" of the Pan Pacific Hotel, this "sleeper" is "one of the better-kept secrets in SF"; the "polished" Cal–New French menu paired with "professional, yet unobtrusive service" rivals some of the best in town; while being "pleasantly easy to get into", however, the dining room "lacks the vibrant energy of a busy" hot spot due to the fact that "it's in a hotel lobby (practically)."

## Pacific Café S M                    19 | 13 | 16 | $28

*7000 Geary Blvd. (34th Ave.), 415-387-7091*

◪ This "1970s fish shack" in the Richmond "keeps 'em lined up" thanks to its "simple" "grilled-all-the-way-through hefty steaks of fresh Pacific seafood" ("the cost of which includes a tasty salad or soup"); the "free wine while you wait" "helps cover a lot of sins", but a dip in the Service score suggests that diners would just as soon skip the "cheap" Chardonnay in exchange for their "taking reservations."

## Pacific's Edge S M                    24 | 26 | 23 | $65

*Highlands Inn, 120 Highland Dr. (Hwy. 1), Carmel, 831-622-5445*

◪ "Check the weather report for fog" and "time your reservation for the sunset", because the raison d'être of this *très* "romantic" destination in Carmel is the "stunning view" of the coast (far nicer than the "'80s flashback decor" inside); although the Pacific has the edge, the "delicious" "Cal–New French tasting menu", paired with an "exquisite wine list", "never fails to be a highlight"; wallet-watchers wince that at these prices "they should be arrested for thievery", but those who got it say it's "worth every penny."

## Pairs L S M                    ▽ 16 | 14 | 15 | $35

*4175 Solano Ave. (Wine Country Ave.), Napa, 707-224-8464*

◪ Up Valley residents had high hopes for this Cal-"Asian fusion" joint that moved in 2001 to this "rather mundane" "mini strip mall" in the town of Napa; while many newcomers find the "educated cuisine" (replete with suggested wine pairings for each course), sake drinks and "enchanting" patio "exceed expectations", old-timers opine it's still "a little rough around the edges", declaring the food and service "were better in the old location in St. Helena."

### Pakwan ⚡🇸Ⓜ⊅          22  6  10  $14
*501 O'Farrell St. (Jones St.), 415-776-0160*
*3182 16th St. (bet. Guerrero & Valencia Sts.), 415-255-2440*
■ "Whether money is a concern or not", this "cheapo" set of "no-frills Indian-Pakistanis" in the Tenderloin and Mission "is a must"; "buy your beer across the street" ("it's BYO"), "then order at the counter, get your own dishes and pick up your food when they announce your number"; caveat emptor: "even the 'mild' dishes require frequent doses of mango lassi" drinks or "fluffy and scrumptious" naan bread to cool the tongue.

### Palatino ⚡🇸Ⓜ          ∇ 19  17  19  $30
*803 Cortland Ave. (Ellsworth St.), 415-641-8899*
■ "Out-of-the-ordinary regional Italian specialties" and "special events (e.g. the Roman Chanukah menu)", along with "engaging waiters" who cause a "crowded, small room" to seem "cozy", "make Bernal the eighth hill of Rome" and this "unpretentious" yearling "the new default restaurant" for locals "in the neighborhood."

### Palio d'Asti ⚡Ⓜ          20  19  22  $38
*640 Sacramento St. (bet. Kearny & Montgomery Sts.), 415-395-9800*
■ This Italian "stallion of a restaurant" (named for the famed Asti bareback horse race) runs circles around the other Downtown "power-lunch eateries"; the cuisine is "stylish and well executed" and served by the "most professional staff" in SF ("the kind that remembers your name"); "the convivial atmosphere" gallops at lunch, but the "occasional wine-and-white-truffle dinners" are strong finishers too.

### Palomino ◑⚡🇸Ⓜ          18  21  17  $35
*345 Spear St. (bet. Folsom & Harrison Sts.), 415-512-7400*
☑ "Even though it's a chain", this Embarcadero "yuppie haunt" is "a horse of a different color" because it "has lots of tables on the patio" and a "fantastic view of the Bay"; since the Cal-Med menu can be "hit-or-miss", discriminating diners primarily horse around with the appetizers (the "gorgonzola fries – an absolute must"); still, it's considered "*the* place to mingle with singles" before a Pac Bell Park game – though "getting the waiter's attention could be an Olympic event."

### Pancho Villa Taqueria ⚡🇸Ⓜ          24  9  15  $10
*3071 16th St. (bet. Mission & Valencia Sts.), 415-864-8840 ◑*
*365 S. B St. (bet. 3rd & 4th Aves.), San Mateo, 650-343-4123*
■ At the risk of Villafying its competitors, Panchophiles proclaim "when all the arguing about the best burrito in the Mission is done, this Mexican is the winner" – thanks to "succulent, flavorful meats" and a "smorgasbord of tasty salsa" that "put the 'o' in olé" and make up for "assembly-

line" service, "cafeteria-style" seating and "security persons serving as doormen"; N.B. the San Mateo branch also offers a *muy bueno* juice bar.

### Pane e Vino L S M

24  17  19  $35

*3011 Steiner St. (Union St.), 415-346-2111*

◪ This "tiny trattoria" in Cow Hollow is "a coveted spot to carbo-load" on "just what [the name] says – bread and wine" and "amazing homemade pastas" while "spotting local celebrities"; even if the "small, crowded rooms" make "conversation difficult", "the food speaks loudly enough" and the "fun" "waiters make you feel as if you're in Northern Italy"; still, the belligerent bay *basta* with those lines and "reservations that continue to be a mirage."

### Pangaea S

▽ 27  21  24  $44

*250 Main St. (Eureka Hill Rd.), Point Arena, 707-882-3001*

■ "You'll be amazed at the extremely creative and expertly prepared fare" at this "inviting" restaurant "in the middle of nowhere" (aka Point Arena); the husband-and-wife owners whip up "zaftig flavors in an ever-changing menu" "that covers the globe" and add a "carefully selected wine list" that features organic bottlings from around the world; while fans warn it's "not traditional", it's "maybe the best food" and "most fun on the North Coast."

### Panta Rei L S M ⊄

–  –  –  I

*431 Columbus Ave. (Stockton St.), 415-591-0900*

Named for Heraclitus' theory of constant change, this modestly priced North Beach Italian is located in a space that's housed three restaurants in the last three years; chef Fabrizio Laudati and co-owner Alessandro Iacobelli (of Baldoria and Bella Trattoria) hope to slow the revolving door with Roman specialties like pasta with rabbit sauce and gnocchi with lamb.

### Paragon L M

14  17  15  $32

*701 Second St. (Townsend St.), 415-537-9020*

◪ "Marvelous warehouse architecture", supremely "skilled bartenders" and "a great patio for a sunny day" are the draws at this "popular Pac Bell Park gathering place", part of a chain whose New American food "isn't bad, but just isn't memorable"; sports fans say it's "decent for the ballpark scene . . . until baseball season, when the place turns into hell."

### Paragon Bar & Cafe L S M

▽ 15  26  18  $33

*Claremont Resort & Spa, 41 Tunnel Rd. (Domingo St.), Berkeley, 510-549-8510*

◪ It's "about time a high-end bar opened for professionals in the East Bay" cry quenched quaffers at this "really chic in a 1960s-Audrey-Hepburn-kind-of-style" eatery; "on a clear evening you can't beat the view of the Bay and SF", but unfortunately the Californian fare "doesn't match up", and "if you're used to getting the classic Claremont Resort, service, you may be disappointed."

### Parcel 104 🄻🅂Ⓜ     ▽ 27 | 26 | 23 | $51 |
*Santa Clara Marriott, 2700 Mission College Blvd. (Great America Blvd.), Santa Clara, 408-970-6104*
◪ "Wowza" warble wowed diners who have visited this "excellent newcomer to the Silicon Valley scene"; "in a lovely room" within the Santa Clara Marriott, partners "Bradley Ogden and chef Bart Hosmer capture the market-fresh attitude" with a seasonal New American menu that features "local ingredients" "pulled from the ground, picked from the ocean"; "live jazz" nightly helps makes it a place to "impress colleagues and clients", even if some say the service, while rated highly, is still "a bit sketchy."

### Park Grill 🄻🅂Ⓜ     ▽ 22 | 20 | 23 | $45 |
*Park Hyatt Hotel, 333 Battery St. (Clay St.), 415-296-2933*
◼ VPs and VCs assure us there's no better place "for power breakfast and lunch" than this "exceptional" eatery in the Downtown Hyatt thanks to the "quietest room" that "lets you talk and relax" and "excellent servers" who know their job; however, despite its renown as "an old standby for the business crowd", gourmets insist the often "terrific" New American food and "decor far surpass that reputation."

### Parma Ⓜ     22 | 14 | 22 | $27 |
*3314 Steiner St. (bet. Chestnut & Lombard Sts.), 415-567-0500*
◼ This "true neighborhood" trattoria delivers an "all-around authentic Northern Italian experience" ("in the Marina of all places") with "frescoes on the wall", "service that makes you feel like a regular" and "delicious" "garlic-infused" standards that "are a way of life here"; reservations aren't accepted, but locals assure us "dinner with Pietro Elia" (the "extremely friendly" owner) "makes the wait for a table worth it."

### Passage to India 🄻🅂Ⓜ     18 | 14 | 15 | $22 |
*1991 W. El Camino Real (bet. Escuela & Rengstorff Aves.), Mountain View, 650-969-9990*
◼ Silicon Valley techies are relieved to see that their beloved poori purveyor has made safe passage to Mountain View in this "sparse" but still "nicer" locale; although the "amazingly tasty" curries and signature chicken tikka masala are deemed Delhicious, regulars suggest the weekend and Tuesday night "buffets are the best deal"; "informed service" rounds out the journey.

### Passionfish 🅂Ⓜ     ▽ 26 | 17 | 25 | $35 |
*701 Lighthouse Ave. (Congress Ave.), Pacific Grove, 831-655-3311*
◼ Chef/co-owner "Ted Walter delights" a *petit,* passionate passel of Pacific Grove patrons with his many "unique

preparations" comprised of "the freshest fish and produce available"; while "wonderful service" creates a "welcoming atmosphere", this Californian's "crowing glory is the sensational wine list priced at retail."

### Pasta Moon LⓈⓂ    22 | 19 | 19 | $36 |
*315 Main St. (Mill St.), Half Moon Bay, 650-726-5125*
■ Bearing pedigrees from NYC's Le Cirque and Chez Panisse respectively, "the chef and the pastry chef are a divine couple, at least in the kitchen" at this "small-town Italian cafe" in Half Moon Bay where "wonderfully inventive pastas" and "mouthwatering" desserts "are everyday occurrences" – as is "a nice little selection of wines by the glass"; so go ahead, stop and "spoil yourself for lunch" "on a drive down the coast."

### Pasta Pomodoro ⓈⓂ    15 | 12 | 15 | $17 |
*2027 Chestnut St. (Fillmore St.), 415-474-3400* Ⓛ
*598 Haight St. (Steiner St.), 415-436-9800*
*816 Irving St. (9th Ave.), 415-566-0900* Ⓛ
*2304 Market St. (Castro St.), 415-558-8123* ◐Ⓛ
*1865 Post St. (Fillmore St.), 415-674-1826* Ⓛ
*4000 24th St. (Noe St.), 415-920-9904* Ⓛ
*655 Union St. (Columbus Ave.), 415-399-0300* Ⓛ
*1875 Union St. (Laguna St.), 415-771-7900* Ⓛ
*5500 College Ave. (Lawton Ave.), Oakland, 510-923-0900* Ⓛ
*421 Third St. (Irving St.), San Rafael, 415-256-2401* Ⓛ
◪ "People like to pooh-pooh Pasta P", but the truth is "locals on a budget" as well as those "who don't want to cook" confess they like this "ubiquitous Bay Area chain" for its "winning formula": "reliable", if "dumbed-down, Italian" fare, "speedy service" and "unbelievable value."

### Pastis LⓂ    23 | 19 | 20 | $41 |
*1015 Battery St. (Green St.), 415-391-2555*
■ On "the edge of the Financial District", chef/co-owner Gerald Hirigoyen's "classic Basque" bistro with Gallic influences is "the real deal" – "French chefs, French waiters" (some replete with same French "impatience"), plus a "really long" zinc bar that serves pastis; regulars declare it's "just as good as" "its more famous sister" Fringale, "but less expensive and easier to get into" – plus, there's an "open terrace" for "people-watching."

### Pauline's Pizza    24 | 13 | 16 | $21 |
*260 Valencia St. (bet. Duboce & 14th Sts.), 415-552-2050*
■ "In a town where pizza is certainly not king", "this venerable institution" reigns as queen thanks to its "fresh, inventive toppings" (who knew Meyer lemon and figs were "good on pizza"?) and "stellar cornmeal crusts"; "build your own masterpiece" or defer to "the daily veggie special", but don't forget to eat your greens ("refreshing salads") or save room for the "fabulous sorbets"; despite

the "crazy edge-of-cracktown location" in the Mission, the only addiction visible is to the signature pesto, which "multitudes" "have gotten hooked on."

### paul K 🅂     19 | 16 | 19 | $36
*199 Gough St. (Oak St.), 415-552-7132*
■ The wild card of Hayes Valley's "pre-concert spots", this "stylish" address is "more than just a place to eat before" a performance, thanks to the "close-knit servers" who "exhibit a passion for the food" – an "exotic" assemblage of "inventive", "well-presented" Med meals ("like mom used to make if she was from the Middle East") paired with "a list of clever cocktails" (pomegranate martini, anyone?).

### Pazzia 🅛🅜     23 | 13 | 21 | $26
*337 Third St. (bet. Folsom & Harrison Sts.), 415-512-1693*
■ "Don't let the strip-mall" location "in the shadow of the Moscone Center" "deter you" from experiencing some of the "most authentic Italian food" "in SoMa"; the secret lies in the "incredible pastas" and thin-crust pizzas baked with *amore* in a wood-burning oven and the "heartwarming", heartstoppingly "beautiful" staff whose welcome gives the sense of "being back in Italy"; speaking of which, "dress for Sicilian weather" because this tiny place really heats up.

### Pearl 🅛     ▽ 22 | 15 | 21 | $30
*1339 Pearl St. (bet. Franklin & Polk Sts.), Napa, 707-224-9161*
■ This pearl of a place with an "enticing patio" is prized for chef/co-owner Nicki Zeller's "excellent Californian homestyle cooking, plus its casual atmosphere and skillful service" ("with a reasonably priced wine list to boot"); savvy locals say go now, because "as the neighborhood around it undergoes a long-overdue face-lift", it won't be Downtown Napa's "best-kept secret anymore."

### Pearl Alley Bistro 🅛🅢🅜     22 | 18 | 20 | $35
*110 Pearl Alley (Cedar St.), Santa Cruz, 831-429-8070*
◪ The "fearless" kitchen of this Santa Cruz Cal-International offers some "startling creations"; but fear not, "if the constantly changing menu" "isn't to your liking one week, you can always go with the Mongolian barbecue" or drown your sorrows at the "awesome" wine bar that features rotating "guest staffing from some of the local vineyards"; although "the service is good until they get busy", that fails to dampen the "fun, fun, fun" scene.

### Pelican Inn 🅛🅢🅜     14 | 24 | 17 | $30
*10 Pacific Way (Hwy. 1), Muir Beach, 415-383-6000*
◪ "If you don't have time to get to" the UK and are craving "an authentic Guinness on tap", then a trip to this "cozy British inn" (complete with "roaring fire in the dining room") "in the middle of Marin" is just the ticket; while "the scene is so convincingly English that only the American accents

seem out of place", the "traditional pub grub" "unfortunately is comparable" to what you'd find in London "as well", so most visitors "avoid the restaurant and have a pint in the pub" or out back on the patio.

### Peninsula Fountain & Grill L S M  17 | 15 | 16 | $17

*Stanford Shopping Ctr., 180 El Camino Real (University Ave.), Palo Alto, 650-327-3141*
*566 Emerson St. (Hamilton Ave.), Palo Alto, 650-323-3131*
■ Palo Alto's "archetypal diner" on Emerson (El Camino opened in 2001) serves burgers, "breakfast all day" and a "broad selection of blue-plate fare that might make you think of mom", but its real claim to fame is the "malted shakes made with their own ice cream" (the soda jerks "even leave the container on the table the old-fashioned way"); it "brings back the '50s", albeit at "'90s prices."

### Perlot S M  – | – | – | E

*Hotel Majestic, 1500 Sutter St. (Gough St.), 415-441-1100*
Sequestered in the Hotel Majestic, this "charming" sleeper "is an insider's secret" for an unrushed romantic rendezvous thanks to a piano's steady tinkling in a "wonderfully quiet" "elegant old room" overseen by "professional service"; although the seasonal New American menu "doesn't match up" to the "sophisticated hotel ambiance", a recent "change in chefs" might change that.

### Perry's L M  12 | 14 | 14 | $27

*Galleria Park Hotel, 185 Sutter St. (bet. Kearny & Montgomery Sts.), 415-989-6895*
*1944 Union St. (bet. Buchanan & Laguna Sts.), 415-922-9022* S
☑ Old-timers opine these "last of the fun bar grills" are a "fine place to grab a beer" and "basic burger" and "watch the game on TV"; however, critics snap "nobody goes here for the food" (which a drop in the score supports) – "it's a habit some people fell into during the swinging '70s", and odds are "if you weren't part of that scene" then, their popularity now "will seem inexplicable"; N.B. a new Palo Alto branch is slated to open around Labor Day.

### Pesce M  ▽ 17 | 13 | 17 | $30

*2227 Polk St. (bet. Green & Vallejo Sts.), 415-928-8025*
■ "Serving straightforward" seafood "at very reasonable prices", this "unpretentious" Polk Street fish house carries piscatory plates with a Northern Italian flavor, thanks to Ruggero Gadaldi ("the owner of Antica Trattoria"); the Decor score may not reflect a recent remodel that has nearly doubled the size and glamorized the "tiny" room.

### Pho Vietnam L S M  ▽ 24 | 6 | 15 | $10

*711 Stony Point Rd. (Sebastopol Rd.), Santa Rosa, 707-571-7687*
☑ This "awesome" Vietnamese in Santa Rosa "is the hole-in-the-wall you always wish to find"; it's the "fragrant",

"super-cheap" "bowls of noodle soup" "that the people come for", which more than "balance out" the "sometimes preoccupied staff" and pho-gettable "storefront decor."

### Phuping Thai Cuisine L S M    – | – | – | M
*Pacific East Mall, 3288 Pierce St. (Central Ave.), Richmond, 510-558-3242*
"Just like Thep Phanom", its big-city sister, this Richmond Thai "provides exciting flavors and textures" ("complete with carved vegetables and fruit") and "friendly, helpful service" to Siamese-seeking East Bayers; bridge-crossers note "it has really easy parking" and, "mall [location] notwithstanding", a "surprisingly relaxing ambiance."

### Piatti L S M    17 | 17 | 17 | $33
*Sixth & Junipero Aves., Carmel, 831-625-1766*
*100 Sycamore Valley Rd. W. (San Ramon Valley Blvd.), Danville, 925-838-2082*
*625 Redwood Hwy./Hwy. 101 (Seminary Dr. exit), Mill Valley, 415-380-2525*
*Stanford Shopping Ctr., 2 Stanford Shopping Ctr. (El Camino Real), Palo Alto, 650-324-9733*
*El Dorado Hotel, 405 First St. W. (Spain St.), Sonoma, 707-996-2351*
*6480 Washington St. (Oak Circle), Yountville, 707-944-2070*
☑ "At all their locations", this suburban string of "formulaic Italians" serves "standard fare" that shows "sparks of creativity" – primarily in "the amazing dipping oil they put on the table with sourdough" – "in now-familiar decor"; although it's "nothing to write home" about and "service can be" maddeningly "inattentive", it's a nice alternative to "higher-priced" options.

### Piazza D'Angelo L S M    18 | 18 | 17 | $32
*22 Miller Ave. (Throckmorton Ave.), Mill Valley, 415-388-2000*
☑ There's no piazza, but this "loud, boisterous" "popular hangout" truly is "Mill Valley's centerpiece", where fortysomethings "crowd the bar for a piece of the action"; strip away the "scene" and it's your "basic neighborhood Italian" (but it's in Marin, "so no checkered oilcloths" please); while it clearly benefits from the lack of local "options", most find the fare "reliable, if not knock-your-socks-off."

### Picante Cocina Mexicana L S M    21 | 12 | 15 | $13
*1328 Sixth St. (bet. Camelia & Gilman Sts.), Berkeley, 510-525-3121*
☑ "Hidden in the industrial district of Berkeley", this "large shack" (owned by Jim Maser of Cafe Fanny fame) "elevates" "solid Mexicano" fare "to a new level" thanks to "top-quality ingredients" and tortillas "made in the lobby!", even if it's ordered and delivered "cafeteria-style"; grown-ups suggest "good margaritas help to overcome the din", but "try the garden" (or takeout) "to escape the hordes of screaming children."

**Picaro** S M ▽ 16 | 11 | 15 | $21

*3120 16th St. (bet. Guerrero & Valencia Sts.), 415-431-4089*

☑ This Mission tapas bar is popular with the indie-flick flock "before seeing a movie at the Roxie" (across the way); the "good" "Spanish food", paired with pitchers of sangria, also makes it "fun for a group"; however, pickier patrons deem it "loud and impersonal", noting the Almodovar-ian "decor could be spruced up somewhat."

**Pier 23 Cafe** L S M 10 | 13 | 10 | $23

*Pier 23, The Embarcadero (Greenwich St.), 415-362-5125*

☑ According to the "twentysomething crowd" that "parties" here, this seafood "shack on the Embarcadero" is the kind of place where you "sit in the sunshine", "throw back a few cold ones" "and relaaax" while listening to "live music"; but even they "stick to the drinks rather than the food" – just "ok" grub served by a "staff that needs an overhaul."

**Pinot Blanc** L S M 22 | 22 | 21 | $47

*641 Main St. (Grayson Ave.), St. Helena, 707-963-6191*

☑ Brought to you by chef Joachim Splichal's Patina group of LA, this "high-class" haven in St. Helena offers "beautiful" surroundings "both indoors and out", "absolutely terrific" Cal–New French fare, a "great wine list and knowledgeable staff" – causing fans to fawn that it's the "best underused restaurant in the Valley"; but a posse of disappointed devotees pout it's "overpriced and overrated" – "Joachim, where are you?"

**Pisces** S M 25 | 22 | 22 | $53

*1190 California Dr. (Broadway), Burlingame, 650-401-7500*

☑ Set in a "renovated railroad station", this "fish bowl-size" seafooder serves up "sublime", "imaginative and stylishly presented" dishes similar to the fare at big sister Aqua, sparking the gratitude of "Valley dwellers who don't have to schlep into SF for a good meal"; however, "the occasional rattle of the Cal Train" passing by is either a "curiosity" or a "drawback", depending on one's liking for locomotives; and some passengers pout about paying "Park Avenue prices at a Burlingame whistle stop."

**Piyassa Restaurant & Bar** L S M – | – | – | M

*1686 Market St. (Gough St.), 415-864-3700*

The young Turks (literally) who run this Hayes Valley haven spice up the narrow, scarlet-red room with a mélange of Mediterranean meze and mains; internationally renowned DJ Aykut (also one of the co-owners) spins world-music dance licks Thursday–Saturday nights.

**Pizza Azzurro** L M ▽ 22 | 14 | 18 | $19

*1400 Second St. (Franklin St.), Napa, 707-255-5552*

■ It's "about time an affordable" source of "awesome" pies slathered with seasonal, regional ingredients "made its way to Downtown" say Napa area natives grateful to this new "little cafe from a chef that used to cook at Tra Vigne"; the "young servers know how to take care of you", and the "upscale pizza-parlor atmosphere" makes it "an honest place to hang" "for that family night out or quick lunch or dinner."

### Pizza Rustica L S M　　　20 | 12 | 15 | $19
*5422 College Ave. (bet. Kales & Manila Aves.), Oakland, 510-654-1601*
◪ Disciples dub this Oakland pizzeria "divine" for its "unique" "gourmet" pies – along with "rarer choices like good rotisserie chicken" – which it delivers, unlike a certain rival down the street; some folks do eat on the premises (there's an "upstairs tiki bar"), but "brusque service" and "the hustle" of the atmosphere cause many to "order to go."

### Pizzetta 211 L S ⌀　　　▽ 24 | 16 | 15 | $20
*211 23rd Ave. (California St.), 415-379-9880*
◪ This "toony tiny" storefront "is the talk of the town" thanks to its thin-crusted pizzas, "a slice of heaven" topped with "top-quality produce"; while the "ever-changing small menu" and "homemade desserts" keep pie-d pipers "coming back" to the Richmond, many prefer to eat "in the comforts of home" due to limited seating (inside and out), and an often "apathetic" attitude.

### PJ's Oyster Bed S M　　　20 | 14 | 17 | $31
*737 Irving St. (bet. 8th & 9th Aves.), 415-566-7775*
◪ "The Dixie beer is cold, the jambalaya will get you hoppin'" and "the zydeco beat" never stops at this "fun, Cajun-style fish house" (we'll "give you a wild guess what their specialty is") in the Inner Sunset; with its "so-so service", "overwhelming din" and "spring break" mentality, it's "the kind of place my mama warned me about" wink Bayou boys and girls who confess "I go often."

### Plearn Thai Cuisine L S M　　　21 | 14 | 15 | $20
*2050 University Ave. (bet. Milvia St. & Shattuck Ave.), Berkeley, 510-841-2148*
◪ "Pleasing pad Thai, classic curries and bright flavors at low prices" "pack them in" to this 20-year-old bite of Bangkok in Downtown Berkeley; but while the "food's still good", "the decor has not held up as well" and foes feel it has become "overconfident", especially given that "service is not as attentive as one might hope."

### Plouf L M　　　22 | 16 | 17 | $35
*40 Belden Pl. (bet. Bush & Pine Sts.), 415-986-6491*
■ "I almost thought I had to get my passport stamped upon entry" declare disoriented Downtowners, since everything about this bistro "makes you feel you're in Marseilles", from

the "fabulous shellfish and frites" to the "heavily accented" "cute waiters in nautical stripes"; the "closely set tables" make it a bit of "a madhouse", but it's "a must for mussels" (and masculine muscles); P.S. the "alleyway" turned outdoor dining room is the place to sit "on a warm sunny day" ("they do happen").

**Plumed Horse** Ⓜ    24 | 24 | 25 | $55 |

*14555 Big Basin Way (4th St.), Saratoga, 408-867-4711*
■ "Classy, conservative" and catering to the "over-50-year-old set" since 1975, this rather "romantic" Saratoga stalwart "is excellent for entertaining or celebrating in posh style"; "you will fall in love with the overly attentive yet unobtrusive staff", the extensive "wine list that reads like a good book" and the "old-fashioned" but "highly satisfying" Californian–New French menu; if you prefer to "save your gold", "eat in the lively bar", which features catchy dance music.

**PlumpJack Cafe** Ⓛ Ⓢ Ⓜ    24 | 21 | 22 | $48 |

*3127 Fillmore St. (bet. Filbert & Greenwich Sts.),*
*415-563-4755*
*PlumpJack Squaw Valley Inn, 1920 Squaw Valley Rd. (Hwy. 89),*
*Olympic Valley, 530-583-1576*
◪ Run by celebrities, this Cow Hollow cafe and its Lake Tahoe branch are "big with the ladies who lunch" and oenophiles who salivate over the "incredible wine list"; "pick something you'd never splurge on" ("you can get it at cost!"), then ask the "knowledgeable servers" to help choose from the "innovative Cal-Med menu" ("don't miss the signature seafood cones") "to pair with it"; however, even worshipers wish they could jack up the seating (it's so "tight", it "feels like dining with the next table").

**Pomelo** Ⓢ Ⓜ    21 | 14 | 18 | $18 |

*1793 Church St. (30th St.), 415-285-2257*
*92 Judah St. (6th Ave.), 415-731-6175* Ⓛ
◪ 'Noodles and grains of the world, unite!' might be the slogan at these "inexpensive" "holes-in-the-wall" in the Sunset and Noe Valley serving an International "scattering of delectable dishes" "named after cities"; "food cooked right before your eyes" creates what little ambiance these "cramped" "tiny haunts" have.

**Ponzu** ● Ⓢ Ⓜ    22 | 22 | 18 | $37 |

*Serrano Hotel, 401 Taylor St. (bet. Geary & O'Farrell Sts.),*
*415-775-7979*
■ Nowadays the "Pan-Asian tapas" thing "seems to be done a little too much, but they manage to do it well" (no surprise, as chef John Beardsley is a Betelnut vet) at this "funky and hip purple" dining room in the Serrano Hotel; the food is "best enjoyed" "when several choices are shared" "family-style" and washed down with a 'Spiritual

Sparkler' or other cocktails – which are reduced twice nightly during 'Double Happiness Happy Hours' (making this a "great place before or after the theater").

### Pork Store Cafe L S M  20 | 8 | 14 | $12

*1451 Haight St. (bet. Ashbury St. & Masonic Ave.), 415-864-6981*

■ "Work off your hangover" at this Haight Street haunt – arguably the "best greasy spoon in the city" – which serves American "comfort food and breakfast all day"; semantic stylists question the name ("cafe? – that implies charm"), but what do you want when the "yummy" eats are "cheap as hell"?

### Postino S M  21 | 23 | 21 | $41

*3565 Mt. Diablo Blvd. (Oak Hill Rd.), Lafayette, 925-299-8700*

■ "The design of the old Lafayette post office lends a certain charm to" this East Bayer whose "luscious brick" walls and tiled floors seem "reminiscent of a Tuscan wine cellar"; but while fans say the "vibrant" Northern Italian–Mediterranean menu really "sings" and appreciate the "suburban prices", another posse won't ring twice for this postman, citing "uneven food" and service that ranges from "gracious" to "only fair."

### POSTRIO L S M  24 | 24 | 22 | $56

*Prescott Hotel, 545 Post St. (bet. Mason & Taylor Sts.), 415-776-7825*

■ This Downtown "classic" remains a "favorite stop for the stars" and "visitors from far and near who are entertained" first by that "elegant entry staircase" and then by the "inventive combinations" of New American–Far Eastern fare and "the show in the [open] kitchen"; a few claim it's "coasting on its laurels" – in particular, the "late '80s decor" "needs a face-lift" – but most say it "still has it"; P.S. "the Wolfgang Puck pizzas are not to be missed."

### Powell's Place L S M  17 | 6 | 11 | $13

*511 Hayes St. (bet. Laguna & Octavia Sts.), 415-863-1404*

■ Gospel singer Emmit Powell's Hayes Street "storefront" offers spiritual nourishment in the form of "no-frills, Southern-style" "home cookin'"; the "yummy fried chicken" is the main event for disciples who ignore the "lukewarm sides" and "sparse decor", enlivened primarily by a jukebox and "head shots" of famous black entertainers.

### Prima L S M  23 | 20 | 21 | $39

*1522 N. Main St. (bet. Bonanza St. & Lincoln Ave.), Walnut Creek, 925-935-7780*

■ An "abundant selection of wines" "at fair prices" ("they also own a wine store next door") is the primo reason for this "beautiful" "see-and-be-seen scene in Walnut Creek"; but thanks to chef Peter Chastain's "use of more and more fresh seasonal ingredients" on the "delightful" Northern Italian menu, "the food is starting to catch up"; now some sniff "the weak link" is the "snobby staff" (maybe "success has gone to their heads").

### Primo Patio Cafe ⓁⓈⓂ    _ | _ | _ | M

*214 Townsend St. (bet. 3rd & 4th Sts.), 415-957-1129*
"Delicious Caribbean food" (if you don't order the signature jerk chicken, then you surely are one) is primo at this "fun" daytime cafe whose "great sunny back patio" constitutes the only seating area; its proximity to Pac Bell Park makes it a "hidden gem "for pre–ball game grub" too.

### Puerto Alegre Restaurant ⓁⓈⓂ ▽ 13 | 9 | 13 | $13

*546 Valencia St. (bet. 16th & 17th Sts.), 415-255-8201*
☑ Yes, it's a Mission "dive", so "why do [scenesters] keep going back, you ask?" – because this Mexican's "perfect for those boozy occasions of large birthday parties with a bunch of friends", a place to order a "cheap" "combo plate and soak up some" "magnificent margaritas"; in fact, it's always best "to go with a group" because "you can't make a reservation" otherwise, and it's "always packed."

### Q ⓈⓂ    20 | 16 | 15 | $21

*225 Clement St. (bet. 3rd & 4th Aves.), 415-752-2298*
■ 'Q' stands for "quirky" at this "funky", "easy-on-the-wallet" spot doling out "huge portions" of New American grub that's a welcome "antidote to the slew of Asian restaurants in the neighborhood"; the "raucous", arty warehouse decor brings a little bit of "SoMa to the Inner Richmond", but "the macaroni and cheese [topped] with tater tots" and "other comfort foods make it feel like home"; N.B. the brunch menu is served every day till dinner.

### Ramblas ⓈⓂ    17 | 15 | 16 | $23

*557 Valencia St. (bet. 16th & 17th Sts.), 415-565-0207*
☑ "In a neighborhood saturated with tapas joints", amigos report that this "fun", "loud" Mission Spanish presents small plates, plus a plethora of paellas, that equal "the others, and without the long wait and attitude"; but the libationary prefer to ramble in just for some "good sangria" and mojitos, skipping what they call "uninspired" dinner.

### R & G Lounge ⓁⓈⓂ    24 | 12 | 15 | $26

*631 Kearny St. (bet. Clay & Sacramento Sts.), 415-982-7877*
☑ It may "sound like a smoker's den", but the come-on at this two-story Chinatown haunt is the swimmingly "fresh seafood" (direct from the fish tanks down below) and "fabulous soups" that have "visitors from Hong Kong" "heading here as soon as they get into town"; don't "be afraid to order by the pictures in their menu", otherwise

you'll miss out on the "really special 'specials'"; try to ignore the often "overbearing service" and decor that, while "renovated", is "a bit too fluorescent."

### Rasselas Ethiopian 🄂🄼    ▽ 14 | 11 | 13 | $21

*2801 California St. (Divisadero St.), 415-567-5010*
*1534 Fillmore St. (bet. Geary Blvd. & O'Farrell St.), 415-346-8696* ●
☑ Swingers say "the combination of couches", "super jazz" and "delicious piles of saucy meat" "makes for good dates" at these Pacific Heights and Western Addition supper clubs; but other scenesters are simply "not hip on Ethiopian food", especially when it's served in "bare-bones decor."

### Ravenous 🄂    24 | 18 | 19 | $40

*420 Center St. (North St.), Healdsburg, 707-431-1302*
### Ravenette 🄻🄂⊄
*117 North St. (bet. Center St. & Healdsburg Ave.), Healdsburg, 707-431-1770*
☑ Last year the owners of this Healdsburg "haunt" moved their main eatery Ravenous to a larger location, saving the original site for midday meals; but while "lunch in Ravenette is still the best", some are "disappointed in dinner at the new place": yes, the Cal cuisine can be "truly ambrosial" and the setting, an "old house that glows with candles" and a patio "with twinkle lights in the trees", "all charm"; but long waits ("even with reservations") and "uneven service" suggest it needs time "to adjust" to the move.

### Ravens, The 🄂🄼    ▽ 19 | 19 | 17 | $38

*Stanford Inn by the Sea, 44850 Comptche-Ukiah Rd. (Coast Hwy. 1), Mendocino, 707-937-5615*
■ "If you are – or ever have been – a vegetarian", this Mendocino coast inn eatery "will knock your socks off"; but even if you aren't, the "unusual preparations" (e.g. sea palm strudel), paired with a "nice view" of the organic gardens and "enchanting sea", guarantee a good time.

### Red Herring 🄻🄂🄼    19 | 18 | 17 | $39

*Hotel Griffon, 155 Steuart St. (bet. Howard & Mission Sts.), 415-495-6500*
☑ "Try to get a seat at one of the tables by the window overlooking the Bay Bridge" suggest old sea-hands of this Embarcadero fish house that also "roasts chickens over the fireplace"; supporters say it's "solid fun", but while the signature "lobster-mango cones are excellent, the other food is mediocre" snap cynics, who wonder if the "slow" staff looks "bored, why should I be excited?"

### Red Rock Cafe &    ▽ 23 | 9 | 16 | $17
### Backdoor BBQ 🄻🄂🄼

*1010 Lincoln Ave. (Main St.), Napa, 707-226-2633*
■ "Big messy burgers", "fantastic BBQ" and "family-size portions" of "fried stuff (fish 'n' chips, onion rings, etc.)" all

rock at this "blue-collar locals'" tavern in Downtown Napa; it gets "crowded at prime time, so watch for an open" "gingham-cloth"-topped "table and run for it", or better still, head to the back door carry-out window "and take it home."

### Redwood Park 🄻Ⓜ                                     25 | 24 | 25 | $74

*Transamerica Pyramid, 600 Montgomery St. (Battery St.), 415-283-1000*
■ "Another George Morrone miracle" burble believers about the former Fifth Floor chef's latest "over-the-top, in a good way" venture Downtown; "from the moment you enter" the "architecturally exciting" art-filled dining room, "every gorgeous detail comes together effortlessly", from the "stellar" "modern French" cuisine to "service that matches it toe-to-toe"; small wonder guests "want to go back immediately – as soon as my loan clears."

### Rendezvous Inn & Restaurant Ⓢ    24 | 19 | 23 | $41

*647 N. Main St. (Bush St.), Fort Bragg, 707-964-8142*
■ "Out of all the restaurants that dot the magnificent Mendocino coast, there are few that" "can beat chef-owner Kim Badenhop's passion for food"; "rich in game", his "creative, delicious" New French fare paired with the "exemplary" yet "modestly priced wine list" makes this "high-class" Fort Bragg hostelry "one of the best deals" in the area.

### Restaurant at                                        23 | 25 | 23 | $55
### Meadowood, The ⓈⓂ

*Meadowood Resort, 900 Meadowood Ln. (Howell Mountain Rd., off Silverado Trail), St. Helena, 707-963-3646*
■ "This place is heaven on earth and where the angels must eat" purr the pampered staying at St. Helena's "most luxurious inn"; set "amongst beautiful scenery" ("overlooking the golf course and croquet field"), the "service is exceptional", the Californian "tasting menu is generous" and the Napa Valley–oriented wine selection "fabulous"; it's also "very expensive", but aren't all those above-mentioned factors "worth it"?

### RESTAURANT AT                                       26 | 24 | 24 | $54
### STEVENSWOOD, THE ⓈⓂ

*Stevenswood Lodge, 8211 Shoreline Hwy./Hwy. 1 (2 mi. south of Mendocino), Little River, 707-937-2810*
■ "Chef Marc Dym has raised the culinary bar on the North Coast" with his "high standards" and "stellar Continental gastronomy" that "is as good as SF's finest" (and "you will pay as much" for it); the combination of the "cozy", "art gallery-esque dining room on the side of the [lodge's] sculpture gardens" coupled with "perfectly orchestrated service" and arguably "the best wine list in the area" "makes you hate to leave"; "fortunately, it is customary to linger for hours fireside."

### Restaurant LuLu ⓁⓈⓂ　　　21　19　17　$39
*816 Folsom St. (bet. 4th & 5th Sts.), 415-495-5775*

◪ "Boy meets grill" at SoMa's "best-smelling restaurant" where a mélange of "loft dwellers", "Folsom Street leather daddies and Nob Hill society" goes "to get loud and stuffed" on "solid, simple French Provençal" fare served "family-style"; maybe "the buzz has died off since it first opened", but most feel it "still holds its own against the new kids in town"; however, do "wear ear protectors" and ear muffs, since the wood-fired ovens "add a distinctive flavor to the food" but do little for the "cavernous", literally "cool digs."

### Restaurant Peony ⓁⓈⓂ　　　23　16　12　$22
*Pacific Renaissance Plaza, 388 Ninth St. (bet. Franklin & Webster Sts.), Oakland, 510-286-8866*

◪ "You'll be searching your pockets for your passport" when you enter "this gigantic dim sum house" that's "as authentic as it gets" thanks to the "varied array of dumplings" that "don't pander to Western tastes" (though often "you have to chase down the carts to get any" from the non–English speaking staff); "plan on waiting a long time for a table" on weekends, as "all of Oakland's Chinatown locals are on the list in front of you."

### Restaurant 301 ⓈⓂ　　　▽ 25　22　25　$43
*The Carter House, 301 L St. (3rd St.), Eureka, 707-444-8062*

■ "If you're passing through Eureka" you'll be "wonderfully surprised" to find "fine dining" in a "pleasant" Victorian inn; while it features "unusual and well-prepared" New French–New American fare (specializing in ingredients grown on the grounds) and "attentive service", it's the 3,500-bottle-rich wine list ("arguably the greatest cellar in the U.S.") "that's the star in this place."

### Restaurant Umunhum Ⓢ　　　23　16　20　$46
*699 Almaden Expwy. (Via Valiente), San Jose, 408-927-8773*

◪ "San Jose's SF-style dining haunt" is an "odd mix of urban decor and trendy-ish Eclectic food" in "sleepy suburban Almaden"; "highly professional service" and a "strong" choice of global wines put it on many locals' "short list"; however, the unimpressed yawn ho-hum, the "expensive", "weird combinations" fail to live up to their "potential."

### Rice Table Ⓢ　　　▽ 22　17　23　$29
*1617 Fourth St. (G St.), San Rafael, 415-456-1808*

◪ It "feels like you are in another land" when eating at San Rafael's long-running Indonesian; loyalists still love "the traditional rice-table menu that offers a nice variety" of "fantastic" recipes "passed down from the mother" of the chef-owner; but the unsentimental snap this "limited" veteran is now "a long way from the *rijsttafels* of Amsterdam, both literally and figuratively."

### Rick & Ann's L S M    21 | 14 | 15 | $19
*2922 Domingo Ave. (bet. Ashby & Claremont Aves.), Berkeley, 510-649-8538*

■ "Grab your *Chronicle* and stake out a bench to wait your turn" at this "popular, quaint Berkeley breakfast joint" that's "as crunchy-granola as it gets"; it's also "perfect [and easier to get into] for an American comfort food dinner", but breeders beware: "the very kid-friendly [ambiance] can cause happy couples to put off baby-making for years."

### Rick's S M    ▽ 18 | 16 | 19 | $25
*1940 Taraval St. (30th Ave.), 415-731-8900*

■ This "funky" Sunset Hawaiian offers "above-average American" "comfortable food" and "outstanding" Island BBQ in servings so "humongous" that "most are enough for a family, including nieces and nephews"; ok, so the monthly luaus and "live singers" on weekends are "like a bad lounge act come to life", but somehow it all "combines magically" (with a little help from that "Flaming Pele rum drink") to offer "a great cheap SF thrill."

### Rio Grill L S M    22 | 19 | 20 | $35
*Crossroads Shopping Ctr., 101 Crossroads Blvd. (Rio Rd.), Carmel, 831-625-5436*

☑ "Southwestern meets hip" at this "casual" Californian cafe hidden away in a shopping mall; the "interesting combinations and flavors" (that usually work), "a wine list that makes any enthusiast see double" and "a friendly but not intrusive staff" "make it a primo pick in Carmel" for those hoping to spot "off-duty celebrities"; however, "go early or you won't be able to hear yourself think."

### Ristorante Bacco S M    21 | 19 | 21 | $34
*737 Diamond St. (bet. Elizabeth & 24th Sts.), 415-282-4969*

☑ When Noe Valleyites "want Italiano", they head to this "authentic" "neighborhood trattoria" that "runs circles around newcomers with amazing pastas", a wine list with offerings "even an oenophile has not heard of" and a "wonderful", "all-Italian staff" that "makes you feel like you're in" the mother country; while a "strange layout" doesn't help the "too-close-together" seating, all is forgotten when the "rock shrimp gnocchi rocks your world."

### Ristorante Fabrizio L M    20 | 14 | 20 | $34
*455 Magnolia Ave. (Cane St.), Larkspur, 415-924-3332*

■ "Always-available host Fabrizio" Martinelli's "family-run eatery" "has been feeding Marin County palates for years" with "Northern Italian food you'd expect your grandmother to make" (actually it's his mama) "at good prices"; it's "well loved by Larkspur locals", particularly for 'Monday Night Lobster Dinners' – so "reservations are suggested for that event."

### Ristorante Ideale 🅂   20  14  19  $34

*1309 Grant Ave. (bet. Green & Vallejo Sts.), 415-391-4129*

■ "If you're looking for the 'real deal' in Italian food" among the North Beach "sea of tourist joints", *via vai* to this "shining star", situated in an "ideale" location in the center of Grant Avenue and serviced by a "charming" "all-Italian staff" (no, those are not "faux accents"); the score for the "sterile-feeling decor" may not reflect a recent remodeling.

### Ristorante Milano 🅂   24  15  22  $33

*1448 Pacific Ave. (bet. Hyde & Larkin Sts.), 415-673-2961*

■ Although this ristorante is located "up on Russian Hill", you might easily feel like you're eating on one of Rome's famous seven, what with the "tasty cucina" ("reminds me of grandma's") and "authentic Italian waiters offering insight and attentiveness"; some call it "intimate", others call it "cramped", but you can call your "search for the perfect tiramisu over" once you've sampled it here.

### Ristorante Umbria 🅛🅜   17  14  17  $27

*198 Second St. (Howard St.), 415-546-6985*

◪ "Bustling with business lunchers by day", this corner storefront in SoMa "slows down at night", making it "a great place before a performance at Yerba Buena Center"; chef/co-owner "Guilio and his friendly staff make" fans feel they're "eating with family – if your family serves Montepulciano"; however, the "disappointed" downgraded scores this year, noting they "expect more from a place with such authentic Umbrian roots."

### RITZ-CARLTON DINING ROOM   28  26  27  $78

*Ritz-Carlton Hotel, 600 Stockton St. (bet. California & Pine Sts.), 415-773-6198*

■ When you really "want to impress him or her", this "old-world" "sumptuous" "sophisticate" "is the place to go"; chef "Sylvain Portay regales his audience with fantastic" "cuisine comparable to the best in France", while the nearly "flawless, without any snobbish attitude" staff "treats you like royalty"; it helps if you're among "the new rich of Silicon and the wine valleys" to afford it, but most feel "heaven cannot be as divine as dining at the Ritz"; P.S. "afternoon tea in the lobby lounge" "sets the standard."

### Ritz-Carlton Terrace 🅛🅂🅜   24  24  25  $46

*Ritz-Carlton Hotel, 600 Stockton St. (bet. California & Pine Sts.), 415-773-6198*

■ "Dress to impress" when you come to this "casually elegant", "blissfully quiet" hotel haunt, because while it's "the low-cost cousin to the main restaurant", "the fine Med cuisine" and "pampering", "leisurely paced" service "live up to the Ritz-Carlton name"; "Sunday jazz brunch on the veranda, if the weather cooperates, is simply "*le ne plus ultra*" (we "dare you to find a better" alternative).

### RIVOLI 🆂Ⓜ　　　　26　22　23　$40

*1539 Solano Ave. (bet. Neilson St. & Peralta Ave.), Berkeley,
510-526-2542*

■ While there are "no fancy foods" on the ever-changing
Cal-Med menu of this "fun, relaxed" East Bay jewel, chef/co-
owner Wendy Brucker "does magic with simple ingredients
and is able to keep the prices" "much lower than other
comparable-quality" places; the "longtime staffers" "are
tops" too say riveted reviewers who "have never had a bad
meal here – and neither have the cats and raccoons that
gather outside" in the "spellbinding" "backlit garden."

### Robata Grill & Sushi 🅛🆂Ⓜ　　22　16　18　$30

*591 Redwood Hwy./Hwy. 101 (Seminary Dr. exit), Mill Valley,
415-381-8400*

■ Gourmands get two places for the price of one at this
"large" popular Mill Valleyite where "families, couples and
singles co-exist harmoniously"; those looking for a raw deal
are rewarded with "appealing", "fresh-tasting sushi", while
those seeking the real deal in cooked "country Japanese"
fare are granted "robata that's just about perfect."

### Robert's Bistro 🆂Ⓜ　　▽ 25　22　24　$46

*Crossroads Shopping Ctr., 217 Crossroads Blvd. (Rio Rd.),
Carmel, 831-624-9626*

■ Though it's "tucked away in a mall", you'd be hard-
pressed to find a more "romantic setting" in Carmel than
Robert Kincaid's "warm, firelit, cozy-on-a-cold-night" dining
room, which offers "outstanding French bistro food" (think
Dover sole boned tableside), an "excellent wine list" and
"generally great service"; it's a bit "pricey" perhaps, but
the "early-bird prix fixe is a bargain."

### Rock Soup 🆂　　　–　–　–　I

*3299 Mission St. (29th St.), 415-641-7687*

This groovy outer Mission newcomer in a renovated old
bank whips up "homey New American eats" (meatloaf,
chicken pot pie, biscuits and – what else? – "comfort
soups") at rock-bottom prices, precisely the perfect
prescription "for those pink-slip doldrums"; nightly acoustic
music at no cover charge aims to create a communal
atmosphere, in line with the old 'Stone Soup' fable.

### RoHan Lounge ◗🆂　　　–　–　–　M

*3809 Geary Blvd. (bet. 2nd & 3rd Aves.), 415-221-5095*

SF's first and only "Soju bar" introduces Korea's answer
to tequila to Richmond lounge lizards who knock back
"refreshingly different" "specialty cocktails" featuring the
liqueur (distilled from rice, barley and sweet potato); to
accompany, chef Jen Solomon (ex Asia SF) woks up Pan-
Asian small plates and an array of kimchi, while the red-
washed Seoul-phisticated dining room pumps with DJ beats
on the weekends.

### Roosevelt Tamale Parlor L S ⊄   17   6   12   $14
*2817 24th St. (bet. Bryant & York Sts.), 415-550-9213*

◼ When "craving authenticity", head to this "unrepentantly unhip" Mission Mexican that's been "part of SF history" since 1922; "the homemade tamales are outstanding", but amigos insist the "huge portions" of other basics – rice, enchiladas, mole poblano – provide a benchmark for "what [such eats are] supposed to taste like"; "don't be put off" by the "funky" decor that's as worn as a favorite Teddy bear.

### Rosamunde Sausage Grill L S M ⊄   ▽ 22   10   17   $11
*545 Haight St. (Fillmore St.), 415-437-6851*

◼ This bite-size Lower Haight wursteria is "one of the only places in Frisco offering your basic grilled sausage, and a damn good one at that" (actually, there are 13 damn "good varieties"); with practically "no place to sit except" eight stools, it's "like a hot-dog stand only much tastier" (better "mustard selection" too), but you're welcome to grab your brat "and take it to the Toronado beer bar next door."

### Rose Pistola L S M   21   20   18   $41
*532 Columbus Ave. (bet. Green & Union Sts.), 415-399-0499*

◼ Reed Hearon's "raucous" hot-as-a-pistola place offers "a touch of class in the heart of schlocky Columbus Avenue"; "beautiful people abound here", "but what's more beautiful is" the "amazing, fresh" Ligurian-style seafood, which you can "watch being made"; however, those for whom "the bloom is definitely off the rose" warn "be prepared to speak loudly" and carry a lot of patience, because the "I'm-doing-you-a-favor" service "really detracts."

### Rose's Café L S M   17   16   14   $28
*2298 Union St. (Steiner St.), 415-775-2200*

◼ "A rose by any other name wouldn't taste as good" quoth converts who happily munch at brunch or lunch on this Cow Hollow cafe's "wonderful wood-burning-oven pizzas"; however, after-dark diners can't "figure out what and who" this blossom is, as the Northern Italian–New French dinner menu "still lacks refinement and choice" and "the staff seems in a constant state of harriedness."

### Ross Valley Brewing Company L S M   ▽ 19   16   15   $25
*765 Center Blvd. (Pastori Ave.), Fairfax, 415-485-1005*

◼ "Most people come" to this "handsome" "happening brewpub" "to try the handcrafted beer, which is excellent", "but once you've tasted the" "upscale" New American eats that are "much better than the average brewery's", "you have two reasons to return"; given its suburban setting "in sleepy Fairfax", it's no surprise that the place is hospitable to families and "socializing singles" alike.

### Rotunda 🅛🅢🅜    ▽ 21 │ 23 │ 22 │ $34 │
*Neiman Marcus, 150 Stockton St. (Geary St.),
415-362-4777*
■ Attention shoppers, the storied picture windows over
Union Square at this "ultimate ladies-who-lunch" and
"afternoon-tea" venue should be unveiled by the time the fall
collection hits the runway; sure the New American fare "is
pricey (what do you expect? it's in Neiman Marcus)", "but
the complimentary popovers and consommé set the perfect
mood" and "even a hamburger becomes a gastronomic
event" when it's presented under a spectacular glass
rotunda by "top-notch servers."

### Roux    ▽ 26 │ 19 │ 24 │ $45 │
*1234 Main St. (Hunt Ave.), St. Helena, 707-963-5330*
■ A "stunningly simple interior with white plates suspended
on the [red] wall marks the scene of a stunningly wonderful
restaurant" decree the culinary cognoscenti who come to
this St. Helena sophomore; order the "four-course tasting
menu" (with pairings from local boutique vintners) and
your cup will runneth over with a series of "awesome"
French-inspired American dishes (punctuated with "a
series of *amuse-bouches* throughout") "served flawlessly
by a fun group of people."

### Roxanne's 🅢    ▽ 24 │ 23 │ 22 │ $45 │
*320 Magnolia Ave. (King St.), Larkspur, 415-924-5004*
■ "If you're feeling adventurous", attend this "astonishing"
Larkspur 'living foods' restaurant, that eschews meat,
dairy and even stoves (using low-temperature baking, and
blending and straining instead) in order to retain the
vegetables' full nutritional value; it sounds "extremist", but
"truly marvelous" chef-owner Roxanne Klein "pulls it off",
and the converted crow that the experience, in a solar-
powered room fashioned from ecologically sustainable
materials, "may change your eating habits forever."

### Royal Thai 🅛🅢🅜    21 │ 16 │ 17 │ $22 │
*951 Clement St. (11th Ave.), 415-386-1795*
*610 Third St. (Grand Ave.), San Rafael, 415-485-1074*
◩ While "San Rafael houses a number of Thai" eateries, this
princeling located in a "charming old house" is "consistently
the most popular" (by contrast, "its sister" in the Inner
Richmond is refreshingly undiscovered); "dark and pretty
dining rooms" make them "good picks for a cheap date",
and the menus feature specialties that are "different yet
full of flavor" ("the sea bass is a knockout"); however, the
"service is not [nearly as] impressive."

### Roy's 🅛🅢🅜    22 │ 22 │ 21 │ $44 │
*101 Second St. (Mission St.), 415-777-0277*
◩ The SoMa "franchise" of chef Roy Yamaguchi's Hawaiian
Fusion chain is set in a "duel-level dining room" that offers

a "great" "getaway" "without the schlep to Maui"; acolytes admire the "island-inspired treats" that are "thrilling for the taste buds" (though "not for the faint of tongue") and say the "staff, while not perfect, shows more effort than any other place in SF"; but the Roy-ally disappointed declare this branch's "overpriced", "overflavored" fare "pales in comparison" to others in his archipelago.

### Roy's at Pebble Beach ⬛🅛🆂🅜   25 | 25 | 22 | $50
*The Inn at Spanish Bay, 2700 17 Mile Dr. (Congress Rd.), Pebble Beach, 831-647-7423*

■ "If you don't love this place, nothing on this earth is going to please you" exclaim enraptured Roy-als who lap up "fabulous Hawaiian Fusion cuisine" while gazing at the "spectacular views" "of the Pacific Ocean"; go for lunch after a round of golf at Pebble Beach or "plan your dinner around the sunset" and the "serenading bagpipes", but do "get there" because, with the aid of "superior service", most feel the ever-expanding chef-restaurateur "lives up to his reputation here."

### Rubicon 🅛🅜   23 | 19 | 22 | $55
*558 Sacramento St. (bet. Montgomery & Sansome Sts.), 415-434-4100*

🿣 "Who cares if DeNiro and Coppola own a partial share" in this Downtowner? – the "real star here" is "the unmatched wine list" of "Larry Stone, the master sommelier of master sommeliers", though chef Denis Leary's "complex yet not precious" New French–Californian cuisine delivers a strong supporting performance; the "civilized" service ensures it's a top spot "for adults" doing "business lunch and dinner", but "roaring '90s" prices prevent some "young people" from crossing a river they deem "corporate" and "bland."

### Ruen Pair 🅛🆂🅜   – | – | – | M
*1045 San Pablo Ave. (Marin Ave.), Albany, 510-528-2375*

"Gorgeous Thai objects contribute to the pleasure of dining at this" "great find on San Pablo Avenue"; "the attentive staff" "tries very hard to please", serving consistently "fresh tasting" Siamese specialties; but regulars warn the kitchen is "oriented to Western palates", so "if you want your food spicy, you have to strongly emphasize 'hot.'"

### Rutherford Grill 🅛🆂🅜   22 | 18 | 19 | $31
*1180 Rutherford Rd. (Hwy. 29), Rutherford, 707-963-1792*

🿣 "If you've been indulging too much at the wineries", this "casual" Rutherford reliable is "a good place to overload on" all-American "iron-skillet cornbread" and "terrific ribs"; the no-reservations policy "really stinks", but "no corkage fee" is sweeter than the "Oreo cookie dessert", and while there are "better places in Napa Valley", none can compete with the dog-friendly patio here (awarded "four paws" by our canine critics).

### Ruth's Chris Steak House ⑤Ⓜ   23 | 19 | 21 | $50

*1601 Van Ness Ave. (California St.), 415-673-0557*

☑ Carnivores "know it's a chain, but when you want real red meat" ("on the rare side") "this is mecca" "located amid the Van Ness bustle"; though the "sizzling-in-butter" bit is "not for steak purists", the "large portions" doled out by an "old-world, attentive staff" ensure a full belly – "too bad your pockets are empty when you leave."

### Sake Tini Ⓛ⑤Ⓜ   ▽ 14 | 8 | 13 | $24

*Bel Aire Plaza, 3900 Bel Aire Plaza (Trancas St.), Napa, 707-255-7423*

☑ This hip sake specialist was "promising in its beginning" in 2000; but while many still think it's "fun to find" "interesting Asian food" "in an old bowling alley", others huff "there's not much atmosphere, sitting in a strip mall", saying it seems solely "to exist so that Napa twentysomethings can have a pick-up bar."

### Salute Ristorante Ⓛ⑤Ⓜ   16 | 15 | 15 | $30

*Marina Bay, 1900 Esplanade Dr. (Melville Sq.), Richmond, 510-215-0803*
*706 Third St. (Tamalpais Ave.), San Rafael, 415-453-7596*

☑ Locals salute this set of "consistent and friendly" Italian-Meds for fare that's "dependable", if "nothing inventive"; while the "great view" of the Bay overshadows the dining at the Point Richmond branch, it's still considered "a beacon in that middle-of-nowhere" neighborhood; its older sister "in the heart of San Rafael" is "worth a visit if you're in the area."

### Sam's Anchor Cafe Ⓛ⑤Ⓜ   13 | 18 | 13 | $25

*27 Main St. (Tiburon Blvd.), Tiburon, 415-435-4527*

☑ "Sitting out on the sunny deck" of this "Tiburon institution" drinking a brew and "soaking up the amazing view of the city" while "surrounded by wind-chapped sailors and pert sorority sisters" is the "ultimate California experience"; sure, the American "food is pretty average" and "the staff indifferent", but the legions of "seagulls sharing your fries" "aren't deterred", so neither should you be.

### Sam's Grill & Seafood Restaurant Ⓛap Ⓜ   22 | 17 | 19 | $36

*374 Bush St. (bet. Kearny & Montgomery Sts.), 415-421-0594*

☑ "The city's oldest fish house" (circa 1867 – talk about "staying power") Downtown sets "the standard for the vanishing business lunch" replete with "private booths"; "those who cherish the tradition" of "old SF" find solace in the "same" "straightforward" seafood (crab Louis, sand dabs), "crusty sourdough French bread" and "grumpy but classy waiters" who "are still there"; however, the "men's-club" attitude is also "the same as it ever was", as is the dog-eared decor.

### Sanraku Four Seasons L S M     23   14   15   $30
*Sony Metreon Ctr., 101 Fourth St. (Mission St.), 415-369-6166*
*704 Sutter St. (Taylor St.), 415-771-0803*
◪ Maki mavens maintain that the "unbelievable sushi" (plus
other "outstanding" options such as "buttery beef teriyaki")
"makes the lackluster decor", "gruff service" and "long
queues" at this Japanese duo "all but disappear"; their
respective locations also make 'em convenient before a
movie at the Sony Metreon or a show Downtown.

### Santé S M     –   –   –   E
(fka Restaurant at Sonoma Mission Inn & Spa)
*Sonoma Mission Inn & Spa, 18140 Sonoma Hwy./Hwy. 12
(Boyes Blvd.), Sonoma, 707-939-2415*
While few seem to recognize the Sonoma Mission Inn's
recently rechristened eatery (amazing what these spa
getaways can do), those who have say the "new chef
succeeds" with a santé-oriented cuisine that jettisons
butter and cream for soupçons of olive oil and wine; of
course, you can still indulge in more standard Californian
fare, much of it coaxed out of clay ovens.

### Santi L S M     23   18   21   $39
*21047 Geyserville Ave. (Hwy. 101), Geyserville, 707-857-1790*
■ Northern Sonoma County visitors are "impressed" by
this "SF caliber" "sleeper" that showcases "hearty but
elegant Italian cuisine" with a "strong" Cal-Ital "wine list
to match" (most of the 'Cal' part is made up of local valley
wines); "perfectly friendly and attentive" servers move
through an area that boasts a "welcoming fireplace in
cooler months and a relaxing patio for the summer"; in short,
"Geyserville may be the next Yountville if this keeps up."

### Sardine Factory S M     22   23   22   $48
*701 Wave St. (Prescott Ave.), Monterey, 831-373-3775*
■ Despite being a "tourist hangout", this "Monterey staple"
"manages to capture the spirit of [Steinbeck's] Cannery
Row" and be "impressive enough for clients and hard-to-
please" locals; "check out the differently decorated rooms
before deciding where to settle", then tuck into some "top-
notch" seafood and a bottle off the "awesome wine list";
although the "formal service" "will knock you back to the
'60s", "that shouldn't stop you from enjoying it."

### Sassafras Restaurant & Wine Bar L S M     ∇ 23   20   21   $36
*Santa Rosa Business Park, 1229 N. Dutton Ave. (College Ave.),
Santa Rosa, 707-578-7600*
■ Veteran restaurateur Michael Hirschberg has "nicely
reincarnated" his Santa Rosa haunt, Mistral, with a little
help from his friends: old chef Scott Synder, now turning out
regional New American specialties (including a venison-
pork terrine masquerading as a meatloaf sandwich), and

returning wine director Laura Kudla, who oversees the exclusively born-in-the-USA list; already patrons praise the patio as a "great place to people-watch."

### Saul's Restaurant & Delicatessen L S M  18 15 15 $17

*1475 Shattuck Ave. (bet. Rose & Vine Sts.), Berkeley, 510-848-3354*

◪ "In this neck of the woods, a good Jewish deli is like manna from heaven", which explains why "homesick East Coasters" kvell over the "NY-style pastrami and corned beef sandwiches" that are "larger than many studio apartments" in Manhattan; despite the coffee-shop looks and "abrupt service", it may not be 100 percent "authentic", but "rain or shine, there's always a line", so apparently "it'll do for Waspy North Berkeley."

### Savoia Ristorante S M  – – – I

*2355 Chestnut St. (bet. Divisadero & Scott Sts.), 415-346-6623*
Another Italian stallion (named for Italy's last royal family) has entered the Marina stall "where Zinzino used to be"; while the open kitchen and wood-burning stove remain, the interior has been transformed with modern Milano motifs, and the menu lists regional specialties from around The Boot; the expansive bar specializes in Prosecco cocktails.

### Savor L S M  18 15 16 $20

*3913 24th St. (bet. Noe & Sanchez Sts.), 415-282-0344*
◪ "Artful crêpes" "with an international twist and American proportions" are what "keep the [Noe Valley] neighborhood happy on weekend mornings" at this French-Med, especially if folks can savor the moment on the "unbeatable patio out back"; some skeptics sniff it's "not deserving of the stupidly long waits that clog the sidewalk."

### Scala's Bistro ◑ L S M  22 20 20 $40

*Sir Francis Drake Hotel, 432 Powell St. (bet. Post & Sutter Sts.), 415-395-8555*
◼ Although this continuously serving "restaurant in the Sir Francis Drake Hotel" is often "overlooked", it's "one of the hottest and best spots" before or after "Downtown shopping and plays"; the room rollicks with "great energy", the Italian-French "flavors are right on" and the "beautiful" decor evocative "of an old redwood lacquer cigar room" belies the "fairly moderate" prices; just pace yourself with the "enormous portions" or you'll "walk out looking and feeling like Pavarotti."

### Schroeder's L M  15 16 16 $30

*240 Front St. (bet. California & Sacramento Sts.), 415-421-4778*
◪ This "antediluvian" "authentic German" Downtowner (dated 1893) is so "nostalgic" "it's gotten cool again"; "Bavarian pretzels on the tables", "brews as fresh as those

in Munich", "wonderfully Teutonic waiters" and the occasional "polka night" beckon Berlin wanna-bes to bellow "what more do you need?" when sauer-pusses snipe "it's seen better days."

### Scoma's L S M   20 | 16 | 18 | $37

*Pier 47 (bet. Jefferson & Jones Sts.), 415-771-4383*
*588 Bridgeway (Princess St.), Sausalito, 415-332-9551*
◪ It's "the smell of the good ole sea", plus the sight of Fisherman's Wharf or "the Bay (from the Sausalito branch)" that are the lures at this set of "unpretentious" "old-school" seafarers; fans find the fin fare "wonderfully fresh" and feel "you can't beat the views of the water", but raggers reply "you can't eat the views" either and carp these "tourist traps" are "overpriced" and "ordinary."

### Sea Ranch
### Lodge Restaurant L S M   ▽ 16 | 21 | 19 | $37

*Sea Ranch Lodge, 60 Sea Walk Dr. (Hwy. 1), The Sea Ranch, 707-785-2371*
■ Visitors who venture to this "remote" Sea Ranch resort are swept up by the "fabulous views and sunsets" "from any table in the house"; while the "landmark architecture" has long been the draw here, the kitchen offers "well-executed" Californian cuisine "emphasizing [coastal] ingredients", complemented by "friendly service."

### Sears Fine Food L S M ⌿   16 | 8 | 14 | $16

*439 Powell St. (bet. Post & Sutter Sts.), 415-986-1160*
◪ Although "'Fine Food' is stretching things a bit", "locals and natives" alike insist this diner Downtown, seemingly serviced for six decades by the same "grumpy", "blue-haired waitresses", is "worth the wait in line" – at least for its "wonderful silver dollar" "Swedish pancakes"; but a drop in the Decor score confirms a dining room "face-lift" is "most needed."

### Seasons L S M   ▽ 26 | 28 | 28 | $58

*Four Seasons Hotel, 757 Market St. (bet. 3rd & 4th Sts.), 415-633-3838*
■ Sporting a "wonderful view of the Financial District" from its discreet perch on the fifth floor of the Four Seasons Hotel, this "beautiful" newcomer glows with pale-wood paneling, plush amber banquettes and golden lighting; though it's "yet to be discovered", it already seems well-seasoned, judging by reports of chef Christophe Guibert's (ex Paris' Le Cinq) "great" Californian–New French fare "and an attentive staff" that makes "you feel pampered."

### Sent Sovi S   – | – | – | M

*14583 Big Basin Way (5th St.), Saratoga, 408-867-3110*
At press time, the owners have announced their decision to morph this previously pricey prix fixe French into a more

moderate bistro (think slow-braised lamb shank over roasted polenta); the "romantic, European atmosphere" will remain, however, so Silicon Valleyites may well find their longtime favorite remains "a treat in a cottage" "tucked away in the quaint village of Saratoga."

### 71 Saint Peter L M   22 | 18 | 21 | $34

*71 N. San Pedro St. (bet. Santa Clara & St. John Sts.), San Jose, 408-971-8523*

■ A shining beacon "in Downtown San Jose", this "little place has a big sensibility of what makes a great meal" – "nicely prepared" Med classics "with a focus on seafood", "helpful service" and a "reasonably priced wine list"; while the "funky", "rustic interior" is found "lacking compared with" everything else, the patio is downright "romantic."

### SHADOWBROOK L S M   19 | 27 | 20 | $39

*1750 Wharf Rd. (Capitola Rd.), Capitola, 831-475-1511*

◪ The "gorgeous setting, a series of built-on Swiss Chalet–style dining rooms that flow down a verdant hillside", and the "romantic" approach on a "tiny cable car" make this 55-year-old "icon" "ensconced on Soquel Creek" a "popular local celebration spot"; not surprisingly the Continental-American cuisine is "not as good" as the view, but at the very least, "go for drinks" in the "beautiful" handcrafted bar.

### Shalimar ◐ L S M ≠   24 | 4 | 8 | $13

*532 Jones St. (Geary St.), 415-928-0333*
### Shalimar Gardens L S M
*417 O'Farrell St. (bet. Jones & Taylor Sts.), 415-447-4041*

◪ "In a super-sketchy" stretch of the Tenderloin, this Indian-Pakistani may look like "a truck stop in middle hell", but the "phenomenal", "feisty and fast" "fragrant kebabs" and "bread right out of the tandoor" "at absurd prices" are among "the best in the city" (and generate naan-stop lines even at 11 PM); P.S. for a few dollars more, "try [newer] Shalimar Gardens just down the street – same recipes and 100 percent improvement in atmosphere."

### Shanghai 1930 L M   17 | 21 | 17 | $39

*133 Steuart St. (bet. Howard & Mission Sts.), 415-896-5600*

◪ "Drenched with Jazz Age" Asian atmosphere, this "glamorous, sexy" SoMa supper club "is a transporting place to stop for a cocktail" and some "haute Chinese" cuisine; however a drop in the Food score supports sentiments about "so-so fare", and other shafted surveyors feel "shanghaied" by slow service, suggesting this may be a "relic of another bygone era – that of the dot-com."

### Sharon's by the Sea L S M   ▽ 21 | 16 | 20 | $28

*32096 N. Harbor Dr. (Hwy. 1), Fort Bragg, 707-962-0680*

■ When Mendocino coasters get "tired of high-class" dining, they "dress down" and go for Northern Italian–

inflected fare, featuring "fish fresh off the boats", at this "seaside cafe" that "sits on the dock" of Noyo Harbor, aka "one of the cutest little working harbors you'll ever see."

### Shen Hua **L S M**   21 19 16 $22
*2914 College Ave. (bet. Ashby Ave. & Russell St.), Berkeley, 510-883-1777*

☑ "Fresh innovative fare", coupled with "Pottery Barn decor", an "open kitchen" and "a top-shelf full bar", makes this popular Berkeleyite "a refreshing change from the same-old Chinese"; less invigorating are the "deafeningly loud dining conditions" and the "rushed service", though all that's understandable "given the hordes that descend on" the place.

### Shoopra **L S M**   - - - I
*3301 Buchanan St. (bet. Chestnut & Lombard Sts.), 415-614-9300*

A cozy, jewel-toned dining room, aglow with candles, sets the stage at this humble, family-run Assyrian, which offers Cow Hollowers a taste of the Near East (Syria, Turkey, Iraq and Iran) with such dishes as *cooba* (semolina dumplings stuffed with meat) and *rizza* (rice soup), as well as the usual Middle Eastern suspects; for dessert, decide between baklava and baklava, prepared two ways.

### SIERRA MAR **L S M**   28 28 27 $76
*Post Ranch Inn, Hwy. 1 (30 mi. south of Carmel), Big Sur, 831-667-2800*

■ When in a place "where heaven appears to meet earth" (Big Sur), why not "play it to the hilt at this" "superluxe tree house" "perched atop a cliff 1,200 ft. above the Pacific"; it's an "awesome setting", but it's "equaled" by the "exquisite", "passionate" Cal–New French menu, "spectacular" service and a "wine list that's 4,000 bottles strong"; "after a meal here you may melt away in utter bliss."

### Silks **L S M**   24 24 23 $56
*Mandarin Oriental Hotel, 222 Sansome St. (California St.), 415-986-2020*

■ This "formal hotel dining room" Downtown "is the consummate corporate lunch" place, with "elegant, refined" decor ("lots of room between tables"), "impeccable service and "creative Asian-inspired" Cal cuisine; many mourn it still "does not get the recognition it deserves" – though that makes it work "for a quiet evening alone with a loved one" as well.

### Skates on the Bay **L S M**   16 23 18 $35
*100 Seawall Dr. (University Ave.), Berkeley, 510-549-1900*

☑ At this New American, a view "from the Berkeley marina" that's "the stuff picture postcards are made of" "wows out-of-towners every time"; while the service is "unexpectedly accommodating", the "decent" seafood "may not take your breath away", so most folks prefer to skate in "for a sunset drink" "and nibbles" ("just order the minimum amount of food to stay at a table").

### SLANTED DOOR, THE 🄻🅂🅼     26 – 20 $37
*100 Brannan St. (The Embarcadero), 415-861-8032*
◪ "The pinnacle of Asian cuisine" proclaim partisans of chef Charles Phan's "extraordinary slant on" "Vietnamese street food made upscale", paired with "the most innovative wine list"; "it's best to go with a group and order family-style", as the "dishes are on the small side"; P.S. the "casual, high-energy atmosphere" has moved to the Embarcadero while the old digs undergo a renovation (scheduled to reopen March 2003).

### Slow Club 🄻🅂🅼     24 19 19 $31
*2501 Mariposa St. (Hampshire St.), 415-241-9390*
■ "For the New York lounge experience without the flight", a "hip" "young crowd" "jams" this "industrial chic" supper club in the Mission's warehouse district; while the "dark, mysterious atmosphere" makes it the "ultimate first-date venue", the "comforting yummy" New American eats on the daily changing menu "exceed expectations"; "since they don't take reservations", be willing to slow down and wait a while.

### Sociale 🄻🅂🅼     22 21 20 $37
*3665 Sacramento St. (bet. Locust & Spruce Sts.), 415-921-3200*
■ This new restaurant/wine bar is quickly becoming a favorite "neighborhood place" for "the ladies who lunch" by day and other Presidio Heights socialites by night, thanks to the "wonderful" "nouveau Italian" menu ("you must try the fried olive salad" and the "orgasmic doughnut-and-gelato shake") meted out by "an energetic staff"; finding the "charming" dining room is a bit tricky (it's "hidden down a narrow walkway"), but that's a large part of the appeal.

### Soizic 🄻🅂     23 19 19 $36
*300 Broadway (3rd St.), Oakland, 510-251-8100*
■ At this "owner-operated" Oakland "sleeper", "don't let the drab exterior" "dissuade you" – the interior brims with "incredible arty decor" that's "elegant but not pretentious" (or noisy), and "the short but focused menu has no weak points", just "Cal cuisine" "full of fresh flavors and old favorites"; in short, "a refreshing alternative in Jack London Square" ("an area otherwise devoid of good" eateries).

### Soléa 🄻🅼     – – – M
*(fka V Restaurant)*
*Orchard Hotel, 665 Bush St. (bet. Powell & Stockton Sts.), 415-837-1680*
Downtown's swank Orchard Hotel now sports a moderate, Californian-influenced French brasserie; although the dining

room's somewhat awkward layout lacks intimacy, chef Bruno Feldeisen (ex executive pastry chef at NYC's Four Seasons) strives for sweet success not just with his famed desserts, but with intricately flavored fare such as a strip loin laced with cardamom jus.

### South Park Cafe 🅛🅜    21 | 16 | 17 | $32
*108 South Park St. (bet. 2nd & 3rd Sts.), 415-495-7275*
◪ "Hidden away in South Park", this "laid-back cafe" "is the closest thing to authentic Parisian" you'll find without leaving Downtown; the bill of fare is "real bistro" and the ambiance (down to the butcher "paper on the tables and chalkboard menu") is pure Gallic "sans pretense"; there's even "great" sidewalk seating, perfect "when the sun is shining" or just to escape the "noisy, tight quarters" inside.

### Spago Palo Alto 🅛🅜    23 | 22 | 20 | $53
*265 Lytton Ave. (bet. Bryant & Ramona Sts.), Palo Alto, 650-833-1000*
◪ "Silicon Valley's version of Wolfgang Puck's" "revered chain" is still "*the* place" to see the "Shallow Alto crowd" dining on "expense accounts" ("if there are any left") in a puckishly designed dining room that's as "pleasing to the eye" as the Californian cuisine is "to the palate"; while some pout it's too much of a "'80s throwback" with "big corporate decor and fussy architectural dishes", even they concede "the scene is always high-energy" – and those "signature pizzas" "admittedly delicious."

### Spenger's 🅛🅢🅜    13 | 16 | 14 | $30
*1919 Fourth St. (bet. Hearst & University Aves.), Berkeley, 510-845-7771*
◪ Nostalgists and families are "hooked on the retro food" and "perfectly preserved", "nautical-themed" atmosphere of Berkeley's "oldest seafood stop" (circa 1890), "known for its 'shrimp scatter'" as much as its scattered service; while schools of surveyors appreciate the "recent remodel" "by the McCormick & Schmick chain", crabs carp this "overpriced", underwhelming "classic has sunk into the sunset."

### Spiedini 🅛🅢    19 | 17 | 17 | $37
*101 Ygnacio Valley Rd. (Oakland Blvd.), Walnut Creek, 925-939-2100*
◪ Named for the Italian word for skewer, this "very 1980s" trattoria indeed "skewers most things well (excellent rotisserie rabbit, lamb and chicken)" and "used to be the measure by which other restaurants in Walnut Creek were judged"; however, these days, it's some surveyors who are doing the spearing, suggesting that the "food's inconsistent" and (in accord with declining scores) the "austere" room is "noisier than ever"; furthermore, certain "arrogant" staffers "need to be beaten with that stick."

### Spoon S    20 | 17 | 15 | $36
*2209 Polk St. (Vallejo St.), 415-268-0140*

☑ With its day-glo green logo, late-night menu and bustling bar that dominates half of the "cramped" dining room, this "funky" newcomer offers a bit of "NYC's SoHo" on SF's Polk Street; chef Erik Hopinger (ex butterfly) "ladles up some decent grub" on his Californian "comfort food" menu that ranges from sea bass with wild mushroom juice to macaroni and cheese; just don't expect spoon-feeding by the "snooty staff."

### Stars L M    20 | 22 | 19 | $46
*555 Golden Gate Ave. (bet. Polk St. & Van Ness Ave.),*
*415-861-7827*

☑ Comments are crossed when it comes to this "classic in the Civic Center Area": fans "thank their lucky stars" for the "artfully prepared Cal cuisine with interesting Med flair" served by a staff that "gets you to the [show] on time", while acidic astronomers argue it "doesn't twinkle anymore"; still, it's "packed with an eclectic mix" of enough movers and shakers to provide plenty of "stargazing" ops.

### Station House Café L S M    18 | 14 | 15 | $26
*11180 Shoreline Hwy./Hwy. 1 (2nd St.), Point Reyes Station,*
*415-663-1515*

☑ This "locals' place in West Marin" "is an excellent stop on the way to Point Reyes Lighthouse" for "relaxed, reasonably priced" New American fare ("try the fresh seafood" or "terrific Niman Ranch burgers"); although the staff "runs hot and cold" and the "inside is pedestrian", you can't miss with "a spot on the stunning garden patio with an explosion of flowers."

### Stinking Rose L S M    14 | 15 | 14 | $28
*325 Columbus Ave. (bet. Broadway & Vallejo St.), 415-781-7673*

☑ "Bring mints, mouthwash and heartburn medication" to North Beach's "kitschy" Northern Italian "shrine to garlic" because everything (and everybody) "reeks" of the fragrant bulb (from an addictive spread for bread to the ice cream); while rose-colored reviewers deem it "touristy but tasty", the sour-mouthed snarl "you'll grow a mustache waiting for your food" and this "cute gimmick" has "gone mediocre" – "unless your significant other is a vampire."

### Stinson Beach Grill L S M    ∇ 17 | 11 | 12 | $26
*3465 Shoreline Hwy./Hwy. 1 (east of Fairfax Bolinas Rd.),*
*Stinson Beach, 415-868-2002*

■ Hugging the Shoreline Highway near Stinson Beach, this Traditional American grill is "the only place where locals go: the menu is more varied than other places", plus they serve all day and offer "nice outdoor seating"; of course, it doesn't hurt that there's also "nothing else until you hit Mill Valley."

### St. Michael's Alley **L S**　　22 | 18 | 20 | $32
*806 Emerson St. (Homer Ave.), Palo Alto, 650-326-2530*
■ While this "cozy" "Palo Alto hideaway" has lots of star power (it was a Clinton "favorite when Chelsea was at Stanford"), the spotlight remains on California's bounty, both with the "seasonally changing menu" and the "good selection of Santa Cruz Mountain wines"; Saints fans come marching in for brunch, lunch and dinner and are treated to "service that can't do enough to please."

### Stokes Restaurant & Bar **L S M**　　23 | 22 | 22 | $41
*500 Hartnell St. (bet. Madison & Polk Sts.), Monterey, 831-373-1110*
■ "The romance of old Monterey lives in this restored adobe" thanks to "chef Brandon Miller, one of the most talented cooks" in the area; his "delicious" Cal-Med menu is sure to stoke your fire, the way he stokes the wood-burning fireplace that dominates the dining room; aided by "fantastic servers", those who believe that "variety" is the spice of life can cobble together "a very affordable meal" from a selection of "small plates and tapas."

### St. Orres **S M ≠**　　24 | 23 | 21 | $50
*36601 Shoreline Hwy./Hwy. 1 (2 mi. north of Gualala), Gualala, 707-884-3303*
☑ "Inspired by a woodland sprite", chef-owner Rosemary Campiformio "passionately forages" for chanterelles and other local goodies that comprise the "unique" Cal menu served in her offbeat hostelry – "where else can you get a salad laced with red hots and jicama stars" while sitting amid a "Russian-style" residence complete with "onion domes and funky cottages"; the jaded find the "quirky" show "tiring", but strong scores side with those who deem this "a wonderful place to eat and stay."

### STRAITS CAFE **L S M**　　22 | 20 | 18 | $33
*3300 Geary Blvd. (Parker Ave.), 415-668-1783*
*3295 El Camino Real (Ventura Ave.), Palo Alto, 650-494-7168*
☑ Chef and cookbook author "Chris Yeo does a wonderful job of bringing a bit of Indonesia and India" (plus China and Malaysia) to the Inner Richmond and Palo Alto at this set of "scrumptious Singaporeans" whose "fresh spin on spicy" "food will blow you away"; some grumble the "annoyingly slow service" needs strait-ening out, but "fun froofy drinks replete with plastic monkeys" can compensate.

### Street Restaurant **L S**　　20 | 16 | 18 | $27
*2141 Polk St. (Vallejo St.), 415-775-1055*
■ This new kid on the street (Polk, that is) "is just what the neighborhood needs" – "a fun, reasonably priced" New American featuring "yummy comfort food with a kick" ("don't miss the [thrice-a-week] buttermilk fried chicken") and "the best bartenders in town"; no reservations are taken

for the "funky industrial" setting ("lots of concrete and hard chairs"), but you can always snare a stool at the eat-in bar.

### Suppenküche ⑤Ⓜ     20 | 16 | 18 | $27 |
*601 Hayes St. (Laguna St.), 415-252-9289*
■ When "you're jonesing for that Jungfrau feeling", "step into" this "raucous" "German country pub" in Hayes Valley that's "like Oktoberfest" every day with its "huge steins" of "hard-to-find" beers (served from a giant boot) and "hearty portions" of sauerkraut, sausage and schnitzel; your rump "might be aching for a cushion planted on the wooden picnic benches", "but your belly will be singing oompah-pah."

### Sushi Groove Ⓜ     22 | 19 | 16 | $34 |
*1516 Folsom St. (bet. 11th & 12th Sts.), 415-503-1950*
*1916 Hyde St. (bet. Green & Union Sts.), 415-440-1905* ⑤
◪ Get into the groove at this Japanese pair that "dares to answer the question 'how trendy can you make your sushi?'"; while both offer "right-off-the-boat" sashimi, "rule-breaking" rolls and "Adonis waiters" "who need a little polishing", the "tiny" outpost "tucked into the folds of Russian Hill" "is trendy and romantic" with an adjoining "wine bar"/waiting room, while "the SoMa branch", with a sake bar and "DJ spinning for the hipster crowd", is simply "trendy and loud."

### SUSHI RAN ⓁⓈⓂ     27 | 20 | 21 | $41 |
*107 Caledonia St. (bet. Pine & Turney Sts.), Sausalito, 415-332-3620*
■ "Run", don't walk to this jam-packed Sausalito Japanese that "doesn't need cartoons or house music" "to draw a crowd" because its "superb" "velvety" "fish that evaporates in your mouth" and "inventive dishes that push the fresh sushi ingredients to new heights" "are the best in Marin" and perhaps "the land"; the extensive "wine and sake bar next door" doesn't make the "looong waits" any shorter, though you can "have a snack there if you can't" tarry.

### SWAN OYSTER DEPOT ⓁⓂ⌀     26 | 11 | 22 | $25 |
*1517 Polk St. (bet. California & Sacramento Sts.), 415-673-1101*
◪ This "old-time SF tradition" on Polk Street is "half raw bar, half floor show" thanks to simply prepared "seafood that's as fresh as it gets" (also available to go) and the bevy of "brothers/owners behind the counter" who "know food and fun"; true "the elbow-to-elbow", "counter-only" "seating is uncomfortable", but mollusk mavens maintain "nothing beats" "sitting at the same oyster bar that my granddad sat at 40 years ago"; N.B. closes at 5:30 PM.

### Syrah Ⓛ     25 | 20 | 21 | $38 |
*205 Fifth St. (Davis St.), Santa Rosa, 707-568-4002*
■ Don't rely on syrah-ndipity to get yourself to this bistro, quickly becoming a Santa Rosa "hot spot" thanks to chef

Josh Silver's "entertaining" personality and "imaginative" Californian-French fixings, "incredibly presented" in a "whimsical" dining room (upside-down colanders serve as lighting fixtures); "the menu changes on a [monthly] basis", but you can count on "friendly service" (overseen by his wife/co-owner Regina) and *beaucoup* half-bottles of syrah (Rhône Valley varietals).

### Tadich Grill 🇱 Ⓜ                              20 | 18 | 18 | $36
*240 California St. (bet. Battery & Front Sts.), 415-391-1849*
◪ At this vintage Downtown "fish house", "old-school" basics (cioppino, sand dabs, the "best damn tartar sauce"), "bantering" "curmudgeonly" waiters and "strong drinks" "still prevail"; younglings yawn it "feels like it's for old people who can't chew as well anymore", and even loyalists admit the coveted private "booths are obtainable and the staff can give polite service, but you have to work at getting either"; still, "it hasn't lasted [over] 150 years for nothing."

### Taiwan 🇱 🇸 Ⓜ                               16 | 6 | 12 | $16
*445 Clement St. (6th Ave.), 415-387-1789*
*2071 University Ave. (Shattuck Ave.), Berkeley, 510-845-1456* ◗
◪ Those homesick for Tapei come to this chainlet of "cheap Chinese" haunts in the Inner Richmond and Berkeley when "craving" "delicious Taiwanese dim sum specialties" served all day; however, they suggest "enjoy the dumplings" ("anything with dough is fantastic") but "dump the rest", which is "not great anymore."

### Takara 🇱 🇸 Ⓜ                         ▽ 19 | 11 | 19 | $26
*22 Peace Plaza (Geary Blvd.), 415-921-2000*
■ Fans of "Japanese classics from sushi to sukiyaki" to shabu-shabu (its specialty) should give this Peace Plaza place a chance; there are no bells and whistles here, just beautifully presented food and "courteous servers" with the best bet "for the money" being the "set-menu options", "served in cute small cups with lids on them."

### Tao Cafe 🇸 Ⓜ                              - | - | - | M
*1000 Guerrero St. (22nd St.), 415-641-9955*
Rising from the crash of the Mission's Flying Saucer comes this Vietnamese cafe run by a husband-and-wife duo; the once-racy bi-level space has been transformed into meditative environs with lots of carved wood, celadon and rattan; the limited menu features Hanoi classics such as pho, plus Kirin on tap.

### Taqueria Cancun ◗ 🇱 🇸 Ⓜ≢             22 | 6 | 13 | $9
*1003 Market St. (6th St.), 415-864-6773*
*3211 Mission St. (Valencia St.), 415-550-1414*
*2288 Mission St. (19th St.), 415-252-9560*
◪ "If you can brave the territory and squeeze between some pretty funky patrons" at this triad of taquerias, you'll

be rewarded by the "biggest and biggest-value vegetarian burritos" as well as a cadre of carnivorous alternatives, the secret of which lies in "the whole chunks of avocado nestled within"; they're "not much to look at, but the jukebox keeps things lively."

**Tarpy's Roadhouse** L S M — 20 | 21 | 20 | $37

*2999 Monterey-Salinas Hwy. (Canyon Del Rey Blvd.), Monterey, 831-647-1444*

■ Located "in the middle of nowhere" outside Monterey, "this rambling" 1917 "fieldstone building" scores for its "charming courtyard seating (tough to get when the weather's clear)", "very friendly service" and "down-home Cal-American" menu (on which "tasty BBQ" and vegetarian options happily coexist) that's "surprisingly good" for "a real roadhouse."

**Tartine Bakery** L S ≠ — – | – | – | I

*600 Guerrero St. (18th St.), 415-487-2600*

Baker extraordinaire Chad Robertson and partner Elizabeth Prueitt have relocated their beloved Bay Village Bread business to this sunny French in the Mission; in addition to their signature hearth-style loaves and pastries, savories such as hot pressed *tartines* (open-faced sandwiches), along with serious coffee drinks coaxed from an antique Italian machine, are available for breakfast and lunch.

**Taste Cafe & Bistro** L S — – | – | – | M

*1199 Forest Ave. (Prescott Ln.), Pacific Grove, 831-655-0324*

This modern Continental bistro offers some of the best value on the Monterey Peninsula; decked out in charming European appointments, with an open kitchen, it's where locals in-the-know go for "high-quality" escargots, grilled marinated rabbit and local wines "without the pretensions or high prices" of the big names around Pacific Grove.

**TASTINGS RESTAURANT** L S M — 26 | 20 | 23 | $50

*505 Healdsburg Ave. (Piper St.), Healdsburg, 707-433-3936*

■ "Up-and-coming chef" Derek McCarthy and wife Sandy Kim's New American Healdsburg hideaway continues to wow "the wine-country set" by "turning out a sophisticated" series of "small tastes" "inventively paired" – as the name implies – with "their unusual vino list"; diners dig the daily tasting menu that "allows them to sample many new things", while "the wonderful staff brings real class" and "warmth" "to a tough location" ("in a parking lot!").

**Taylor's Automatic Refresher** L S M — 24 | 11 | 16 | $14

*933 Main St. (bet. Charter Oak Ave. & Pope St.), St. Helena, 707-963-3486*

■ "If you're driving through St. Helena", don't automatically pass by this "'50s-style" "drive-up diner", a refreshingly "unpretentious" "hamburger stand" with "thick milkshakes" that also "sells wine and takes American Express" (geez, "this is what makes people make fun of California"); the plastic comes in handy, because it may "look like fast food, [but] it costs like white linen."

### Ten-Ichi ⬛⬛⬛   20  13  16  $28

*2235 Fillmore St. (bet. Clay & Sacramento Sts.), 415-346-3477*
◪ Ten-acious regulars roll in to this "reliable" Upper Fillmore Japanese "fallback"; from the udon to the 'guiltless' teriyaki featuring skinless white meat, "it's all good here", but what really reels them in are the "expensive" but "excellent" and eccentrically named rolls, served by a "personable staff."

### TERRA ⬛⬛   27  24  25  $56

*1345 Railroad Ave. (bet. Adams & Hunt Sts.), St. Helena, 707-963-8931*
■ "Your taste buds have not yet been out of the closet until you've tried some of" chef/co-owner Hiro Sone's "absolutely unbelievable" "imaginative" New French fusion fare with Northern Italian and "Asian influences"; "the quiet old stone building" "off the main drag of St. Helena" offers "refuge from the wine country's marauding masses" with "gracious service" and an "out-of-this-world" wine list; so "let everyone duke it out to get reservations" elsewhere – this is a "true must-do" in the Valley.

### Thai House ⬛⬛   20  14  19  $19

*2200 Market St. (bet. 15th & Sanchez Sts.), 415-864-5006* ⬛
*151 Noe St. (Henry St.), 415-863-0374*
■ "Both the boys and the Thai food are hot" at this Castro couple, serving "good, basic" Siamese that's "better than [many] moderately priced Bangkok" eateries; the "staff is as polite as can be", and it's just plain "nice to find a place in the neighborhood where you don't have to wait an hour for a table"; some suggest everything "tastes better at Noe Street, [perhaps] because it's quainter."

### Thanh Long ⬛   25  17  19  $41

*4101 Judah St. (46th Ave.), 415-665-1146*
■ Longtime fans "don't even bother looking at the menu" at this "dressed-down version of its sister Crustacean" "in the outer Sunset", as "there are only two things to get": "orgasmic roasted crab" in "a variety of" Vietnamese sauces and the "secret recipe" garlic noodles; so go get "down and dirty" with the critters, and "be prepared to splurge" (the "tab for crabs will blow you away"); also "give yourself plenty of time to scavenge for parking."

### Thanya & Salee ⬛⬛⬛   ∇ 17  15  15  $23

*1469 18th St. (Connecticut St.), 415-647-6469*
■ "This trendy little Thai tucked away in Potrero Hill" satisfies the neighborhood's itch for "solid" Siamese food,

"impeccably presented" "at reasonable prices"; its "added bonus is the attached Lingba Lounge" "that serves killer drinks while you wait for your table" and stays open till 2 AM, earning it status as a good "local hangout."

**Thep Phanom Thai Cuisine** S M   25 | 15 | 18 | $25
*400 Waller St. (Fillmore St.), 415-431-2526*
◪ Praise for this perennially "packed-to-the-rafters" place in the Lower Haight is "sometimes Phanomenal, sometimes Thepid", but it's usually universal; the "tongue-awakening" bites of Bangkok (particularly those on "the specials boards, which never really change") delivered by "brusque" but "efficient servers" are considered "the gold – perhaps platinum – standard in Thai" cuisine and "make the location, parking [and reservations] hassles worth it."

**Thirsty Bear Brewing Co.** L S M   14 | 13 | 12 | $27
*661 Howard St. (bet. New Montgomery & 3rd Sts.), 415-974-0905*
◪ Although this "noisy" SoMa "meat market" serves "a wide array of" Spanish eats "to share alongside numerous" "homemade beers" in a "post-industrial setting", the profusion of pool-shooting "yuppie dot-commers" proves "that it's more a party place than a dinner place"; the barely impressed insist that it's "time to teach the old bear new tricks", as "there are better breweries" (and "tapas joints") in the Bay Area."

**Three Seasons** S M   23 | 16 | 17 | $28
*3317 Steiner St. (bet. Chestnut & Lombard Sts.), 415-567-9989*
◪ "It isn't the Slanted Door or Betelnut", but "for those in the Marina" "aching for" Vietnamese vittles, this young Asian is nearly "as good", "with fair prices" and "without the wait"; go with "a large group", as "it's hard not to order one of everything" on the "tapas-style" menu and every one of the 10 "spring rolls is delicious"; sore cynics suggest "they'd do us a favor to spend some of our money on more comfortable chairs and a more interesting environment."

**Ti Couz** L S M   21 | 15 | 15 | $20
*3108 16th St. (bet. Guerrero & Valencia Sts.), 415-252-7373*
◪ "In the thick of" the "hipster zone", this crêperie continues to "impress" with "*magnifique*" "square-shaped" *galettes* ("you will inevitably order one from each menu – savory and sweet"); it's "a little piece of Brittany" with "rustic decor" and hard Celtic ciders sipped "from [ceramic] bowls", but it's dogged by "long lines", "turn-and-burn service" and "parking that continues to be a Mission impossible"; P.S. now serving "Breton-style" seafood after 5 PM.

**Timo's** S M   19 | 15 | 17 | $23
*842 Valencia St. (bet. 19th & 20th Sts.), 415-647-0558*
◼ Diners desperately seeking Spanish snacks "count on this" colorful Missionite, as the "inspired" small plates

"are not your run-of-the-mill tapas" and there's "rarely a wait"; "copious amounts of" "good sangria" and flamenco music "help one deal with the cramped quarters", plus "flirty bartenders will create personalized libations if you flirt back."

### Tin-Pan Asian Bistro L S M      18 ｜ 18 ｜ 18 ｜ $25

*2251 Market St. (bet. Noe & Sanchez Sts.), 415-565-0733*
◪ With "a Cosmo in one hand and chopsticks in the other", partying patrons panning for Pan-Asian fare pack this "Castro scene" "catering to all cravings, from flatbreads to" "delish noodles" to chocolate-raspberry won tons; however, critics can the joint, crying "while the portions are huge, the dishes look better than they taste" and insisting "if it weren't for the location, it wouldn't stand a chance."

### Tita's S      ▽ 16 ｜ 11 ｜ 19 ｜ $19

*3870 17th St. (bet. Noe & Sanchez Sts.), 415-626-2477*
■ "While poi is nowhere to be had", this "homey" "slice of Hawaii" in the Castro offers a "true taste of *o'hana* (home cooking)" "for displaced Polynesians or the culturally curious"; such staples as "the best *malasadas*" [fried doughnuts] "made to order" "this side of Oahu" "put the 'o' in ono (good)", and "the staff exudes [such an] aloha spirit" that "you can almost feel the island breeze."

### Tokyo Go Go S      23 ｜ 22 ｜ 18 ｜ $34

*3174 16th St. (bet. Guerrero & Valencia Sts.), 415-864-2288*
■ "You expect Barbarella to be the sushi chef" at this Mission scene exuding "1960s James Bond cool" and packed "with more black-clad folks than you'd see at a funeral"; "thankfully [quieter than] its sister Ace Wasabi", it's ideal when you want "innovative" Japanese fusion fare, sake cocktails and "a party atmosphere altogether", the latter two Go-ing far to ease the often "long waits."

### Tomatina L S M      15 ｜ 10 ｜ 11 ｜ $19

*3127 Mission College Blvd. (Great America Pkwy.), Santa Clara, 408-654-9000*
*Inn at Southbridge, 1016 Main St. (bet. Charter Oak Ave. & Pope St.), St. Helena, 707-967-9999*
*1325 W. Main St. (Mt. Diablo Blvd.), Walnut Creek, 925-930-9999*
■ The fun, free-wheeling atmosphere of its namesake tomato food fight captures the spirit behind this trio of "self-serve" Italian-Meds; the "rockin'" *piadines* ("yummy flatbreads with a huge salad on top") and "chewy" pizzas are the best bets for "budget meals" *con famiglia.*

### Tommaso's S      24 ｜ 16 ｜ 19 ｜ $23

*1042 Kearny St. (bet. Broadway & Pacific Ave.), 415-398-9696*
■ "Located off North Beach's main drag", this "laid-back" Southern Italian "landmark" attracts "an interesting mix of politicos, locals" and tourists for its "most divine pizza"

("dare we say the best in the metropolis?") emerging from SF's "original wood-burning oven" (circa 1935); your hosts, "the Crotti family", and "the communal seating guarantee a good time", just "arrive early to beat the crowds" or plan on "doing a little adult-book shopping next door" while you wait.

### Tommy Toy's Cuisine Chinoise L S M
23 | 23 | 22 | $55

*655 Montgomery St. (bet. Clay & Washington Sts.), 415-397-4888*

◪ Tommy doesn't toy around at his "posh" (jacket and tie required) eponymous Downtowner whose "slinky '50s Hong Kong movie"-set decor, "different but superb" "New French take on Chinese dishes" and "gorgeous presentations" "cater to the quasi-famous" and expense-accounters; while "almost blinded by the dazzling silverware", some feel sidelined by the "pushy service that tries to make you order the tasting menu" – though it does make for "a meal you won't forget."

### Tonga Room S M
11 | 23 | 14 | $32

*Fairmont Hotel, 950 Mason St. (California St.), 415-772-5278*

◪ Bring a group of friends and "a sense of humor" to this "tiki-tacky" cocktail lounge on Nob Hill whose "Polynesian kitsch is right out of a '60s Elvis movie"; "go for the trippy-dippy, retro" "umbrella drinks" and the "cheesy band-on-a-floating-barge" (and "don't tell" about the "artificial monsoons" "that take place every 30 minutes"); however, "take a pass on the ho-hum" Cal-Asian fare, since "you can easily chow down" on the all-you-can-eat buffet for $6 "during happy hour."

### Ton Kiang L S M
25 | 12 | 17 | $24

*5821 Geary Blvd. (bet. 22nd & 23rd Aves.), 415-387-8273*

◪ "Bring your little dumpling" to this "white-tablecloth" Chinese in the "foggy outer Richmond" that gives even Chinatown's best "a run for its money", thanks to its "friendly folks wheeling around carts brimming with fried or steamed everything you can imagine"; while the "dim sum sparkles" all day long, "the Hakka specialties [at dinnertime] are also worth a try"; "the only downsides are long waits on weekends" and "scarce parking."

### Townhouse Bar & Grill L M
19 | 17 | 18 | $28

*5862 Doyle St. (bet. 59th & Powell Sts.), Emeryville, 510-652-6151*

■ This "hip" haunt is "a bright spot in the [culinary] ghost town of Emeryville" thanks to an Eclectic mix of Cal eats, from "inventive and tasty salads" to "fabulous garlic fries", served amid a "woody decor" (including a "spacious, sunny deck") that's "a nice surprise in such an industrial" quarter; "subtle jazz" and "minty mojitos" from the late-serving bar lure the "post-graduate" "younger set."

### Town's End Restaurant & Bakery L S
20 | 14 | 17 | $24

*2 Townsend St. (The Embarcadero), 415-512-0749*

◪ Townies insist "heaven must be sitting at a sunny table having brunch" at this New American cafe/bakery directly on The Embarcadero; both man and women "can live on the" "bread basket alone" "that comes with every order", which explains why there's "always a crowd on Saturday and Sunday mornings", despite a "blasé staff"; but "don't bother going on a weeknight unless you prefer eating alone."

### Trader Vic's L S M
18 | 21 | 19 | $40

*9 Anchor Dr. (Powell St.), Emeryville, 510-653-3400*
*Dina's Garden Hotel, 4269 El Camino Real (San Antonio Ave.), Palo Alto, 650-849-9800*

◪ This "kitschy" set of "tiki-themed" huts are a "page out of the past", "when Cadillac was the car to own" and service was "chivalrous"; though "better than expected", the pseudo-Polynesian–Asian fare (bongo-bongo soup and "cheese bings – need I say more?") "greatly improves with the number" of "paper-umbrella-topped" cocktails drunk; the "spectacular" Aboriginal art in the new Palo Alto outpost and "magnificent sunset" views from the Emeryville branch legitimize the "prices bordering on criminal."

### Trattoria Contadina S M
23 | 16 | 21 | $29

*1800 Mason St. (Union St.), 415-982-5728*

◼ Although this "cute little family-run" trattoria is "slightly away from congested Columbus Avenue", its "delectable dishes" are "heads above the overrated restaurants" there; the "charming Italian waiters" "make you feel as warm on the outside as the pasta makes you feel inside", which more than makes up for the "elbow-to elbow" environs.

### Trattoria La Siciliana S ⌀
23 | 16 | 17 | $24

*2993 College Ave. (Ashby Ave.), Berkeley, 510-704-1474*

◪ Berkeleyites gladly wait at this "cozy" family-run spot serving "down-home Southern Italian cooking at its best" (laced with things "that you won't find in most" places); although the two-tiered trattoria seems "too small", going in groups is "recommended", as everything is served "family-style"; "just don't fill up on bread and the garlicky olive oil", and don't be put off by the "slow, rude" service.

### TRA VIGNE L S M
25 | 25 | 21 | $46

*1050 Charter Oak Ave. (Hwy. 29), St. Helena, 707-963-4444*

◪ Chef "Michael Chiarello is gone", but "this Napa Valley tradition" still "shines" with "absolutely glorious", "daring combinations" of Cal-Italian food; despite somewhat "haughty" hosts, the "knowledgeable staff is friendly and will help you choose" from the "impeccable" wine list; the dining room "is reminiscent of an Italian cathedral", but "you may need to genuflect to" snare "a table in the summer" on the "idyllic outdoor patio among the vines" (if you can't, "try eating at the bar and catch up on all the vineyard dirt").

### Truly Mediterranean  L S M          23  5  12  $11
*3109 16th St. (Valencia St.), 415-252-7482* ●✄
*627 Vallejo St. (Columbus St.), 415-362-2636*
◪ Truly, fans are happy to "forsake decor" at this set of "cheap" Med–Middle Easterners ("mainly take-out places with some seating") for the "fine falafels" and "succulent" schwarma sandwiches that are "enough for two meals" and a "great alternative in the Mission" or North Beach; go ahead, "spend the extra dollar and get the deluxe" versions "with eggplant and potatoes."

### Tu Lan  L M✄                        19  2  8  $13
*8 Sixth St. (Market St.), 415-626-0927*
◪ You got to applaud this SoMa "soup kitchen" with "bus-stop decor" for ladling out "enormous portions of fantastic fried rice" and other Saigon savories at rock-bottom prices; but while "you'll be hard-pressed to find a better deal", be warned of the "super-skanky setting" (those who "need a Vietnamese food fix" aren't the only addicts around, so "the squeamish" should stay away – or order takeaway).

### Tuscany  L S M                       16  20  15  $37
*1005 First St. (Main St.), Napa, 707-258-1000*
◪ Now into its second season, this Downtown Napa trattoria continues to fill up with "wine-country locals" who find it "fun to sit at the counter and watch" the "masters of the wood-fired oven" at work; however, while the "beautiful large room" "is inviting" and "smells good", "nothing sparkles" on the Northern Italian menu, and "they still don't take reservations."

### 2223 Restaurant  S M                22  20  20  $35
*2223 Market St. (bet. Noe & Sanchez Sts.), 415-431-0692*
■ "In the Castro – who'd a thunk it?"; this "upscale", "no-name" New American "redefines comfort food" with its "outrageous" signature "towering roast chicken with garlic mashed potatoes, onion rings and blue lake beans"; regulars are "not sure which is prettier" – the "desserts, described as oral ecstasy", or the "servers, both attentive and knowledgeable"; P.S. the "buzzing" "bar is a great spot to start the evening", but "the fantastic Sunday brunch" affords a "more leisurely experience."

### 231 Ellsworth  L M                   23  20  22  $56
*231 S. Ellsworth Ave. (bet. 2nd & 3rd Aves.), San Mateo, 650-347-7231*
◪ This San Mateo New American "destination restaurant" is praised by the pleasantly pampered for "explosive flavors", "fantastic wine selection" (700 bottles deep) and – "what really makes it special" – formal service; however, "younger-

than-50" folks find the five- and seven-course "tasting menus a bit on the steep side" and the "dark", wood-paneled room "stuffy."

### Universal Cafe S M 　　　　22 | 18 | 17 | $34

*2814 19th St. (bet. Bryant & Harrison Sts.), 415-821-4608*

■ "Despite the out-of-the-way locale", this "hipper-than-hip" Missionite "is always buzzing" with its "deconstructed atmosphere" and "well-constructed" New American menu ("the pan-seared beef was the death of my life as a vegetarian"); the neighborhood crowd "enjoys eating outside when the weather heats up, indoors to watch the chefs do their magic"; but the universal question is not whether the servers are "friendly" or "catty" but if they are model-thin so as "to fit between the tables."

### Uva Trattoria Italiana L S 　　　 – | – | – | M

*1040 Clinton St. (Main St.), Napa, 707-255-6646*

The name remains the same, but a dynamic duo of Italian-blooded Napa natives intends to transform this affordable trattoria into a more lively Downtown destination; new chef Jude Wilmouth (ex Tra Vigne) has begun to introduce classic Southern Italian items such as pan-roasted Chianti-marinated rabbit; an enlarged bar serves a new small-plates menu too.

### Uzen L M 　　　　　　　　21 | 14 | 16 | $29

*5415 College Ave. (bet. Hudson St. & Kales Ave.), Oakland, 510-654-7753*

☑ The Zen-like report they "reach a certain calm when eating here" at this Oaklander, while zealots hiss "stay away from my favorite"; either way, it's clear that the "delicate sushi" "and other Japanese specialties" served in this "simple environment" are "much better than" others in the East Bay; service that's "surprisingly unresponsive to special requests" just doesn't cut it, however.

### Valhalla L S 　　　　　▽ 19 | 21 | 17 | $46

*201 Bridgeway (Main St.), Sausalito, 415-331-9463*

☑ Flamboyant madam-cum-restaurateur "Sally Stanford would be pleased as punch (or something stronger)" by the "beautiful renovation" and reopening of her historic Sausalito establishment where nearly every table is afforded "amazing views" of the Bay and the SF skyline; the satisfied say if the vistas "don't pull you in, the "contemporary Californian" menu and "bargain wine list" will; but unhappy suitors snap the "sophomoric service and food" indicate this freshman "isn't there yet."

### Venezia L S M 　　　　　　20 | 22 | 20 | $28

*1799 University Ave. (Grant St.), Berkeley, 510-849-4681*

■ Berkeleyites who have "been going to this" "reasonably-priced" "family favorite since it opened in 1980" get a kick out of the "novel atmosphere" – an Italian piazza complete with "working fountain", "plastic pigeons", "murals of city scenes" and "real laundry on the balconies"; thankfully, the "clothes overhead alternate" and so do the "remarkable" "homemade pastas" that the "inventive kitchen kicks out."

### Venticello  S M   23 | 23 | 20 | $40 |
*1257 Taylor St. (Washington St.), 415-922-2545*
☑ "Those in-the-know" who are "too young for the Ritz and too tired of the Tonga Room" "slip into this" "upscale but unstuffy" "Northern Italian on Nob Hill"; "the superb food", served in "intimate surroundings" replete with a "peekaboo view" of the Bay, makes it a "perfect place for a romantic date or a meal with close friends" (and we do mean "close"); the "uneven service" "has caused a lot of venting recently", but the "valet parking is a godsend."

### Venus  L S M   20 | 16 | 16 | $21 |
*2327 Shattuck Ave. (Durant Ave.), Berkeley, 510-540-5950*
☑ The "out-of-this-world" morning meals delivered by this young Berkeley Downtowner are "definitely in my orbit" moon mavens who admire the "small but endearing Californian menu", served under "not too fussy and very friendly" auspices; most don't "venture beyond breakfast", though, and warn "service takes a nosedive if a large group comes in."

### Verbena  L M   ▽ 20 | 16 | 18 | $30 |
*Walter Shorenstein Bldg., 1111 Broadway (11th St.), Oakland, 510-465-9300*
■ Urban renewalists regale this "classy" "much-needed addition" to "restaurant-devoid Downtown Oakland", whose "beautifully executed Med-influenced" Cal cuisine seems "very similar to Gordon's House of Fine Eats in SF" (no surprise, as Gordo himself is the co-chef here); the "warm, professional" staff and "slightly corporate, yet pleasant ambiance" make it especially "swell" for "an elegant business lunch" or as a "martini meeting place."

### Via Centro  L S   22 | 18 | 20 | $36 |
*2132 Center St. (bet. Oxford St. & Shattuck Ave.), Berkeley, 510-981-8373*
■ "Everyone should have a neighborhood Italian as good and innovative as this midpriced" Med-influenced Tuscan trattoria in Berkeley; while there's "welcoming service" and "stylish, modern decor", an address that provides "easy access to campus events" and Downtown theaters is centro to its success.

### Viaggio Ristorante  L S   19 | 21 | 18 | $40 |
*14550 Big Basin Way (4th St.), Saratoga, 408-741-5300*
☑ This "pretty place" in Saratoga with a live "piano player" (Wednesday–Saturday) and a patio out back also features

a lively (read: noisy) "see-and-be-seen bar" scene and a locally oriented wine list that's (gasp) "not overpriced"; optimists opine the quality of the "globe-trotting" but mainly Med menu "is picking up", but others suggest the kitchen and service "still lag" behind the nearby competition.

### Via Vai Trattoria 🄻🅂🅼    20  16  18  $29
*1715 Union St. (bet. Gough & Octavia Sts.), 415-441-2111*
■ There's a good vai-bration at this "friendly Cow Hollow" trattoria that's both "easier to get into than sister Pane E Vino" and "better for the lira" (or Euro), making it a viable proposition for "yummy thin-crust pizzas" and "flavorful pastas"; although the dining room "is a comfortable setting, it can be loud", so go for a table "on the back [heated] patio."

### Vicolo 🄻🅂🅼    19  9  13  $18
*201 Ivy St. (bet. Franklin & Gough Sts.), 415-863-2382*
☒ Seasoned season-ticket holders "would hate to be without" this Hayes Valley "old reliable" Italian that's "great before the symphony" (though "hard to find", as it's "hidden in an alley"); its "inexpensive" but "excellent" signature "cornmeal-crusted" pizzas and "super salads" make a "perfect simple meal", however the "coldish cafeteria-style" digs hit a low note for some.

### Vic Stewart's 🅂🅼    22  21  20  $46
*850 S. Broadway (bet. Mt. Diablo Blvd. & Newell Ave.), Walnut Creek, 925-943-5666*
☒ Providing "*the* Republican hangout for the East Bay" as well as "prime rib so good it brings tears to the eyes", this Walnut Creek steakhouse also offers a late-1800s "railroad depot setting" that includes a "private room" in the form of a Pullman car; though the "outrageous" prices prompt weeping of a different sort, its choo-choosy champions counter "no complaints."

### Victorian Gardens 🅂    ▽ 29  28  30  $65
*Victorian Gardens, 14409 S. Hwy. 1 (south of Elk, 8 mi. north of Pt. Arena), Manchester, 707-882-3606*
■ "An evening spent" at this "exquisitely restored Victorian" inn on the Mendocino coast is an "opulent affair" to "be remembered for years"; chef/co-owner Luciano Zamboni prepares a five-course tasting menu featuring Italian wines and "food from a Roman nonna's kitchen" (and "harvested from his incredible garden" and livestock farm), while his wife Pauline "gives you the most personal service you've ever encountered"; plus there's only one seating a night, so you can linger as long as Victoria's reign.

### Vik's Chaat Corner 🄻🅂    25  3  8  $11
*724 Allston Way (bet. 4th & 5th Sts.), Berkeley, 510-644-4412*
☒ "Chaat chewers" chow down on "cheap", "astoundingly delicious" paper-platefuls of "authentic Indian" "street

nibbles"; the "bare-bones-as-it-comes" "warehouse setting" in Berkeley, "lack of eating space" and "6 PM closing time" don't deter the "crowds", 'cause the "food's all that counts here."

### Villa Corona ⬛⬛　　　▽ 20 | 9 | 16 | $14

*Bel Aire Plaza, 3614 Bel Aire Plaza (Trancas St.), Napa, 707-257-8685*
*1138 Main St. (bet. Pope & Spring Sts.), St. Helena, 707-963-7812* Ⓜ

■ "If you're hungry for authentic Mexican food" when traveling through wine country, these "family-run" cantinas in Napa and St. Helena provide a *Like Water for Chocolate* experience with "awesome guacamole", "carnitas burritos that are almost all meat" and "addictive enchiladas"; "speedy counter ordering" is the crowning touch.

### Village Pub, The ⬛⬛Ⓜ　　25 | 24 | 22 | $51

*2967 Woodside Rd. (Whiskey Hill Rd.), Woodside, 650-851-9888*

■ Don't let the "name deceive" you – this "excellent reincarnation of an established gathering place" on the Peninsula "is certainly no pub"; the "stylish" setting featuring "warm fireplaces and cool red-upholstered chairs" is "unlike the other 'woodsy' Woodside" restaurants, and rising-star chef Mark Sullivan's "outstanding" seasonal New American fare would never be mistaken for grub (despite the burger on the menu); fervent villagers vow that though it's "expensive", it's "worth the splurge."

### Viognier ⬛⬛Ⓜ　　　23 | 21 | 22 | $47

*Draeger's Mkt., 222 E. Fourth St. (bet. B St. & Ellsworth Ave.), San Mateo, 650-685-3727*

☑ Located on the top floor of "Draeger's mega-gourmet superstore", this San Matean appropriately offers "top-drawer everything"; the "unexpectedly" "quiet dining room" provides a "classy" backdrop for the "creative" Med cuisine and "service to match"; a few feel it's "pricey for what you get", but acolytes who do indulge also "leave time for shopping" at "the food temple."

### Vi's ⬛⬛Ⓜ⇄　　　▽ 20 | 10 | 13 | $16

*724 Webster St. (bet. 7th & 8th Sts.), Oakland, 510-835-8375*

☑ "Great bowls" of "steaming", "world-class" "pho and duck noodle soup" "can be had for a song" sing savvy surveyors who get their Vietnamese fix at this "good-value" venue in Oakland's Chinatown; while the service is "attentive" and there's rarely a wait, the "somewhat sterile" setting's not winning any pho-to contests.

### Vivande Porta Via ⬛⬛Ⓜ　　23 | 14 | 20 | $33

*2125 Fillmore St. (bet. California & Sacramento Sts.), 415-346-4430*

☑ "A storefront window hides this gem" in Upper Fillmore run by cookbook author Carlo Middione, who purveys "fresh cheeses, salamis and desserts" to take home, along with "pasta without equal" and other "exceptional Italian" fare for those who stay; there's "not a lot of atmosphere" and the "seating arrangements" aren't the most "comfortable", but the "exceptional" food and "charming staff" make it a "standard-bearer in a city of high standards."

### Wappo Bar Bistro 🅛🆂🅜     21 | 21 | 19 | $33

*1226 Washington St. (Lincoln Ave.), Calistoga, 707-942-4712*

☒ An "interesting blend of cuisines" "adds up to a delightful" meal at this International "find in Calistoga", complemented by a "good wine list with a few lesser-known labels" but without the whopping markups; "sitting outside under the grape arbor for lunch" (and on summer nights) "is divine" and is a superior alternative to the "crowded" digs inside, but be warned: "service can be a bit flaky."

### Wasabi & Ginger 🆂🅜     ▽ 21 | 15 | 18 | $24

*2299 Van Ness Ave. (Vallejo St.), 415-345-1368*

☒ Devotees who've discovered this Van Ness Japanese love to make conversation with the "friendly sushi chefs" who whip up "amazing", "original" rolls and other fare (and cheapskates fall for "free edamame and green-tea ice cream"); whiners who wonder whassup with the "interior that leaves much to be desired" feel it's "best for takeout."

### Waterfront     18 | 22 | 18 | $43
### Restaurant & Cafe 🅛🆂🅜

*Pier 7, The Embarcadero (Broadway), 415-391-2696*

☒ "The name says it all" at this behemoth on Pier 7 that "commands attention on the Embarcadero" and offers two different "waterfront dining options"; the "formal Cal-French upstairs" sports "views of the stratosphere" (and a "bill in the same range") while the "casual downstairs cafe" serves lighter fare emphasizing seafood; in both cases, the "good, not great" vittles and "rushed service" are trumped by the "knockout" Bay vistas.

### Watergate 🆂🅜     24 | 19 | 20 | $38

*1152 Valencia St. (bet. 22nd & 23rd Sts.), 415-648-6000*

☒ For a "surprising change of pace in the hectic Mission", try this "fancy-ish", "quiet", "overlooked" gem; there's no smoking gun here, just "brilliantly executed" French–Asian fusion fare on a "fantastic three-course prix fixe menu" that may offer the "best value in the city"; however, "plan on a long dinner", as "friendly service" can also be "slow."

### Water Street Bistro 🅛🆂🅜⊘     – | – | – | M

*100 Petaluma Blvd. N. (Western Ave.), Petaluma, 707-763-9563*

This French bistro facing "the Petaluma River" and run by Stephanie Rastetter (the "excellent chef" from the now-shuttered Babette's in Sonoma) offers "fabulous", "fresh" sandwiches, soups and salads in a "pleasant", "casual" setting; N.B. although the kitchen closes at 5 PM, it serves summertime weekend suppers and monthly theme dinners.

### We Be Sushi 🛇 Ⓜ  17 | 9 | 16 | $17

*3226 Geary Blvd. (bet. Parker & Spruce Sts.), 415-221-9960*
*94 Judah St. (6th Ave.), 415-681-4010*
*538 Valencia St. (bet. 16th & 17th Sts.), 415-565-0749* 🛇
*1071 Valencia St. (22nd St.), 415-826-0607* 🛇

☑ The fact that this chainlet of budget Japanese "almost named itself McSushi" "says it all" for penny-pinchers who purport these "nothing-fancy" fin-fare factories "take care of your craving" and leave you with "cash for cocktails later"; devotees declare the fish "fresh" and "good", though thrill-seekers think "we be boring" is more like it.

### Wente Vineyards 🛇 Ⓛ Ⓜ  23 | 25 | 21 | $48

*5050 Arroyo Rd. (Wetmore Rd.), Livermore, 925-456-2450*

■ "The winding road" that leads to the Livermore Valley also leads to arguably "the best restaurant east of Berkeley"; "snuggled in the hills and vineyards", this stunning spot showcases chef Kimball Jones' "superbly executed California-fresh" fare (his signature "smoked pork chops are a must") paired with a "great wine list" and delivered by "unrushed" service, making it a "nice, quick getaway"; P.S. try "brunch alfresco."

### Wild Hare 🛇 Ⓜ  23 | 21 | 21 | $46

*1029 El Camino Real (bet. Menlo & Santa Cruz Aves.),*
*Menlo Park, 650-327-4273*

■ "Personable" Joey Altman's (host of the *Bay Cafe* TV show) Menlo Park "wild" adventure commands "kudos" for its "excellent" "exotic game"–heavy menu, "city style" and "top-notch" service; however, at press time, the restaurant is gearing up to switch over to a more casual, general American bistro, as yet unnamed, with a new lounge and entranceway.

### Willow Wood Market Cafe 🛇 Ⓛ 🛇 Ⓜ  21 | 13 | 16 | $22

*9020 Graton Rd. (bet. Brush & Edison Sts.), Graton, 707-522-8372*

■ "Tucked" away "in a funky little grocery store" "in the one-horse town of Graton", this "eclectic" eatery whipping up "country comfort food" and International eats ("great polenta") is the "locals' favorite" for "non-traditional breakfasts" and "creative sandwiches"; you've got to be "willing to wait", because it doesn't take reservations and the service can be as "relaxed" as the "atmosphere."

### Wine Spectator Greystone 🛇 Ⓛ 🛇 Ⓜ  22 | 23 | 20 | $47

*Culinary Institute of America, 2555 Main St. (Deer Park Rd.),*
*St. Helena, 707-967-1010*

☑ This "stately château" in St. Helena is "as much a tourist attraction as the wineries" surrounding it; the "cavernous" interior features an "open kitchen" where "delightful seasonal" Cal fare is prepared; since it's "run by CIA" (the cooks, "not the spies"), you can expect a "knowledgeable" staff; however, bi-coastal bashers deem it "disappointing compared with its Hyde Park, NY, counterpart."

### Woodward's Garden　　24　15　20　$42
*1700 Mission St. (Duboce St.), 415-621-7122*
■ "Come hungry" and bring your map to find this "tiny", "hidden gem" in the Mission that provides a "quiet", "romantic" rendezvous despite being located off "a highway exit ramp" (think "*Blade Runner* meets Merchant Ivory"); fans find the "phenomenal" New American comfort food and "attentive yet unobtrusive service" "match what you find in larger, more well-known establishments."

### Xyz ⓁⓈⓂ　　17　20　14　$46
*W Hotel, 181 Third St. (Howard St.), 415-817-7836*
◪ "If you badly want to be hip", this "too-cool-for-school" spot in "the swanky W Hotel" offers a "stylish", "inspiring" setting for dinner before a movie at the Metreon or after SF MOMA; however, culture vultures variously assess the Californian cuisine as "creative" or "boring", and the "snobby" staff "needs to get over themselves" ("we had to call the hostess from our cell phone to ask for the check").

### Yabbies Coastal Kitchen ⓈⓂ　　23　19　20　$39
*2237 Polk St. (bet. Green & Vallejo Sts.), 415-474-4088*
■ You gotta "try this place, mate" assert Aussies and "pescetarians" about this Polk Street "off-the-beaten-track" New American–seafooder that lures locals with "fresh" "fantastic fish" and its "superior raw bar" complemented by "an amazing wine list"; if you factor in the "bright, refreshing" digs ("not too stiff, not too casual") and "friendly staff", it's "surprising it isn't harder to get into."

### Yankee Pier ⓁⓈⓂ　　19　16　18　$31
*286 Magnolia Ave. (bet. King St. & William Ave.), Larkspur, 415-924-7676*
◪ Bradley Ogden's "paean to Cape Cod" on "Larkspur's burgeoning restaurant row" "is a winner" for homesick Yankees craving "classic New England" seafood and "informal", "shack"-y "Eastern-seaboard atmosphere" ("pier in to see" local Marin celebs); regulars reveal "stick to the biscuits, chowder and fish fry and you'll be happy as a clam", but the "steep" prices are harder to swallow.

### Yank Sing ⓁⓈⓂ　　24　16　17　$29
*Rincon Ctr., 101 Spear St. (bet. Howard & Mission Sts.), 415-957-9300*
*49 Stevenson St. (bet. 1st & 2nd Sts.), 415-541-4949*
■ If shu mai mavens "had to choose their last meal", they'd flag down a "feast" from one of the "carts constantly rolling

past" proffering "traditional and creative" dim sum "and then some" at these SoMa Chinese "addictions"; both branches are "more upscale" and "user-friendly" than "the various Stockton Street dumps", so the only caveat is to "pace yourself" – "you can spend big bucks" here.

### Yianni's S | – | – | – | I |
*1708 Church St. (29th St.), 415-647-3200*
From spanakopita to souvlaki and taramasalata to tzatziki, it's all Greek to us (including the wines) at this wallet-friendly neighborhood spot in Noe Valley; while the sunny back patio is great for brunching, the comfy blue-and-white dining room has its own attraction, namely the brandy-soaked kasseri cheese that is lit on fire at the table to accompany the fresh, handmade pita bread.

### Yokoso Nippon L M⊘ | ∇ 19 | 5 | 11 | $18 |
*314 Church St. (15th St.), no phone*
■ Nobody knew the moniker of the Castro's beloved 'No Name Sushi' "until the owners put up a handwritten sign"; but there's still a lot to 'no' about this "tiny", "dilapidated" budget Japanese: "no liquor license" and "no reservations", "as there's no phone" ("so be prepared to wait"), but it's all no problem because what it does have is "one hard-working chef" rolling out more "great" raw fish "than you can shake your wallet at."

### Yoshi's at
### Jack London Square L S M | 18 | 21 | 16 | $33 |
*Jack London Sq., 510 Embarcadero W. (Washington St.), Oakland, 510-238-9200*
◪ In Jack London Square, "jazz and Japanese may seem like an odd combo", "but it works" at this "concept facility" where "stellar" music is booked into an adjacent theater; though the "pricey" sushi's "decent but not memorable", other fare fares better ("flavorful teriyaki", "excellent tempura"), and the setting's certainly "pleasing", so have a "leisurely" repast and "stay for the show."

### Yuet Lee ●L S M⊘ | 21 | 5 | 11 | $18 |
*1300 Stockton St. (Broadway), 415-982-6020*
◪ The "delicious, cheap specialties" including "fresh seafood", "Hong Kong noodles and salt-and-pepper anything" served "until 3 AM" make this "gritty" cash-only Chinatown dive a "late-nighter's dream" ("why else are there so many Asians", off-work chefs and revelers "in the place"?); but beware, the "fluorescent lighting makes you feel like you're being x-rayed" and is highly "unflattering."

### Yukol Place Thai Cuisine S M | 24 | 14 | 20 | $22 |
*2380 Lombard St. (bet. Pierce & Scott Sts.), 415-922-1599*
■ Marina locals lumbering along Lombard looking for "excellent", "authentic Thai" "in a serene, comfortable

setting" would do well by this "favorite" (especially since "it's never difficult to get into"); in fact, the reason it seems like there's "never a soul in the place" is that it's become a "great standby for take-out orders" for the neighborhood.

### Yumma's L S M ▽ 20 10 17 $13
*721 Irving St. (bet. 8th & 9th Aves.), 415-682-0762*
■ "There's nothing fancy about this order-first-then-sit-down" Mediterranean in the Inner Sunset – just "cheap", "awesome falafel" and "great" (dare we say yummy?) schwarma "served by some of the nicest people in the neighborhood"; P.S. "don't miss the backyard patio" on those rare fog-free days.

### Z L M ▽ 18 21 17 $45
*127 First St. (bet. Edith & State Sts.), Los Altos, 650-917-2000*
■ Although it's zee "third restaurant in this location in three years", Los Altans feel that Noah Cooper's (ex Spago Palo Alto) "recent reincarnation" featuring an Asian-influenced French menu (served throughout the day, with lighter lounge fare available between lunch and dinner) is "the first one with good food"; still, zero-sum slammers say it's not "quite up to the high prices" or "high style" of the opulent environs.

### ZACHARY'S 25 11 14 $18
### CHICAGO PIZZA L S M ⊄
*1853 Solano Ave. (The Alameda), Berkeley, 510-525-5950*
*5801 College Ave. (Oak Grove Ave.), Oakland, 510-655-6385*
■ "Calling it 'just pizza' is like calling the Hope Diamond 'just a rock'" attest advocates of the sustenance slung by these "East Bay institutions" consisting of "ooey, gooey, cheesy" "Chicago-style deep-dish pies that are better than you get" in the Windy City (and arguably "why real estate is so high" here); bring cash and "expect to wait", or if you want to avoid the "rowdy", "college-bar atmosphere", "call ahead for a half-baked to go."

### Zaika L S M 19 18 15 $26
*1700 Shattuck Ave. (Virginia St.), Berkeley, 510-849-2452*
■ Berkeleyites could not live on Breads of India alone, so this "dressed-up version" has opened in North Berkeley with a larger menu that features a "creative", "rotating" mix of regional offerings plus "solid standards"; unlike its sibling, it offers a "very attractive room", reservations and bottles of Singha to help extinguish the "spicy" fare ("but expect to pay for it" all).

### Zante's Indian 17 5 9 $17
### Cuisine & Pizza L S M
*3489 Mission St. (30th St.), 415-821-3949*
■ "Unbelievable" ("don't knock it till you try it") "Indian pizza" "full of spices" on a naan crust "that's the best (and

only) in the city" is the pull at this quirky curry palace in Bernal Heights that also doles out "zesty" Subcontinent standards; aesthetes eschew the "cafeteria-like" interior and "have it delivered."

### Zao Noodle Bar 🅛🅢🅜  14 | 13 | 14 | $17

*2406 California St. (Fillmore St.), 415-345-8088*
*2031 Chestnut St. (Fillmore St.), 415-928-3088*
*3583 16th St. (bet. Market & Noe Sts.), 415-864-2888*
*261 University Ave. (bet. Bryant & Ramona Sts.), Palo Alto, 650-328-1988*
◪ For those days "when you feel a cold coming on" or simply "yearn for a comforting" bowl of broth, this chain of Pan-Asian "noodle joints" (also serving "inventive rice dishes") is just what the doctor ordered; though "it's fast" and ladles out "good portions", those who find the fare pho-ny prefer to head elsewhere "for the real thing."

### Zaré 🅛🅜  23 | 20 | 23 | $43

*568 Sacramento St. (bet. Montgomery & Sansome Sts.), 415-291-9145*
■ The secret ingredient of "this secret little place" is chef-owner Hoss Zaré, a "charmer" who "makes you feel like a million bucks every time you walk in"; his constantly "changing", "imaginative" Mediterranean oeuvre is equaled only by the "doting" service; in addition, the "cozy" room is "elegant" and "romantic", making it a "gem hidden in the grayness of the Financial District."

### Zarzuela  22 | 16 | 19 | $30

*2000 Hyde St. (Union St.), 415-346-0800*
■ Armchair travelers indulge their "Spanish culinary fantasies" at this "stylish" spot serving "superb paella" and "authentic tapas" that prompt patrons to "say *olé* and over-order"; you may be in for a "long wait", but meantime "the sangria flows" and the "cheerful staff" "welcomes you like an old friend"; "it's a real find" on Russian Hill – and so is parking, so you're better off "taking the bus."

### Zax  24 | 18 | 23 | $40

*2330 Taylor St. (Columbus Ave.), 415-563-6266*
■ "Don't tell anyone about this great sleeper at the end of the cable car line" in North Beach, where "the freshness and preparation" of the Cal-Med fare "rivals" the city's top spots ("luscious goat-cheese soufflé is a must-try"); it's "made all the better by sane prices", and the "charming", "intimate" interior provides an "oasis" where "adults can converse without shouting."

### Zazie 🅛🅢🅜  20 | 18 | 17 | $23

*941 Cole St. (bet. Carl St. & Parnassus Ave.), 415-564-5332*
◪ "While lunch and dinner" at this French bistro "have their highlights", the "amazing" "brunch is the real reason to

head to" (and "wait" at) this "neighborhood sweetheart" enchanting Cole Valley with "incredible gingerbread pancakes"; supper also offers "hearty" helpings in a "charming space with a beautiful little garden out back", although the "tables are so close together you're likely to accidentally use someone else's fork."

### zazu S
(fka zuzu)　　　　　　　　　　▽ 26 | 19 | 24 | $43
*3535 Guerneville Rd. (Willowside Rd.), Santa Rosa, 707-523-4814*
■ Although this Santa Rosa spot was forced to change its name, that hasn't stopped its "talented" owners from creating "memorable", "unfussy, yet sophisticated" Italian–New American dishes with an "extensive local wine selection"; the "cozy, easygoing atmosphere" makes you feel comfortable enough to "go in jeans or Chanel."

### ZIBIBBO L S M
　　　　　　　　　　　　　　21 | 22 | 19 | $40
*430 Kipling St. (bet. Lytton & University Aves.), Palo Alto, 650-328-6722*
◪ Furnishing "power meals for the surviving Silicon Valley elite", this bustling boîte (a "decibel-laden sister to SF's LuLu") "is still the hippest" place in Palo Alto; its "eclectic Med menu that generally fires on all pistons", "unusual wine list" and "reasonable prices" lure loyalists, and though sensitive sorts feel snubbed by "snobby service", more feel the "enjoyable environment" makes it "lots of fun."

### Zin L S M
　　　　　　　　　　　　　　20 | 17 | 20 | $37
*344 Center St. (North St.), Healdsburg, 707-473-0946*
◪ "Zin is in" at this viticultural venue located just off Healdsburg Square showcasing "an extensive Sonoma Zinfandel list" and "hearty", "zinful" New American food to pair with it; while "not for light eaters", "it's honest" and "fun", much like the "friendly staff"; however, the "industrial decor" gives the zin-sation of an "empty warehouse."

### Zinsvalley L M
　　　　　　　　　　　　　　－ | － | － | M
*Browns Valley Mkt., 3253 Browns Valley Rd. (bet. Austin & Larkin Sts.), Napa, 707-224-0695*
This sophomore may not be the best-known in Browns Valley, but it has "quickly become one of the area's favorites" thanks to the deft touch of its Mustards-alumni management; the converted home offers Eclectic-American eats served in two cozy rooms with loads of brick, wood and fireplaces or on a large patio overlooking a creek; true to its name, the wine list features 60 Zinfandels, many from small vintners.

### Zucca L S M
　　　　　　　　　　　　　　▽ 21 | 22 | 18 | $37
*186 Castro St. (bet. Central & Villa Sts.), Mountain View, 650-864-9940*
■ Mountain Viewers "welcome" "this fine addition" to Castro Street, where executive chef (and Gary Danko

protégé) Paul Cohen offers a refreshingly affordable culinary romp through the cuisines of Italy, Greece and Turkey ("the real deal, without a twist"), irrigated by an international wine list specializing in bottles under $20; locals just pray it doesn't become "too popular for its own good."

### ZUNI CAFE ⬤ 🅛 🅢          23 | 20 | 18 | $40

*1658 Market St. (bet. Franklin & Gough Sts.), 415-552-2522*
▨ Judy Rodgers' Hayes Valley "legend" is the "embodiment of SF" dining; her now-"classic" roasted chicken and "best" whole-leaf Caesar salad are the apotheosis of "simple, impeccable" Italian-Med fare, and the "long", "convivial" bar is *the* place to "rub elbows with the 'in' crowd"; while non-believers opine it's "as overrated as the New Economy was", "there's a reason" this "quietly cool" "treat" is "still a locals' favorite."

### Zuzu 🅛 🅢 🅜          22 | 20 | 22 | $34

*829 Main St. (bet. 2nd & 3rd Sts.), Napa, 707-224-8555*
■ Arriving just in time for the revitalization of old-town Napa, this "happening" "hot spot" is "a nibbler's dream" offering an array of affordable traditional Spanish tapas along with "innovative" "small dishes" from South and Central America; a wormwood bar, sultry Corona-red plaster walls and "dimly lit" Moroccan lamps lend a lived-in feel to the bi-level "hangout"; N.B. don't confuse this with Santa Rosa's zazu, which bore the same name for a short time.

# Indexes

**CUISINES**
**LOCATIONS**
**SPECIAL FEATURES**

Indexes list the best of many within each category.

# CUISINES

## Afghan
Helmand

## American (New)
Alexis Baking Co.
A.P. Stump's
A Tavola
bacar
Basin
Big Four
Bistro at Glen Ellen
Bistro Ralph
Boonville Hotel
Brannan's Grill
Cafe Esin
Cafe La Haye
Cafe Lolo
Celadon
Chaz Rest.
Chenery Park
Chez TJ
Cobalt Tavern
Cosmopolitan Cafe
Deuce
Dry Creek Kitchen
Duck Club
Eulipia
Feast
First Crush
Flea St. Café
Fog City Diner
French Laundry
Gary Danko
Ginger Island
Globe
Gordon's Hse./Fine Eats
Indigo
Infusion Bar
Jianna
Jocco's
John Bentley's
Kenwood
Kingfish

Lark Creek Inn
Liberty Cafe
Lion & Compass
Martini Hse.
MatrixFillmore
Maurice Rest.
Mecca
Mendo Bistro
Miramonte
Mirepoix
Miss Millie's
MoMo's
Mustards Grill
955 Ukiah
Olema Inn
One Market
Paragon
Parcel 104
Park Grill
Perlot
Postrio
Q
Restaurant 301
Rick's
Rock Soup
Ross Valley Brew.
Rotunda
Roux
Sassafras
Skates on the Bay
Slow Club
Station Hse. Café
Street Rest.
Tastings Rest.
Town's End
2223 Restaurant
231 Ellsworth
Universal Cafe
Village Pub
Wild Hare
Woodward's Garden
Yabbies
zazu

Zin
Zinsvalley

### American (Traditional)
Anzu
Autumn Moon
Balboa Cafe
Beach Chalet
Bette's Oceanview
BIX
Blue Plate
Boulevard
Brazen Head
Buckeye Roadhse.
Buck's
Cafe Flore
Cafe For All Seasons
Calistoga Inn
Casa Orinda
Chloe's Cafe
Cityscape
Cliff House
Curve Bar
Daily Grill
Delancey St.
Dine
Dipsea Cafe
Dottie's True Blue
Eastside West
Ella's
FatApple's
Felix & Louie's
FlatIron Grill
Fly Trap
Gordon Biersch
Gordon's
Hard Rock Cafe
Hayes St. Grill
Home
It's Tops Coffee
Jimtown Store
JoAnn's Cafe
Julia
Kate's Kitchen
Kelly's Mission Rock

Lark Creek
Lark Creek Inn
Lauren's
Mama's Royal Cafe
Mama's/Washington Sq.
Max's Diamond
Meetinghouse
Mel Hollen's Bar
Moose's
Mo's Grill
Moss Beach
Nepenthe
Original Joe's
Peninsula Fountain
Perry's
Pork Store Cafe
Rick & Ann's
Rutherford Grill
Sam's Anchor
Sam's Grill
Sears Fine Food
Shadowbrook
Stinson Beach
Tarpy's Roadhse.
Taylor's Automatic
Yankee Pier

### Asian
AsiaSF
Azie
Betelnut Pejiu Wu
Bridges
butterfly
Carême Room
Chaya Brasserie
Citrus Club
Compass Rose
Crustacean
E&O Trading Co.
Eos Rest.
Flying Fish Grill
Grasshopper
Hawthorne Lane
House
La Mooné

## Cuisine Index

Lisa Hemenway's
Mandalay
Marica
Ma Tante Sumi
Pairs
Ponzu
RoHan Lounge
Sake Tini
Silks
Straits Cafe
Three Seasons
Tin-Pan Asian
Tonga Room
Trader Vic's
Watergate
Z
Zao Noodle Bar

### Bakeries
Alexis Baking Co.
Boulange
Citizen Cake
Costeaux Bakery
Downtown Bakery
Emporio Rulli
Gayle's Bakery
Liberty Cafe
Model Bakery
Town's End

### Barbecue
Bo's Barbecue
Brother-in-Law's
Brother's Korean
Buckeye Roadhse.
Coriya Hot Pot City
Everett & Jones
Flint's BBQ
Foothill Cafe
Geyserville Smokehse.
Juban
Koryo
Memphis Minnie's
Red Rock Cafe

### Belgian
Frjtz Fries

### Burmese
Mandalay
Nan Yang Rockridge

### Cajun/Creole
Alcatraces
Elite Cafe
Le Krewe
Nola
PJ's Oyster

### Californian
Ahwahnee Din. Rm.
Albion River Inn
Alcatraces
All Season's Cafe
Applewood Inn
A.P. Stump's
AsiaSF
Asqew Grill
Avenue 9
Bay Wolf
Bistro Elan
Blackhawk Grille
Blue Plate
Boonville Hotel
Breads of India
Bridges
Brix
Bucci's
butterfly
Cafe Beaujolais
Cafe Kati
Cafe Lucy
Caffe Centro
Carnelian Room
Carneros
Charcuterie
Charles Nob Hill
Charlie's
Chateau Souverain
Chez Panisse
Chez Panisse Café
Citizen Cake
Cool Café
Cozmo's
Desiree

Domaine Chandon
Duarte's Tavern
Eldo's Grill
Enrico's
Erna's Elderberry
Eulipia
Farmhouse Inn
Flea St. Café
Flying Fish Grill
Foothill Cafe
Fork
Fournou's Ovens
Gabriella Café
Garden Court
Garibaldis
General's Daughter
Glen Ellen Inn
Grand Cafe
Grasing's Coastal
Hawthorne Lane
Higashi West
Italian Colors
Jardinière
Jimmy Bean's
John Ash & Co.
Julia's Kitchen
JZ Cool
Lalime's
Ledford House
Le Krewe
Little River Inn
Lucy's Rest.
MacCallum Hse.
Madrona Manor
Manka's Inverness
Marinus
Ma Tante Sumi
mc$^2$
Meadowood Grill
Mikayla/Casa Madrona
Mistral
Mixx Rest.
Moosse Cafe
Napa Valley Grille
Napa Valley Wine

Night Monkey
Osake
Oswald's
Pacific
Pacific's Edge
Pairs
Palomino
Paragon Bar
Passionfish
Pearl
Pearl Alley Bistro
Pinot Blanc
Plumed Horse
PlumpJack Cafe
Ravenous
Rest. at Meadowood
Rio Grill
Rivoli
Rubicon
Santé
Sea Ranch Lodge
Seasons
Sierra Mar
Silks
Soizic
Soléa
Spago Palo Alto
Spoon
Stars
St. Michael's Alley
Stokes Rest.
St. Orres
Syrah
Tarpy's Roadhse.
Tonga Room
Townhouse B&G
Tra Vigne
Valhalla
Venus
Verbena
Waterfront Rest.
Wente Vineyards
Wine Spectator
XYZ
Zax

## Cambodian

Angkor Borei
Angkor Wat
Battambang
Cambodiana

## Caribbean

Cha Cha Cha
Charanga
Primo Patio

## Cheese Steaks

Jay's Cheese Steak

## Chinese

Alice's
Brandy Ho's
Chef Chu's
Dragon Well
Eliza's
Eric's
Firecracker
Fook Yuen
Fountain Court
Gary Chu
Great China
Great Eastern
Happy Cafe
Harbor Village
Hong Kong Flower
House of Nanking
Hunan
Hunan Home's
Jade Villa
Koi Palace
Little Shin Shin
Mandarin
Mayflower
Mei Long
Omei
R & G Lounge
Restaurant Peony
Shanghai 1930
Shen Hua
Taiwan
Tommy Toy's

Ton Kiang
Yank Sing
Yuet Lee

## Coffee Shops/Diners

Bette's Oceanview
Caffe Centro
Downtown Bakery
FatApple's
It's Tops Coffee
JoAnn's Cafe
Mama's Royal Cafe
Mel's Drive-In
Mo's Grill
Peninsula Fountain
Sears Fine Food

## Continental

Anton & Michel
Bella Vista
Caprice
Compass Rose
Dal Baffo
Maddalena's/Café Fino
Rest. at Stevenswood
Shadowbrook
Taste Cafe

## Delis/Sandwich Shops

Downtown Bakery
East Coast West
Gayle's Bakery
Jimtown Store
JZ Cool
Max's
Moishe's Pippic
Rosamunde Sausage
Saul's Rest.

## Dim Sum

Fook Yuen
Harbor Village
Hong Kong Flower
Jade Villa
Koi Palace
Mayflower
Restaurant Peony

Taiwan
Ton Kiang
Yank Sing

## Eclectic/International
Andalu
Bistro at Glen Ellen
Bloo
Britt-Marie's
Cafe Cuvée
Cafe Kati
Cafe La Haye
Cafe Prima
Carta
Central Park
Chow
Firefly
Hayes & Vine Wine
House
Lauren's
Montrio
Olive Bar
Pangaea
Pearl Alley Bistro
Pomelo
Restaurant Umunhum
Townhouse B&G
Wappo Bar
Willow Wood
Zinsvalley

## English
Lovejoy's Tea Rm.
Pelican Inn

## Eritrean
Massawa

## Ethiopian
Axum Cafe
Blue Nile
Rasselas Ethiopian

## French
Ana Mandara
Auberge du Soleil
Basque Cultural Ctr.

Cafe Beaujolais
Café Fanny
Cafe Jacqueline
Campton Place
Carême Room
Casanova
Chantilly
Chateau Souverain
Chez Papa
Chez Spencer
Costeaux Bakery
El Paseo
Emile's
French Laundry
Fresh Cream
Galette
Gervais Rest.
Jardinière
Julius' Castle
La Forêt
L'Olivier
Luna Park
Ma Tante Sumi
Merenda
Plouf
Restaurant LuLu
Scala's Bistro
Soléa
Ti Couz
Waterfront Rest.

## French (Bistro)
Absinthe
À Côté
Alamo Square
Anjou
Baker St. Bistro
Bistro Clovis
Bistro Elan
Bistro Jeanty
Bistro Vida
Bizou
Black Cat
Bocca Rotis
Bouchon
Brava Terrace
Butler & The Chef

Cafe Bastille
Café Claude
Cafe Lucy
Café Marcella
Café Rouge
Chapeau!
Charcuterie
Christophe
Clémentine
Florio
Foreign Cinema
Fringale
girl & the fig
Hyde St. Bistro
Jojo
K&L Bistro
L'Amie Donia
La Note
Le Bistrot
Le Central Bistro
Le Charm
Left Bank
Le Petit Robert
Le Zinc
Nizza La Bella
Robert's Bistro
Savor
Sent Sovi
South Park Cafe
Syrah
Tartine Bakery
Water St. Bistro
Zazie

## French (New)

All Season's Cafe
Applewood Inn
Azie
Bistro Liaison
Boulange
Charles Nob Hill
Chaya Brasserie
Chaz Rest.
Chez TJ
Citron

Club XIX
Domaine Chandon
Elisabeth Daniel
Erna's Elderberry
Fifth Floor
Fleur de Lys
Fork
Gary Danko
Grand Cafe
Guernica
Isa
Jeanty at Jack's
Julia's Kitchen
Kenwood
La Folie
La Mooné
La Toque
Le Colonial
Le Papillon
Lisa Hemenway's
Madrona Manor
Marché
Marché aux Fleurs
Marica
Marinus
Masa's
$mc^2$
Mirepoix
955 Ukiah
Pacific
Pacific's Edge
Pastis
Pinot Blanc
Plumed Horse
Redwood Park
Rendezvous Inn
Restaurant 301
Ritz-Carlton Din. Rm.
Rose's Café
Roux
Rubicon
Seasons
Sierra Mar
Terra
Tommy Toy's
Watergate
Z

# Cuisine Index

## Fusion
Brix
Eos Rest.
House
Mei Long
Roy's
Roy's at Pebble Beach
Straits Cafe

## German
Matterhorn Swiss
Schroeder's
Suppenküche

## Greek
Evvia
Kokkari Estiatorio
Yianni's

## Hamburgers
Balboa Cafe
Barney's
Burger Joint
Hard Rock Cafe
Liverpool Lil's
Marin Joe's
Mel's Drive-In
Mo's Grill
Perry's
Red Rock Cafe
Taylor's Automatic

## Hawaiian
Rick's
Roy's
Roy's at Pebble Beach
Tita's

## Indian
Ajanta
Amber India
Breads of India
Gaylord India
Indian Oven
Lotus Cuisine
Maharani
Pakwan

Passage to India
Shalimar
Vik's Chaat Corner
Zaika
Zante's

## Indonesian
Rice Table

## Italian
(N=Northern; S=Southern;
N&S=includes both)
Acquerello (N)
Albona Rist. (N)
Alioto's (S)
Allegro (N&S)
Antica Trattoria (N&S)
Aperto (N&S)
A Tavola (N&S)
Baldoria (N&S)
Bella Trattoria (N&S)
Bistro Don Giovanni (N&S)
Bocca Rotis (N&S)
Bruno's (N&S)
Buca di Beppo (S)
Buca Giovanni (N&S)
Cafe Citti (N)
Cafe 817 (N)
Café Fanny (N)
Café Marcella (N)
Café Niebaum-Coppola (S)
Cafe Pro Bono (N&S)
Cafe Riggio (N&S)
Café Tiramisu (N)
Caffe Delle Stelle (N)
Caffè Greco (N&S)
Caffe Macaroni (S)
Caffe Sport (S)
Capellini (N)
Capp's Corner (N&S)
Casanova (N)
Casa Orinda (N&S)
Chantilly (N)
Cucina Paradiso (S)
Cucina Viansa (N)

Dal Baffo (N)
D'Asaro (N&S)
Delfina (N&S)
Della Santina's (N)
E'Angelo (N)
Emmy's (N&S)
Emporio Rulli (N&S)
Faz (N&S)
Felix & Louie's (N&S)
Fior d'Italia (N)
Florio (N&S)
Frantoio (N)
Gabriella Café (N)
Giorgio's Pizza (N&S)
Gira Polli (N&S)
Graziano's (N&S)
Green Valley Cafe (N)
I Fratelli (N&S)
Il Davide (N)
Il Fornaio (N)
Incanto (N&S)
Italian Colors (N&S)
Jackson Fillmore (N&S)
Julius' Castle (N)
Kuleto's (N)
La Felce (N)
La Ginestra (S)
Little Joe's (N&S)
LoCoCo's (S)
L'Osteria del Forno (N)
Luna Park (N&S)
Maddalena's/Café Fino (N&S)
Mangiafuoco (N)
Marin Joe's (N&S)
Mario's Bohemian (N)
Merenda (N)
Mescolanza (N)
Mezza Luna (S)
Michelangelo (N&S)
Nob Hill Café (N&S)
North Beach Rest. (N&S)
Oliveto Cafe (N)
Original Joe's (N&S)

Osteria (N)
Palatino (N&S)
Palio d'Asti (N&S)
Pane e Vino (N)
Panta Rei (N)
Parma (N)
Pasta Moon (N&S)
Pasta Pomodoro (N&S)
Pazzia (N&S)
Pesce (N)
Piatti (N&S)
Piazza D'Angelo (N&S)
Postino (N)
Prima (N)
Ristorante Bacco (N&S)
Ristorante Fabrizio (N)
Ristorante Ideale (N&S)
Ristorante Milano (N)
Ristorante Umbria (N&S)
Rose Pistola (N)
Rose's Café (N)
Salute Rist. (N&S)
Santi (N&S)
Savoia Rist. (N&S)
Scala's Bistro (N&S)
Sharon's by the Sea (N)
Sociale (N&S)
Spiedini (N)
Stinking Rose (N)
Terra (N)
Tomatina (N&S)
Tommaso's (S)
Tratt. Contadina (N&S)
Tratt. La Siciliana (S)
Tra Vigne (N&S)
Tuscany (N)
Uva Trattoria (N&S)
Venezia (N&S)
Venticello (N)
Via Centro (N)
Via Vai (N&S)
Vicolo (N&S)
Victorian Gardens (N&S)
Vivande Porta Via (N&S)

zazu (N)
Zuni Cafe (N)

### Japanese
Ace Wasabi's
Anzu
Blowfish, Sushi
Deep Sushi
Ebisu
Fuki Sushi
Godzila Sushi
Grandeho's Kamekyo
Hamano Sushi
Hana Japanese
Higashi West
Hotei
Juban
Kabuto Sushi
Kirala
Kyo-Ya
Le Poisson Japonais
Maki
Mas Sake
Mifune
Minako
Moki's Sushi
Norikonoko
O Chamé
Osake
Ozumo
Robata Grill
Sanraku Four Seasons
Sushi Groove
Sushi Ran
Takara
Ten-Ichi
Tokyo Go Go
Uzen
Wasabi & Ginger
We Be Sushi
Yokoso Nippon
Yoshi's

### Jewish
East Coast West
Moishe's Pippic
Saul's Rest.

### Korean
Brother's Korean
Koryo

### Mediterranean
Auberge du Soleil
Bay Wolf
Bistro Aix
Bucci's
Cafe Esin
Cafe Gibraltar
Cafe Pro Bono
Caffè Museo
Carneros
Carrara's
Celadon
Cetrella Bistro
Chez Nous
Chez Panisse
Chez Panisse Café
downtown
Enrico's
Fandango
Faz
F.I.G.S.
42 Degrees
Fournou's Ovens
Frascati
Garibaldis
Insalata's
Lalime's
La Mediterranée
Lapis Rest.
La Scene Café
Ledford House
Lucy's Rest.
Manzanita
Maurice Rest.
Mendo Bistro
Mezze
Mikayla/Casa Madrona
Mistral
Ondine
Palomino
paul K

Piyassa
PlumpJack Cafe
Postino
Ritz-Carlton Terrace
Rivoli
Salute Rist.
Savor
71 Saint Peter
Stokes Rest.
Tomatina
Truly Mediterranean
Verbena
Via Centro
Viaggio Rist.
Viognier
Yumma's
Zaré
Zax
Zibibbo
Zucca
Zuni Cafe

### Mexican/Tex-Mex

Cactus Taqueria
Cafe Marimba
Doña Tomás
El Balazo
El Palomar
Guaymas
Joe's Taco
Juan's Place
La Cumbre
La Rondalla
Las Camelias
La Taqueria
Mas Sake
Maya (SF)
Maya (Sonoma)
Pancho Villa
Picante Cocina
Puerto Alegre
Roosevelt Tamale
Taqueria Cancun
Villa Corona

### Middle Eastern

Kan Zaman
La Mediterranée
Maykedah
Shoopra
Truly Mediterranean

### Moroccan

Aziza

### Noodle Shops

Citrus Club
Hotei
Mifune
Tin-Pan Asian
Zao Noodle Bar

### Nuevo Latino

Alma
Asia de Cuba
La Luna

### Pacific Rim

Jordan's
Moki's Sushi

### Pakistani

Pakwan
Shalimar

### Persian

Maykedah

### Pizza

Amici's
Café Niebaum-Coppola
Capellini
Felix & Louie's
Frantoio
Giorgio's Pizza
Il Fornaio
La Ginestra
LoCoCo's
L'Osteria del Forno
Mescolanza
Nob Hill Café
North Beach Pizza

# Cuisine Index

Pauline's Pizza
Pazzia
Pizza Azzurro
Pizza Rustica
Pizzetta 211
Postrio
Spago Palo Alto
Tommaso's
Via Vai
Vicolo
Zachary's Chicago
Zante's

## Polynesian
Tonga Room
Trader Vic's

## Portuguese
LaSalette

## Pub Food
Calistoga Inn
Liverpool Lil's
Pelican Inn

## Russian
Katia's Russian Tea

## Seafood
Alamo Square
Alioto's
Aqua
A. Sabella's
Barbara's Fishtrap
Crustacean
downtown
Eastside West
Farallon
Great Eastern
Hayes St. Grill
Hong Kong Flower
Koi Palace
Mayflower
McCormick & Kuleto's
Navio

Ondine
Pacific Café
Passionfish
Pesce
Pier 23 Cafe
Pisces
PJ's Oyster
Plouf
Red Herring
Rose Pistola
Sam's Grill
Sardine Factory
Scoma's
Sharon's by the Sea
Skates on the Bay
Spenger's
Swan Oyster Depot
Tadich Grill
Thanh Long
Ti Couz
Yabbies
Yankee Pier
Yuet Lee

## Senegalese
Bissap Baobab

## Singaporean
Straits Cafe

## South African
Joubert's

## South American
Destino
girl & the gaucho
Miramonte
Zuzu

## Southern/Soul
Catahoula Rest.
Everett & Jones
Kate's Kitchen
Kingfish
Memphis Minnie's
Powell's Place

## Southwestern
Eldo's Grill
Nola
Rio Grill

## Spanish
Alegrias
B44
César
Esperpento
Iberia
Lorca
Picaro
Ramblas
Thirsty Bear
Timo's
Zarzuela
Zuzu

## Steakhouses
Acme Chop Hse.
Alfred's Steak
Cole's Chop Hse.
Harris'
House of Prime Rib
Izzy's Steak
John's Grill
Morton's
Ruth's Chris
Vic Stewart's

## Swiss
Matterhorn Swiss

## Taiwanese
Coriya Hot Pot City
Taiwan

## Tapas
À Côté
Alegrias
Andalu
AsiaSF
César
Cetrella Bistro
Cha Cha Cha
Charanga

Chez Nous
Destino
Esperpento
girl & the gaucho
Grasshopper
Iberia
Isa
Lorca
Picaro
Ramblas
Thirsty Bear
Timo's
Zarzuela
Zuzu

## Tearooms
Frjtz Fries
Lovejoy's Tea Rm.
O Chamé

## Thai
Basil
Cha Am Thai
Dusit Thai
Khan Toke
King of Thai
Manora's
Marnee Thai
Neecha Thai
Phuping Thai
Plearn Thai
Royal Thai
Ruen Pair
Thai House
Thanya & Salee
Thep Phanom
Yukol Place

## Tibetan
Lhasa Moon

## Vegetarian
Flea St. Café
Fleur de Lys
Greens
Herbivore

# Cuisine Index

Joubert's
Millennium
Ravens
Roxanne's

## Vietnamese
Ana Mandara
Golden Turtle
La Vie
Le Cheval

Le Colonial
Le Soleil
Pho Vietnam
Slanted Door
Tao Cafe
Thanh Long
Three Seasons
Tu Lan
Vi's

# LOCATIONS

## SAN FRANCISCO

### Bernal Heights
Angkor Borei
Blue Plate
Dusit Thai
Emmy's
Liberty Cafe
Moki's Sushi
Palatino
Taqueria Cancun
Zante's

### Castro
Cafe Cuvée
Cafe Flore
Chow
Home
La Mediterranée
La Mooné
Ma Tante Sumi
Pasta Pomodoro
Thai House
Tin-Pan Asian
Tita's
2223 Restaurant
Yokoso Nippon
Zao Noodle Bar

### Chinatown
Brandy Ho's
Great Eastern
House of Nanking
Hunan Home's
R & G Lounge
Yuet Lee

### Civic Center
Indigo
Max's
Mel's Drive-In
Millennium
Stars

### Cow Hollow
Amici's
Baker St. Bistro
Balboa Cafe
Betelnut Pejiu Wu
Brazen Head
Charlie's
Eastside West
Liverpool Lil's
MatrixFillmore
Merenda
Night Monkey
Pane e Vino
Perry's
PlumpJack Cafe
Rose's Café
Shoopra
Via Vai

### Downtown
Alfred's Steak
Anjou
Anzu
Aqua
Asia de Cuba
B44
BIX
Cafe Bastille
Café Claude
Café Tiramisu
Campton Place
Carnelian Room
Cha Am Thai Express
Cityscape
Compass Rose
Daily Grill
E&O Trading Co.
Elisabeth Daniel
Farallon
Faz

Fifth Floor
First Crush
Fleur de Lys
Garden Court
Gaylord India
Globe
Gordon Biersch
Grand Cafe
Harbor Village
Hunan
Jeanty at Jack's
John's Grill
King of Thai
Kokkari Estiatorio
Kuleto's
Kyo-Ya
La Scene Café
Le Central Bistro
Le Colonial
L'Olivier
Masa's
Max's
mc$^2$
Morton's
Pacific
Palio d'Asti
Park Grill
Pastis
Perry's
Plouf
Ponzu
Postrio
Redwood Park
Rotunda
Rubicon
Sam's Grill
Sanraku Four Seasons
Scala's Bistro
Schroeder's
Sears Fine Food
Seasons
Silks
Soléa
Tadich Grill
Taqueria Cancun
Tommy Toy's
Zaré

### Embarcadero
Boulevard
Chaya Brasserie
Delancey St.
Fog City Diner
Il Fornaio
Lapis Rest.
North Beach Pizza
One Market
Ozumo
Palomino
Pier 23 Cafe
Red Herring
Town's End
Waterfront Rest.

### Excelsior
North Beach Pizza

### Fisherman's Wharf
Alioto's
Ana Mandara
A. Sabella's
Frjtz Fries
Gary Danko
Gaylord India
Grandeho's Kamekyo
Mandarin
McCormick & Kuleto's
Scoma's

### Glen Park
Chenery Park

### Haight-Ashbury/ Cole Valley
Asqew Grill
Boulange
Cha Cha Cha
Citrus Club
El Balazo
Eos Rest.
Grandeho's Kamekyo
Kan Zaman

Massawa
North Beach Pizza
Pasta Pomodoro
Pork Store Cafe
Zazie

### Hayes Valley
Absinthe
Bistro Clovis
Caffe Delle Stelle
Citizen Cake
Frjtz Fries
Hayes & Vine Wine
Hayes St. Grill
Jardinière
Moishe's Pippic
paul K
Piyassa
Powell's Place
Suppenküche
Vicolo
Zuni Cafe

### Inner Richmond
Angkor Wat
Bella Trattoria
Brother's Korean
Cafe Riggio
Clémentine
Coriya Hot Pot City
Fountain Court
Giorgio's Pizza
Katia's Russian Tea
King of Thai
Le Soleil
Mandalay
Mel's Drive-In
Q
RoHan Lounge
Royal Thai
Straits Cafe
Taiwan
We Be Sushi

### Inner Sunset
Avenue 9
Ebisu

Eldo's Grill
Hotei
House
Park Chow
PJ's Oyster
We Be Sushi
Yumma's

### Japantown
Cafe Kati
Juban
Maki
Mifune
Pasta Pomodoro
Perlot
Takara

### Lower Haight
Axum Cafe
Bloo
Burger Joint
Indian Oven
Kate's Kitchen
Memphis Minnie's
Rosamunde Sausage
Thep Phanom

### Marina
Ace Wasabi's
Alegrias
Asqew Grill
Barney's
Bistro Aix
Cafe Marimba
Chaz Rest.
Cozmo's
Dragon Well
E'Angelo
Greens
Isa
Izzy's Steak
Lhasa Moon
Marinette
Mas Sake
Mel's Drive-In
Parma

Pasta Pomodoro
Savoia Rist.
Three Seasons
Yukol Place
Zao Noodle Bar

### Mission
Alma
Andalu
Bissap Baobab
Blowfish, Sushi
Bruno's
Burger Joint
butterfly
Cha Cha Cha
Charanga
Chez Spencer
Delfina
Esperpento
Firecracker
Foreign Cinema
Gordon's Hse./Fine Eats
Herbivore
Jay's Cheese Steak
La Cumbre
La Luna
La Rondalla
La Taqueria
Le Krewe
Lorca
Luna Park
Mangiafuoco
Minako
Pakwan
Pancho Villa
Pauline's Pizza
Picaro
Puerto Alegre
Ramblas
Rock Soup
Roosevelt Tamale
Slow Club
Tao Cafe
Taqueria Cancun
Tartine Bakery

Ti Couz
Timo's
Tokyo Go Go
Truly Mediterranean
Universal Cafe
Watergate
We Be Sushi
Woodward's Garden

### Nob Hill
Big Four
Charles Nob Hill
Fournou's Ovens
Le Bistrot
Nob Hill Café
Ritz-Carlton Din. Rm.
Ritz-Carlton Terrace
Tonga Room
Venticello

### Noe Valley
Alcatraces
Alice's
Barney's
Chloe's Cafe
Deep Sushi
Eric's
Firefly
Hamano Sushi
Incanto
Le Zinc
Lovejoy's Tea Rm.
Miss Millie's
Pasta Pomodoro
Pomelo
Ristorante Bacco
Savor
Yianni's

### North Beach
Albona Rist.
Black Cat
Buca Giovanni
Cafe Jacqueline
Café Niebaum-Coppola
Caffè Greco

Caffe Macaroni
Caffe Sport
Capp's Corner
Cobalt Tavern
Enrico's
Fior d'Italia
Gira Polli
Helmand
House
Jianna
Julius' Castle
La Felce
Little Joe's
L'Osteria del Forno
Mama's/Washington Sq.
Mario's Bohemian
Maykedah
Mel Hollen's Bar
Michelangelo
Moose's
Mo's Grill
North Beach Pizza
North Beach Rest.
Panta Rei
Pasta Pomodoro
Ristorante Ideale
Rose Pistola
Stinking Rose
Tommaso's
Tratt. Contadina
Truly Mediterranean
Zax

## Pacific Heights

Eliza's
Godzila Sushi
Julia
Meetinghouse
Neecha Thai
Rasselas Ethiopian

## Potrero Hill

Aperto
Chez Papa
Eliza's
42 Degrees
Kelly's Mission Rock
Thanya & Salee

## Presidio Heights

Desiree
Ella's
Garibaldis
Sociale

## Richmond

Aziza
Beach Chalet
Chapeau!
Cliff House
Kabuto Sushi
Khan Toke
La Vie
Mayflower
Mescolanza
Pacific Café
Pizzetta 211
Ton Kiang

## Russian Hill

Allegro
Frascati
Hyde St. Bistro
I Fratelli
Ristorante Milano
Sushi Groove
Zarzuela

## SoMa

AsiaSF
Azie
bacar
Basil
Bizou
Buca di Beppo
Caffè Museo
Cha Am Thai
Cosmopolitan Cafe
Dine
Fly Trap
Fringale
Hawthorne Lane
Hunan
Le Charm
Manora's

Max's
Maya
Mel's Drive-In
Mo's Burgers
North Beach Pizza
Pazzia
Restaurant LuLu
Ristorante Umbria
Roy's
Sanraku Four Seasons
Shanghai 1930
Slanted Door
Sushi Groove
Thirsty Bear
Tu Lan
XYZ
Yank Sing

### South Beach/ Pacific Bell Park
Acme Chop Hse.
Butler & The Chef
Caffe Centro
Curve Bar
Infusion Bar
Max's Diamond
MoMo's
Paragon
Primo Patio
South Park Cafe

### Sunset
Joubert's
King of Thai
Little Joe's
Marnee Thai
Pasta Pomodoro
Pomelo
Rick's
Thanh Long

### Tenderloin
Carême Room
Dottie's True Blue
Olive Bar
Original Joe's

Pakwan
Shalimar

### Twin Peaks/ West Portal
Bocca Rotis
Cafe For All Seasons

### Upper Fillmore
Chez Nous
Elite Cafe
Florio
Galette
Jackson Fillmore
La Mediterranée
Ten-Ichi
Vivande Porta Via
Zao Noodle Bar

### Upper Market/ Church Street
Carta
Destino
It's Tops Coffee
Mecca

### Van Ness/Polk
Acquerello
Antica Trattoria
Baldoria
Boulange
Crustacean
East Coast West
F.I.G.S.
Golden Turtle
Hard Rock Cafe
Harris'
House of Prime Rib
La Folie
Le Petit Robert
Maharani
Matterhorn Swiss
Pesce
Ruth's Chris
Spoon
Street Rest.
Swan Oyster Depot

Wasabi & Ginger
Yabbies

### Western Addition
Alamo Square
Brother-in-Law's

Herbivore
Jay's Cheese Steak
Maurice Rest.
Rasselas Ethiopian


## EAST OF SAN FRANCISCO

### Albany
Britt-Marie's
Nizza La Bella
Ruen Pair

### Berkeley
Ajanta
Barney's
Bette's Oceanview
Bistro Liaison
Blue Nile
Breads of India
Cactus Taqueria
Café Fanny
Café Rouge
Cambodiana
César
Cha Am Thai
Chez Panisse
Chez Panisse Café
downtown
FatApple's
Ginger Island
Great China
Jimmy Bean's
Jordan's
Juan's Place
Kirala
Lalime's
La Mediterranée
La Note
LoCoCo's
Norikonoko
North Beach Pizza
O Chamé
Paragon Bar
Picante Cocina

Plearn Thai
Rick & Ann's
Rivoli
Saul's Rest.
Shen Hua
Skates on the Bay
Spenger's
Taiwan
Tratt. La Siciliana
Venezia
Venus
Via Centro
Vik's Chaat Corner
Zachary's Chicago
Zaika

### Danville
Blackhawk Grille
Brava Terrace
Bridges
Faz
Piatti

### El Cerrito
FatApple's

### Emeryville
Bucci's
Townhouse B&G
Trader Vic's

### Hayward
Everett & Jones

### Lafayette
Bo's Barbecue
Duck Club
Postino

**Livermore**
Wente Vineyards

**Oakland**
À Côté
Autumn Moon
Barney's
Battambang
Bay Wolf
Cactus Taqueria
Cafe 817
Carrara's
Citron
Doña Tomás
Everett & Jones
Flint's BBQ
Garibaldis
Grasshopper
Italian Colors
Jade Villa
Jojo
Koryo
Le Cheval
Little Shin Shin
LoCoCo's
Mama's Royal Cafe
Marica
Max's
Mezze
Nan Yang Rockridge
Oliveto Cafe
Pasta Pomodoro
Pizza Rustica

Restaurant Peony
Soizic
Uzen
Verbena
Vi's
Yoshi's
Zachary's Chicago

**Orinda**
Casa Orinda

**Pleasant Hill**
Left Bank

**Pleasanton**
Faz

**Richmond**
Phuping Thai
Salute Rist.

**San Ramon**
Cafe Esin

**Walnut Creek**
Il Fornaio
Lark Creek
Prima
Spiedini
Tomatina
Vic Stewart's

**Yosemite-Oakhurst**
Ahwahnee Din. Rm.
Erna's Elderberry

### NORTH OF SAN FRANCISCO

**Calistoga**
All Season's Cafe
Brannan's Grill
Calistoga Inn
Catahoula Rest.
FlatIron Grill
Wappo Bar

**Corte Madera**
Il Fornaio
Izzy's Steak
Marin Joe's
Max's

**Eureka**
Restaurant 301

## Fairfax
Ross Valley Brew.

## Geyserville
Chateau Souverain
Geyserville Smokehse.
Santi

## Glen Ellen/Kenwood
Bistro at Glen Ellen
Cafe Citti
girl & the gaucho
Glen Ellen Inn
Kenwood

## Guerneville
Applewood Inn
Farmhouse Inn

## Healdsburg
Bistro Ralph
Charcuterie
Costeaux Bakery
Downtown Bakery
Dry Creek Kitchen
Felix & Louie's
Jimtown Store
Madrona Manor
Manzanita
Ravenous
Tastings Rest.
Zin

## Lake Tahoe
PlumpJack Cafe

## Larkspur
Emporio Rulli
Lark Creek Inn
Left Bank
Ristorante Fabrizio
Roxanne's
Yankee Pier

## Mendocino County
Albion River Inn
Boonville Hotel

Cafe Beaujolais
Cafe Prima
Lauren's
Ledford House
Little River Inn
MacCallum Hse.
Mendo Bistro
Moosse Cafe
955 Ukiah
Pangaea
Ravens
Rendezvous Inn
Rest. at Stevenswood
Sea Ranch Lodge
Sharon's by the Sea
St. Orres
Victorian Gardens

## Mill Valley
Buckeye Roadhse.
Dipsea Cafe
El Paseo
Frantoio
Gira Polli
Joe's Taco
La Ginestra
Piatti
Piazza D'Angelo
Robata Grill

## Napa
Alexis Baking Co.
Bistro Don Giovanni
Brix
Cafe Lucy
Carneros
Celadon
Cole's Chop Hse.
Foothill Cafe
Julia's Kitchen
Mustards Grill
Napa Valley Wine
Pairs
Pearl
Pizza Azzurro
Red Rock Cafe

## Location Index

Sake Tini
Tuscany
Uva Trattoria
Villa Corona
Zinsvalley
Zuzu

### Olema
Olema Inn

### Petaluma
Cucina Paradiso
Graziano's
Water St. Bistro

### Ross
Marché aux Fleurs

### Rutherford
Auberge du Soleil
La Toque
Rutherford Grill

### San Anselmo
Cucina Jackson
Fork
Insalata's

### San Rafael
Amici's
Cafe Marimba
Dipsea Cafe
Il Davide
Las Camelias
Lotus Cuisine
Pasta Pomodoro
Rice Table
Royal Thai
Salute Rist.

### Santa Rosa
Cafe Lolo
Feast
Gary Chu
Hana Japanese
John Ash & Co.
Lisa Hemenway's

Mirepoix
Mixx Rest.
Osake
Pho Vietnam
Sassafras
Syrah
zazu

### Sausalito
Christophe
Guernica
Mikayla/Casa Madrona
Ondine
Scoma's
Sushi Ran
Valhalla

### Sebastopol/Valley Ford
K&L Bistro
Lucy's Rest.
Willow Wood

### Sonoma
Cafe La Haye
Cucina Viansa
Della Santina's
Deuce
General's Daughter
girl & the fig
LaSalette
Maya
Piatti
Santé

### Sonoma Coast
Duck Club

### St. Helena
Green Valley Cafe
Martini Hse.
Meadowood Grill
Miramonte
Model Bakery
Pinot Blanc
Rest. at Meadowood
Roux
Taylor's Automatic
Terra

## Location Index

Tomatina
Tra Vigne
Villa Corona
Wine Spectator

### Tiburon
Caprice
Guaymas
Sam's Anchor

### West Marin
Manka's Inverness
Pelican Inn

Station Hse. Café
Stinson Beach

### Yountville
Bistro Jeanty
Bouchon
Domaine Chandon
French Laundry
Gordon's
Napa Valley Grille
Piatti

## SOUTH OF SAN FRANCISCO

### Half Moon Bay/Coast
Barbara's Fishtrap
Cafe Gibraltar
Cetrella Bistro
Duarte's Tavern
Mezza Luna
Moss Beach
Navio
Pasta Moon

### Monterey/Carmel
Anton & Michel
Casanova
Club XIX
Duck Club
Fandango
Flying Fish Grill
Fresh Cream
Grasing's Coastal
Il Fornaio
Marinus
Montrio
Nepenthe
Pacific's Edge
Passionfish

Piatti
Rio Grill
Robert's Bistro
Roy's at Pebble Beach
Sardine Factory
Sierra Mar
Stokes Rest.
Tarpy's Roadhse.
Taste Cafe

### Santa Cruz/Aptos
El Palomar
Gabriella Café
Gayle's Bakery
Omei
Oswald's
Pearl Alley Bistro
Shadowbrook

### South San Francisco/ Daly City
Basque Cultural Ctr.
JoAnn's Cafe
Koi Palace

## SILICON VALLEY/PENINSULA

### Burlingame
Il Fornaio
Juban

Kuleto's
Max's
Pisces

## Campbell
Buca di Beppo

## Los Altos
Chef Chu's
Hunan Home's
I Fratelli
Jocco's
Z

## Los Gatos
Café Marcella

## Menlo Park
Bistro Vida
Dal Baffo
Duck Club
Flea St. Café
Gaylord India
Iberia
Juban
JZ Cool
Left Bank
Marché
Wild Hare

## Millbrae
Fook Yuen
Hong Kong Flower

## Mountain View
Amber India
Amici's
Chez TJ
Mei Long
Passage to India
Zucca

## Palo Alto
Bistro Elan
Buca di Beppo
Café Niebaum-Coppola
Cafe Pro Bono
Cool Café
Evvia
Fuki Sushi
Gordon Biersch

Higashi West
Hong Kong Flower
Il Fornaio
L'Amie Donia
Le Poisson Japonais
Maddalena's/Café Fino
Mas Sake
Max's
Nola
Osteria
Peninsula Fountain
Piatti
Spago Palo Alto
St. Michael's Alley
Straits Cafe
Trader Vic's
Zao Noodle Bar
Zibibbo

## Redwood City
Amici's
Chantilly
D'Asaro
Max's
Mistral

## San Carlos
A Tavola

## San Jose
A.P. Stump's
E&O Trading Co.
Emile's
Eulipia
Gordon Biersch
Il Fornaio
La Forêt
La Taqueria
Le Papillon
Original Joe's
Restaurant Umunhum
71 Saint Peter

## San Mateo
Amici's
Capellini
Central Park

# Location Index

Happy Cafe
Kingfish
La Cumbre
Lark Creek
Pancho Villa
231 Ellsworth
Viognier

## Santa Clara
Parcel 104
Tomatina

## Saratoga
Basin
Gervais Rest.

Plumed Horse
Sent Sovi
Viaggio Rist.

## Sunnyvale
Faz
Lion & Compass

## Woodside
Bella Vista
Buck's
John Bentley's
Village Pub

# SPECIAL FEATURES

(Restaurants followed by a † may not offer
that feature at every location.)

## Breakfast
(See also Hotel Dining)
Absinthe
Autumn Moon
Bette's Oceanview
Buck's
Butler & The Chef
Cafe 817
Café Fanny
Cafe Flore
Chez Spencer
Chloe's Cafe
Citizen Cake
Desiree
Dipsea Cafe
Dottie's True Blue
Downtown Bakery
Duarte's Tavern
East Coast West
Ella's
Emporio Rulli
FatApple's
Galette
Gordon's
Harbor Village
Il Fornaio†
It's Tops Coffee
Jimmy Bean's
Jimtown Store
JoAnn's Cafe
Kate's Kitchen
La Mediterranée†
La Note
Mama's Royal Cafe
Mama's/Washington Sq.
Mel's Drive-In†
Model Bakery
Oliveto Cafe
Peninsula Fountain
Pork Store Cafe

Rick & Ann's
Rose's Café
Savor
Sears Fine Food
Station Hse. Café
Ton Kiang
Town's End
Venus
Zazie

## Brunch
Absinthe
Andalu
Autumn Moon
Avenue 9
Bette's Oceanview
Bistro Vida
Buckeye Roadhse.
Buck's
Cafe Cuvée
Cafe La Haye
Cafe Marimba†
Cetrella Bistro
Chloe's Cafe
Citizen Cake
Cityscape
Cozmo's
Dipsea Cafe†
Dottie's True Blue
Elite Cafe
Ella's
Flea St. Café
Fog City Diner
Garden Court
Gaylord India†
General's Daughter
Hong Kong Flower†
Il Fornaio†
Insalata's
Jordan's

Kate's Kitchen
Kelly's Mission Rock
La Luna
La Mediterranée†
La Note
Lark Creek†
Mama's Royal Cafe
Mama's/Washington Sq.
Mayflower
Mel's Drive-In†
Mikayla/Casa Madrona
Miss Millie's
MoMo's
Moose's
Napa Valley Grille
Navio
Pasta Moon
Piazza D'Angelo
Postrio
Primo Patio
Rest. at Meadowood
Restaurant LuLu
Rick & Ann's
Rio Grill
Ritz-Carlton Terrace
Rose's Café
Sam's Anchor
Schroeder's
Sears Fine Food
St. Michael's Alley
Ton Kiang
Town's End
2223 Restaurant
Universal Cafe
Viognier
Waterfront Rest.
Wente Vineyards
XYZ
Zazie
Zibibbo
Zuni Cafe

## Buffet Served

(Check availability)
Ahwahnee Din. Rm.
Amber India
Anzu
Carême Room
Cityscape
Cliff House
Coriya Hot Pot City
Duck Club†
Garden Court
Gaylord India†
Jordan's
Lotus Cuisine
Mikayla/Casa Madrona
Navio
Pacific
Passage to India
Pelican Inn
Rest. at Meadowood
Ritz-Carlton Terrace

## Business Dining

Acme Chop Hse.
Alfred's Steak
Amber India
Anzu
A.P. Stump's
Aqua
Azie
bacar
Basin
Big Four
Bizou
Boulevard
Buck's
Campton Place
Carnelian Room
Cha Am Thai†
Chantilly
Chaya Brasserie
Chef Chu's
Cole's Chop Hse.
Cool Café
Cosmopolitan Cafe
Daily Grill
Dal Baffo
Dine
Duck Club†
E&O Trading Co.†

Emile's
Evvia
Farallon
Faz†
Flea St. Café
Fly Trap
Fournou's Ovens
Fuki Sushi
Gervais Rest.
Gordon's Hse./Fine Eats
Harris'
Hawthorne Lane
Higashi West
House of Prime Rib
Iberia
Il Fornaio†
Infusion Bar
Izzy's Steak†
Jeanty at Jack's
John's Grill
Julius' Castle
Kokkari Estiatorio
Kuleto's†
Kyo-Ya
La Forêt
Lark Creek†
Le Central Bistro
Le Papillon
Lion & Compass
Masa's
Max's†
mc²
Meadowood Grill
Mistral
MoMo's
Moose's
Morton's
One Market
Osteria
Ozumo
Pacific
Palio d'Asti
Paragon
Park Grill
Pastis

Pazzia
Ponzu
Postrio
Red Herring
Redwood Park
Restaurant LuLu
Ristorante Umbria
Ritz-Carlton Din. Rm.
Roy's
Rubicon
Ruth's Chris
Sam's Grill
Sanraku Four Seasons
Seasons
71 Saint Peter
Shanghai 1930
Silks
Soléa
South Park Cafe
Spago Palo Alto
Stars
St. Michael's Alley
Tadich Grill
Thirsty Bear
Tommy Toy's
Townhouse B&G
231 Ellsworth
Verbena
Viaggio Rist.
Viognier
Waterfront Rest.
Yank Sing
Zaré
Zibibbo
Zuni Cafe

**Catering**
Acquerello
Alcatraces
Alma
Aziza
bacar
Basin
Bistro Ralph
Bizou

Boonville Hotel
Bouchon
Breads of India
Cafe Esin
Cafe Kati
Cafe Lolo
Cafe Prima
Carneros
Catahoula Rest.
Central Park
César
Cetrella Bistro
Chaz Rest.
Chenery Park
Chez Nous
Cool Café
Cucina Viansa
Daily Grill
D'Asaro
Destino
Dry Creek Kitchen
Emile's
Evvia
Farallon
Frascati
Gabriella Café
Gayle's Bakery
Gordon's
Grasing's Coastal
Greens
Hyde St. Bistro
Insalata's
Jianna
John Ash & Co.
Kokkari Estiatorio
La Folie
Lalime's
Lapis Rest.
Lark Creek†
Le Charm
Le Cheval
Le Papillon
Le Poisson Japonais
Manzanita
Marché

Maurice Rest.
Maya (SF)
Meetinghouse
Merenda
Millennium
One Market
Ozumo
Pane e Vino
Pasta Moon
Pazzia
Pearl
Pesce
Pinot Blanc
Piyassa
PlumpJack Cafe†
Ravenous†
Restaurant LuLu
Rick & Ann's
Roux
Sassafras
71 Saint Peter
Sociale
Soizic
St. Michael's Alley
Stokes Rest.
Straits Cafe
Tra Vigne
2223 Restaurant
Vivande Porta Via
Wente Vineyards
Yank Sing
Yumma's
zazu
Zibibbo

## Celebrity Chefs

Aqua, *Michael Mina*
Bistro Jeanty, *Philippe Jeanty*
Boulevard, *Nancy Oakes*
Campton Place, *Laurent Manrique*
Catahoula, *Jan Birnbaum*
Chef Chu's, *Lawrence Chu*
Chez Panisse, *Alice Waters*
Citizen Cake, *Elizabeth Falk*
Delfina, *Craig Stoll*
Dry Creek Kit., *Charlie Palmer*
Elisabeth Daniel, *Daniel Patterson*

EOS, *Arnold Eric Wong*
Farallon, *Mark Franz*
Fifth Floor, *Laurent Gras*
Flea St. Café, *Jesse Cool*
Fleur de Lys, *Hubert Keller*
French Laundry, *Thomas Keller*
Fringale, *Gerard Hirigoyen*
Gary Danko, *Gary Danko*
Jardinière, *Traci Des Jardins*
La Folie, *Roland Passot*
Lark Creek Inn, *Bradley Ogden*
La Toque, *Ken Frank*
Martini House, *Todd Humphries*
Masa's, *Ron Siegel*
Mustards Grill, *Cindy Pawlcyn*
Pinot Blanc, *Joachim Splichal*
Redwood Park, *George Morrone*
Rose Pistola, *Reed Hearon*
Roy's at Pebble Beach, *Roy Yamaguchi*
Slanted Door, *Charles Phan*
Terra, *Hiro Sone*
Zuni Cafe, *Judy Rodgers*

## Child-Friendly

(Besides the normal fast-food places; * children's menu available)
Acme Chop Hse.
Alioto's*
Allegro
Anzu*
Asqew Grill
A Tavola*
Autumn Moon*
Barbara's Fishtrap*
Barney's†
Beach Chalet*
Bette's Oceanview
Blue Plate
Bocca Rotis*
Buca di Beppo
Buckeye Roadhse.*
Cactus Taqueria†
Cafe For All Seasons

Cafe Riggio*
Caffe Macaroni
Caffe Sport
Capp's Corner*
Carrara's
Casanova*
Casa Orinda
Chenery Park*
Chez Panisse Café*
Chow
Cityscape*
Cliff House
Coriya Hot Pot City
Deuce*
Dipsea Cafe*
Doña Tomás*
Duck Club†
El Palomar*
Emmy's
FatApple's†
Felix & Louie's*
Firefly
First Crush*
Garden Court*
Ginger Island*
Green Valley Cafe
Guernica*
Hard Rock Cafe*
House of Prime Rib*
I Fratelli*
Il Fornaio†
Insalata's*
Italian Colors*
Jocco's
Jordan's*
Juban
JZ Cool
Koryo
La Ginestra*
Lark Creek*
Lauren's*
Left Bank†
Little Joe's†
LoCoCo's
Marin Joe's*

Max's†
Meadowood Grill*
Mel's Drive-In†
Mistral*
Mixx Rest.*
Montrio*
Moss Beach*
Napa Valley Grille*
Navio*
Nola*
One Market*
Original Joe's†
Oswald's*
Pacific*
Pacific Café
Pacific's Edge*
Pairs*
Park Grill*
Pasta Pomodoro†
Pelican Inn*
Peninsula Fountain
Perry's†
Piatti†
Picante Cocina*
Postino
Primo Patio*
Q
Red Rock Cafe
Restaurant LuLu*
Rick & Ann's*
Rick's
Rio Grill*
Ritz-Carlton Din. Rm.*
Roosevelt Tamale
Rutherford Grill*
Sardine Factory*
Savor*
Scoma's*
Shadowbrook*
Skates on the Bay*
Spenger's
Station Hse. Café*
Stokes Rest.*
Tarpy's Roadhse.*
Tomatina†

Tonga Room*
Townhouse B&G
Town's End
Venezia*
Vic Stewart's*
Viognier
Yankee Pier*
Zao Noodle Bar†

### Critic-Proof
(Get lots of business,
despite so-so food)
Beach Chalet
Cliff House
Gordon Biersch
Hard Rock Cafe
Mel's Drive-In
Pasta Pomodoro
Pier 23 Cafe
Sam's Anchor
Spenger's
Tonga Room
Zao Noodle Bar

### Dancing
AsiaSF
Cityscape
Compass Rose
Curve Bar
Enrico's
Jordan's
Kelly's Mission Rock
Maddalena's/Café Fino
Mas Sake†
Maya (Sonoma)
Piyassa
Plumed Horse
Shanghai 1930
Tonga Room

### Delivery/Takeout
(D=delivery, T=takeout)
Absinthe (T)
Alegrias (T)
Alfred's Steak (T)
Antica Trattoria (T)

# Special Feature Index

Anzu (T)
Asqew Grill (T)
A Tavola (D,T)
Autumn Moon (T)
Aziza (T)
Baker St. Bistro (T)
Barbara's Fishtrap (T)
Basin (T)
Bella Vista (T)
B44 (T)
Bistro Aix (T)
Bistro Don Giovanni (T)
Bistro Liaison (T)
Bistro Ralph (T)
Bistro Vida (D,T)
Bizou (T)
Black Cat (T)
Bloo (T)
Bo's Barbecue (T)
Buckeye Roadhse. (T)
Cafe Beaujolais (T)
Cafe Gibraltar (T)
Cafe La Haye (T)
Cafe Lolo (T)
Café Marcella (T)
Cafe Prima (D,T)
Café Rouge (T)
Casanova (T)
Casa Orinda (T)
Charanga (T)
Chaz Rest. (T)
Chenery Park (T)
Chez Nous (T)
Chow†
Cosmopolitan Cafe (T)
Costeaux Bakery (D,T)
Cucina Paradiso (T)
Delfina (T)
Doña Tomás (T)
downtown (T)
Dry Creek Kitchen (D,T)
E&O Trading Co. (T)
Eastside West (T)
Eulipia (T)
Evvia (D)

Fandango (T)
Flea St. Café (T)
Florio (T)
Flying Fish Grill (T)
Fringale (T)
Garibaldis†
General's Daughter (T)
girl & the fig (T)
girl & the gaucho (T)
Glen Ellen Inn (T)
Globe (T)
Gordon's (D,T)
Gordon's Hse./Fine Eats (T)
Greens (T)
Green Valley Cafe (T)
Helmand (T)
Home (T)
House of Prime Rib (T)
Hunan (T)
Indigo (T)
Insalata's (D,T)
Izzy's Steak†
Jianna (T)
Kingfish (T)
Kokkari Estiatorio (T)
Kyo-Ya (T)
La Forêt (T)
Lark Creek (T)
LaSalette (T)
Left Bank (T)
Le Poisson Japonais (T)
LoCoCo's (T)
Luna Park (T)
Maddalena's/Café Fino (T)
Maya (SF) (D,T)
Maya (Sonoma) (T)
Meadowood Grill (T)
Merenda (T)
Mezza Luna (T)
Millennium (T)
Miramonte (T)
955 Ukiah (T)
Nola (D,T)
Ondine (T)
Pastis (T)

Pearl (T)
Pesce (T)
Pinot Blanc (T)
PJ's Oyster (D,T)
Plouf (T)
Ravenous (T)
Ravens (T)
Restaurant LuLu (T)
Restaurant 301 (T)
Restaurant Umunhum (D,T)
Rivoli (T)
RoHan Lounge (T)
Rose Pistola (T)
Roux (T)
Roy's (T)
Rutherford Grill (T)
Ruth's Chris (T)
Santi (T)
Sassafras (T)
Savoia Rist. (T)
Sea Ranch Lodge (T)
71 Saint Peter (T)
Sierra Mar (T)
Station Hse. Café (T)
St. Michael's Alley (T)
Stokes Rest. (T)
Syrah (T)
Townhouse B&G (T)
Tra Vigne (D,T)
Valhalla (T)
Verbena (T)
Viaggio Rist. (T)
Vic Stewart's (T)
Village Pub (T)
Wappo Bar (T)
Water St. Bistro (T)
Wente Vineyards (T)
Wild Hare (T)
Yabbies (T)
Yankee Pier (T)
Zarzuela (T)
zazu (T)
Zibibbo (T)
Zuni Cafe (T)
Zuzu (T)

## Dining Alone

(Other than hotels and places
with counter service)

Absinthe
Ace Wasabi's
Acme Chop Hse.
Andalu
Asqew Grill
Bette's Oceanview
Bistro Jeanty
Blowfish, Sushi
Burger Joint†
Cafe Bastille
Cafe Citti
Café Claude
Cafe 817
Café Niebaum-Coppola†
Café Rouge
Capp's Corner
César
Chez Papa
Citizen Cake
Dal Baffo
Ebisu
Enrico's
Eos Rest.
Evvia
FatApple's
Firefly
Fog City Diner
Fringale
Frjtz Fries
Galette
Godzila Sushi
Grandeho's Kamekyo
Hamano Sushi
Hana Japanese
Kabuto Sushi
Kirala
L'Amie Donia
La Note
Le Bistrot
Left Bank†
Le Petit Robert
Le Zinc

Liverpool Lil's
Mario's Bohemian
Matterhorn Swiss
Mel's Drive-In†
Mustards Grill
Nizza La Bella
Pasta Pomodoro
Robata Grill
Rose's Café
Sears Fine Food
Suppenküche
Sushi Ran
Swan Oyster Depot
Ti Couz
Tokyo Go Go
Tommaso's
Tra Vigne
Viognier
Vivande Porta Via
Wild Hare
Yank Sing†
Yoshi's
Zazie
Zibibbo

## Entertainment

(Call for days and times of performances)
Albion River Inn (piano)
Alegrias (flamenco/guitar)
Ana Mandara (jazz)
Angkor Wat (dancers)
AsiaSF (gender illusionists)
Azie (DJ)
Aziza (belly dancers)
bacar (jazz)
Beach Chalet (jazz)
Big Four (piano)
Bissap Baobab (Brazilian/jazz)
BIX (jazz)
Black Cat (jazz)
Bo's Barbecue (bands)
Bruno's (jazz)
butterfly (DJ/jazz)
Cafe Bastille (jazz)
Café Claude (jazz)

Cafe Prima (varies)
Carta (jazz/piano)
Central Park (bands)
Cetrella Bistro (jazz)
Chantilly (varies)
Chez Spencer (jazz/piano)
Cityscape (varies)
Clémentine (jazz)
Cobalt Tavern (jazz)
Compass Rose (varies)
Cosmopolitan Cafe (blues/jazz)
Cucina Viansa (bands)
Curve Bar (varies)
Deep Sushi (DJ)
Destino (flamenco/tango)
downtown (jazz)
Duck Club†
E&O Trading Co.†
Eastside West (varies)
El Palomar (mariachi)
Emmy's (DJ)
Enrico's (jazz)
Esperpento (flamenco/vocals)
Everett & Jones†
Faz†
Felix & Louie's (jazz)
Fritz Fries (DJ)
Gordon's Hse./Fine Eats (jazz)
Guaymas (mariachi)
Hard Rock Cafe (pop/rock)
Harris' (jazz/piano)
Hawthorne Lane (piano)
Italian Colors (guitar)
Jardinière (jazz duo)
John's Grill (jazz)
Jordan's (swing)
Kan Zaman (belly dancer)
Katia's (accordion/guitar)
Kelly's Mission Rock (bands/DJ)
Kingfish (blues)
La Mooné (jazz)
La Note (jazz)
Lapis Rest. (jazz)
La Rondalla (mariachi)
LaSalette (fado)

La Scene Café (piano)
Ledford House (jazz)
Left Bank†
Lhasa Moon (Tibetan)
Little River Inn (classical guitar)
Lorca (Spanish)
Lucy's Rest. (guitar/piano)
Maddalena's (jazz trio)
Madrona Manor (jazz)
Mangiafuoco (jazz)
Marin Joe's (jazz/piano)
Marinus (jazz)
Mas Sake†
MatrixFillmore (DJ)
Max's†
Mecca (jazz/R&B)
Mel Hollen's Bar (piano)
Mezze (guitar/jazz)
Mistral (jazz)
Moose's (jazz)
Navio (jazz)
One Market (jazz/piano)
Pacific (piano)
Pacific's Edge (jazz/piano)
Paragon Bar (jazz)
Parcel 104 (jazz)
Perlot (piano)
Piatti†
Pier 23 Cafe (varies)
Plumed Horse (bands/piano)
Ponzu (DJ)
Prima (jazz/piano)
Puerto Alegre (mariachi)
Rasselas Ethiopian†
Restaurant Umunhum (jazz)
Rick's (Hawaiian)
Ritz-Carlton Din. Rm. (harp)
Ritz-Carlton Terrace (jazz)
Rock Soup (varies)
RoHan Lounge (DJ)
Rose Pistola (jazz)
Sake Tini (bands/DJ)
Santé (piano)
Schroeder's (polka)
Seasons (piano)

Shadowbrook (jazz)
Shanghai 1930 (jazz)
Station Hse. Café (jazz)
Stinson Beach (jazz)
Straits Cafe†
Taste Cafe (jazz)
Thanya & Salee (DJ)
Timo's (flamenco/guitar)
Tita's (Hawaiian)
Tonga Room (bands)
Townhouse B&G (jazz)
Trader Vic's†
Uva Trattoria (piano)
Viaggio Rist. (piano)
Vic Stewart's (guitar/piano)
Wappo Bar (Brazilian/jazz)
Yoshi's (jazz)
Zinsvalley (guitar)

## Fireplaces

Albion River Inn
Anton & Michel
Applewood Inn
A. Sabella's
Auberge du Soleil
Autumn Moon
Barney's†
Bella Vista
Betelnut Pejiu Wu
Big Four
Bistro Don Giovanni
Bistro Jeanty
Boonville Hotel
Boulange†
Brannan's Grill
Brix
Cafe Citti
Caprice
Casanova
Casa Orinda
Cetrella Bistro
Chantilly
Chateau Souverain
Chez Panisse Café
Chez TJ

Chow†
Cliff House
Club XIX
Dal Baffo
Della Santina's
Dipsea Cafe†
Domaine Chandon
Duck Club†
El Paseo
Erna's Elderberry
Evvia
Farmhouse Inn
Faz†
Foreign Cinema
French Laundry
Fresh Cream
Gaylord India†
Gervais Rest.
Guaymas
Harris'
House of Prime Rib
Iberia
Il Fornaio†
John Ash & Co.
Joubert's
Kenwood
Kokkari Estiatorio
Kuleto's†
Lark Creek Inn
La Toque
Ledford House
Left Bank†
Lion & Compass
MacCallum Hse.
Madrona Manor
Manka's Inverness
Marin Joe's
Marinus
Martini Hse.
Mezza Luna
Mikayla/Casa Madrona
Moosse Cafe
Navio
Nepenthe
Nola

Oliveto Cafe
Pacific
Pairs
Parcel 104
Pelican Inn
Piatti†
Piazza D'Angelo
Pinot Blanc
Plouf
Plumed Horse
PlumpJack Cafe†
Prima
Ravenous†
Ravens
Red Herring
Redwood Park
Rest. at Meadowood
Rest. at Stevenswood
Rio Grill
Robert's Bistro
Rutherford Grill
Salute Rist.†
Santé
Sardine Factory
Sea Ranch Lodge
Seasons
Shanghai 1930
Sierra Mar
Skates on the Bay
Spago Palo Alto
Stokes Rest.
Tarpy's Roadhse.
Valhalla
Vic Stewart's
Village Pub
Viognier
Wild Hare
Wine Spectator
Zinsvalley

## Historic Places

(Year opened; *building)
1830s  Stokes Rest.*
1848  La Forêt*

1849 Tadich Grill
1850's Gary Chu
1850's Geyserville Smokehse.
1862 Boonville Hotel
1862 General's Daughter*
1863 Cliff House
1864 Jeanty at Jack's
1867 Sam's Grill
1876 Olema Inn
1876 Woodward's Garden*
1880s Meetinghouse
1881 Madrona Manor
1882 Calistoga Inn
1882 MacCallum Hse.*
1882 Wine Spectator*
1884 Terra*
1886 Cole's Chop Hse.*
1886 Fior d'Italia
1890 Deuce*
1890 Spenger's
1893 Cafe Beaujolais*
1893 Schroeder's
1893 Valhalla*
1901 downtown
1902 Chez TJ*
1904 Compass Rose*
1904 Victorian Gardens
1908 John's Grill*
1909 Garden Court*
1910 Mel Hollen's Bar
1912 Capp's Corner*
1912 Carême Room
1912 Swan Oyster Depot
1914 Balboa Cafe
1915 Jordan's*
1916 Pork Store Cafe
1917 Manka's Inverness
1917 Napa Valley Wine*
1917 Tarpy's Roadhse.*
1919 Sardine Factory*
1920 Sam's Anchor
1920s Kingfish
1922 Julius' Castle
1922 Roosevelt Tamale
1923 Martini Hse.

1924 Big Four*
1924 Farallon*
1925 Beach Chalet*
1925 John Bentley's*
1927 Ahwahnee Din. Rm.
1927 Moss Beach
late 1800's Miramonte*
late 1800's Vic Stewart's*

## Hotel Dining

Abigail Hotel
    Millennium
Ahwahnee Hotel
    Ahwahnee Din. Rm.
Auberge du Soleil
    Auberge du Soleil
Bernardus Lodge
    Marinus
Blue Heron Inn
    Moosse Cafe
Bodega Bay Lodge & Spa
    Duck Club
Campton Place Hotel
    Campton Place
Carter House
    Restaurant 301
Casa Madrona Hotel
    Mikayla/Casa Madrona
Claremont Resort & Spa
    Jordan's
    Paragon Bar
Clift Hotel
    Asia de Cuba
Dina's Garden Hotel
    Trader Vic's
El Dorado Hotel
    Piatti
Fairmont Hotel
    Tonga Room
Farmhouse Inn
    Farmhouse Inn
Four Seasons Hotel
    Seasons
Galleria Park Hotel
    Perry's

# Special Feature Index

Highlands Inn
  Pacific's Edge
Hilton San Francisco
  Cityscape
Hotel Griffon
  Red Herring
Hotel Healdsburg
  Dry Creek Kitchen
Hotel Majestic
  Perlot
Hotel Monaco
  Grand Cafe
Hotel Nikko
  Anzu
Hotel Palomar
  Fifth Floor
Hotel Vintage Court
  Masa's
Huntington Hotel
  Big Four
Hyatt Sainte Claire
  Il Fornaio
Inn at Southbridge
  Tomatina
Inn at Spanish Bay
  Roy's at Pebble Beach
Lafayette Park Hotel
  Duck Club
Little River Inn
  Little River Inn
Lodge at Pebble Beach
  Club XIX
Lodge at Sonoma
  Carneros
MacCallum House Inn
  MacCallum Hse.
Madrona Manor
  Madrona Manor
Mandarin Oriental Hotel
  Silks
Manka's Inverness Lodge
  Manka's Inverness
Meadowood Resort
  Meadowood Grill
  Rest. at Meadowood

Monterey Plaza
  Duck Club
Mount View Hotel
  Catahoula Rest.
Olema Inn
  Olema Inn
Orchard Hotel
  Soléa
Pacific Renaissance Plaza
  Restaurant Peony
Palace Hotel
  Garden Court
  Kyo-Ya
Palomar Hotel
  El Palomar
Pan Pacific Hotel
  Pacific
Park Hyatt Hotel
  Park Grill
Pelican Inn
  Pelican Inn
PlumpJack Squaw Valley Inn
  PlumpJack Cafe
Post Ranch Inn
  Sierra Mar
Prescott Hotel
  Postrio
Renaissance Stanford Court
  Fournou's Ovens
Richelieu Hotel
  Mel's Drive-In
Ritz-Carlton Hotel
  Navio
  Ritz-Carlton Din. Rm.
  Ritz-Carlton Terrace
Santa Clara Marriott
  Parcel 104
Sea Ranch Lodge
  Sea Ranch Lodge
Serrano Hotel
  Ponzu
Sir Francis Drake Hotel
  Scala's Bistro
Sonoma Mission Inn & Spa
  Santé

Stanford Inn by the Sea
  Ravens
Stanford Park Hotel
  Duck Club
Stevenswood Lodge
  Rest. at Stevenswood
Villa Florence Hotel
  Kuleto's
Vintners Inn
  John Ash & Co.
Warwick Regis
  La Scene Café
Westin St. Francis Hotel
  Compass Rose
W Hotel
  XYZ

## "In" Places

Ace Wasabi's
Acme Chop Hse.
À Côté
Alma
Ana Mandara
Andalu
A.P. Stump's
Aqua
Asia de Cuba
Azie
Aziza
bacar
Balboa Cafe
Betelnut Pejiu Wu
B44
Bistro Don Giovanni
Bistro Jeanty
BIX
Bloo
Bouchon
Boulevard
Buckeye Roadhse.
butterfly
Café Fanny
Cafe Flore
Café Marcella
Cafe Marimba†

Café Rouge
Caffe Centro
Campton Place
César
Cha Cha Cha†
Charanga
Chaya Brasserie
Chez Nous
Chez Panisse
Chez Panisse Café
Chez Papa
Chez Spencer
Citizen Cake
Cosmopolitan Cafe
Cozmo's
D'Asaro
Deep Sushi
Delfina
Dine
Doña Tomás
downtown
Downtown Bakery
Dry Creek Kitchen
Eastside West
Ebisu
Elisabeth Daniel
Emile's
Emmy's
Enrico's
Eos Rest.
Evvia
Farallon
Fifth Floor
Flea St. Café
Fleur de Lys
Florio
Foreign Cinema
42 Degrees
French Laundry
Fringale
Garibaldis†
Gary Danko
girl & the gaucho
Globe
Gordon's Hse./Fine Eats

Grasshopper
Hawthorne Lane
Il Davide
Isa
Jardinière
Jeanty at Jack's
Jianna
Jojo
Julia
Julia's Kitchen
Kabuto Sushi
Kirala
Kokkari Estiatorio
La Luna
Lark Creek Inn
Le Colonial
Left Bank
Le Petit Robert
Le Poisson Japonais
Lion & Compass
Luna Park
Manzanita
Martini Hse.
MatrixFillmore
mc$^2$
Mecca
Merenda
Miramonte
Moose's
Mustards Grill
Nizza La Bella
Nola
Olive Bar
Oliveto Cafe
One Market
Ozumo
Panta Rei
Parcel 104
Pearl Alley Bistro
Perry's†
Piazza D'Angelo
Plouf
PlumpJack Cafe†
Postino
Postrio

Prima
Redwood Park
Restaurant LuLu
Ritz-Carlton Din. Rm.
Rose Pistola
Rose's Café
Roxanne's
Rubicon
Santi
Scala's Bistro
Slanted Door
Slow Club
Sociale
Spago Palo Alto
Spoon
Sushi Groove
Sushi Ran
Tao Cafe
Three Seasons
Ti Couz
Tokyo Go Go
Trader Vic's
Tra Vigne
Universal Cafe
Valhalla
Verbena
Via Centro
Village Pub
Wild Hare
XYZ
Yankee Pier
zazu
Zibibbo
Zuni Cafe
Zuzu

## Jacket Required
Acquerello
Aqua
Campton Place
Carnelian Room
Chantilly
Club XIX
Elisabeth Daniel
French Laundry

La Folie
La Toque
Masa's
Pacific's Edge

## Late Dining

(Weekday closing hour)
Asia de Cuba (1 AM)
Bouchon (12:30 AM)
Brazen Head (1 AM)
Brother's Korean†
Globe (1 AM)
Great Eastern (1 AM)
It's Tops Coffee (3 AM)
Jeanty at Jack's (1 AM)
King of Thai†
Koryo (2 AM)
La Rondalla (2 AM)
Liverpool Lil's (12:40 AM)
MatrixFillmore (2 AM)
Mel's Drive-In†
North Beach Pizza†
Original Joe's†
Rasselas Ethiopian†
Taqueria Cancun (2:45 AM)
Yuet Lee (3 AM)

## Meet for a Drink

(Most top hotels and the
following standouts)
Absinthe
Ana Mandara
Andalu
AsiaSF
Azie
bacar
Balboa Cafe
Beach Chalet
Betelnut Pejiu Wu
Bistro Clovis
Bistro Don Giovanni
Bistro Vida
BIX
Black Cat
Boulevard
Bruno's

Cafe Bastille
Café Claude
Cafe Flore
Café Niebaum-Coppola†
Café Rouge
Caffè Greco
Carnelian Room
César
Cha Cha Cha†
Charlie's
Cliff House
Cobalt Tavern
Cool Café
Cosmopolitan Cafe
Cozmo's
Curve Bar
Delfina
Doña Tomás
E&O Trading Co.
Eastside West
Elite Cafe
Enrico's
Eos Rest.
Farallon
First Crush
Florio
Foreign Cinema
42 Degrees
Frjtz Fries
Garibaldis†
Gordon's Hse./Fine Eats
Guaymas
Hayes & Vine Wine
Higashi West
Home
Iberia
Infusion Bar
Jardinière
Kan Zaman
Kelly's Mission Rock
Kokkari Estiatorio
Lapis Rest.
La Rondalla
Le Colonial
Left Bank†

Le Petit Robert
Le Zinc
Liverpool Lil's
Maddalena's/Café Fino
Manzanita
Martini Hse.
MatrixFillmore
Maya (Sonoma)
$mc^2$
Mecca
MoMo's
Moose's
Mustards Grill
Nepenthe
Nizza La Bella
Nola
Oliveto Cafe
One Market
Ozumo
Pairs
Palio d'Asti
Pangaea
paul K
Pearl Alley Bistro
Perry's
Picaro
Plouf
Plumed Horse
Puerto Alegre
Ramblas
Rasselas Ethiopian†
Restaurant LuLu
RoHan Lounge
Rose Pistola
Rose's Café
Ross Valley Brew.
Roy's
Sake Tini
Sam's Anchor
Sardine Factory
Shanghai 1930
Skates on the Bay
Slow Club
Spago Palo Alto
Spoon

Stars
Suppenküche
Sushi Groove†
Thanya & Salee
Thirsty Bear
Timo's
Tokyo Go Go
Townhouse B&G
Trader Vic's†
Tra Vigne
2223 Restaurant
Viaggio Rist.
Waterfront Rest.
Wine Spectator
Zibibbo
Zin
Zuni Cafe

## Microbreweries

Beach Chalet
Calistoga Inn
E&O Trading Co.
Eldo's Grill
Gordon Biersch†
Moss Beach
Ross Valley Brew.
Thirsty Bear

## Noteworthy Newcomers

Acme Chop Hse.
Aziza
Bloo
Central Park
Chez Papa
Chez Spencer
Daily Grill
D'Asaro
Deep Sushi
Dry Creek Kitchen
Eldo's Grill
F.I.G.S.
Gervais Rest.
Incanto
Jeanty at Jack's

Julia
Julia's Kitchen
La Luna
Lorca
Marché
Marica
Martini Hse.
MatrixFillmore
Mel Hollen's Bar
Minako
Night Monkey
Olive Bar
Panta Rei
Piyassa
Roxanne's
Santé
Savoia Rist.
Sociale
Soléa
Spoon
Tao Cafe
Tartine Bakery
Trader Vic's
Valhalla
Yianni's
zazu

## Offbeat

Ace Wasabi's
Albona Rist.
Angkor Wat
AsiaSF
Aziza
Blue Nile
Buca di Beppo
Caffe Macaroni
Caffe Sport
Carta
Casa Orinda
Catahoula Rest.
Cha Cha Cha
Destino
Esperpento
Flying Fish Grill
Foreign Cinema
Frjtz Fries
Gaylord India†

girl & the gaucho
Helmand
Jimtown Store
Joubert's
Kan Zaman
Katia's Russian Tea
Khan Toke
La Rondalla
Lhasa Moon
Lovejoy's Tea Rm.
Maharani
Martini Hse.
Matterhorn Swiss
Max's†
Maya (Sonoma)
Maykedah
Millennium
Moss Beach
Pelican Inn
Picaro
Puerto Alegre
Ravens
Rick's
RoHan Lounge
Roxanne's
Schroeder's
St. Orres
Straits Cafe†
Tonga Room
Trader Vic's†
Venezia
Yoshi's
Zante's

## Outdoor Dining

(G=garden; P=patio;
S=sidewalk; T=terrace;
W=waterside)
Acme Chop Hse. (P)
À Côté (P)
Albion River Inn (P,W)
Alioto's (W)
Alma (S)
Anton & Michel (P)
Applewood Inn (T)

A.P. Stump's (P)
Auberge du Soleil (T)
Autumn Moon (P)
Baker St. Bistro (S)
Baldoria (S)
Barbara's Fishtrap (P,S,W)
Barney's (P)
Basin (P)
Bay Wolf (T)
Beach Chalet (W)
Betelnut Pejiu Wu (S)
B44 (P,S)
Bissap Baobab (P)
Bistro Aix (P)
Bistro at Glen Ellen (P)
Bistro Don Giovanni (P,T)
Bistro Elan (P)
Bistro Jeanty (P)
Bistro Liaison (P)
Bistro Vida (S)
Black Cat (P)
Blackhawk Grille (P,T,W)
Blue Plate (G,P)
Boonville Hotel (G,P)
Bo's Barbecue (G)
Bouchon (P)
Boulange†
Bridges (P)
Brix (P)
Bucci's (P)
Buckeye Roadhse. (P)
Butler & The Chef (S)
Cactus Taqueria†
Cafe Bastille (S,T)
Cafe Citti (P)
Café Claude (S,T)
Cafe 817 (S)
Cafe Flore (P,S)
Cafe Lucy (G)
Café Niebaum-Coppola†
Café Rouge (P)
Café Tiramisu (S)
Caffe Centro (S)
Caffè Greco (S)
Caffe Macaroni (S)

Calistoga Inn (P)
Caprice (W)
Carneros (P)
Carrara's (P)
Casanova (P)
Celadon (P,T,W)
César (P)
Cetrella Bistro (T)
Chateau Souverain (P)
Chaya Brasserie (P,S)
Chez Spencer (G)
Chloe's Cafe (S)
Chow†
Citron (P)
Cliff House (W)
Club XIX (P,W)
Cole's Chop Hse. (T,W)
Cool Café (P)
Costeaux Bakery (P,S)
Cucina Paradiso (P)
Cucina Viansa (P)
Deep Sushi (S)
Delancey St. (P)
Della Santina's (G,P)
Deuce (G,P)
Dipsea Cafe†
Domaine Chandon (T,W)
Doña Tomás (P)
Dry Creek Kitchen (G,S)
Duck Club†
E&O Trading Co.†
Eastside West (S)
El Paseo (P)
Emporio Rulli (P,S)
Enrico's (P,S)
Erna's Elderberry (T)
Farmhouse Inn (T)
Feast (P,S)
Felix & Louie's (P)
Flea St. Café (P)
Foreign Cinema (P)
42 Degrees (G,P)
Frantoio (G,P)
French Laundry (P)
Fresh Cream (W)

Frjtz Fries†
Gabriella Café (P)
Galette (T)
Gayle's Bakery (P)
General's Daughter (P)
Gervais Rest. (P)
Ginger Island (P)
girl & the fig (P)
Glen Ellen Inn (P,W)
Gordon Biersch†
Gordon's (P,S)
Grasing's Coastal (P)
Greens (W)
Guaymas (P,W)
Herbivore†
Home (P)
Iberia (P)
Il Davide (P,S)
Il Fornaio†
Isa (P)
Italian Colors (P)
Jianna (S)
Jimtown Store (P)
John Ash & Co. (P)
John Bentley's (P)
Julia's Kitchen (P)
Julius' Castle (T)
Kelly's Mission Rock (P,W)
Kenwood (G)
La Cumbre†
La Forêt (W)
La Mediterranée†
L'Amie Donia (P)
La Note (G)
Lapis Rest. (W)
Lark Creek†
Lark Creek Inn (G,W)
LaSalette (P)
La Toque (P)
Le Charm (P)
Le Colonial (P)
Ledford House (W)
Left Bank†
Le Krewe (S)
Le Petit Robert (S)

Le Zinc (P,T)
Lion & Compass (P)
Lisa Hemenway's (P)
Liverpool Lil's (S)
Lucy's Rest. (P)
Madrona Manor (T)
Marché aux Fleurs (P)
Marin Joe's (P)
Marinus (P,T)
Mario's Bohemian (S)
Martini Hse. (G)
Max's†
Maya (SF) (P)
Maya (Sonoma) (S)
McCormick & Kuleto's (W)
Meadowood Grill (T)
Mel Hollen's Bar (S)
Miramonte (P)
Mirepoix (P)
Miss Millie's (P)
Mistral (P,W)
MoMo's (P)
Moosse Cafe (P,W)
Mo's Grill†
Moss Beach (P,W)
Nan Yang Rockridge (P)
Napa Valley Grille (P)
Nepenthe (P,W)
Night Monkey (G,S)
Nizza La Bella (S)
Nob Hill Café (P,S)
Nola (P)
O Chamé (P)
Olema Inn (G,P)
Ondine (W)
Ozumo (S)
Pacific's Edge (W)
Pairs (P)
Pakwan†
Palomino (P,W)
Paragon (P)
Parcel 104 (P)
Park Grill (T)
Pasta Moon (P,S)
Pastis (P)

# Special Feature Index

Pazzia (P)
Pearl (P)
Pearl Alley Bistro (P)
Peninsula Fountain†
Perry's†
Piatti†
Piazza D'Angelo (P)
Picante Cocina (P)
Picaro (P,S)
Pier 23 Cafe (G,T,W)
Pinot Blanc (P)
Pizzetta 211 (S)
Plouf (S,T)
PlumpJack Cafe†
Pomelo†
Postino (P)
Prima (P,S)
Primo Patio (P)
Q (S)
Ravenous†
Red Herring (S,W)
Rest. at Meadowood (T)
Restaurant Umunhum (P)
Rick & Ann's (P)
Rio Grill (P)
Ristorante Fabrizio (P)
Ritz-Carlton Terrace (T)
Rose Pistola (S)
Rose's Café (S)
Ross Valley Brew. (S)
Roux (P)
Roy's at Pebble Beach (P)
Rutherford Grill (P)
Salute Rist.†
Sam's Anchor (T,W)
Sam's Grill (P)
Santi (P)
Sassafras (P)
Savoia Rist. (P)
Savor (G,P)
Scoma's†
Sea Ranch Lodge (W)
Sent Sovi (P)
71 Saint Peter (P)
Shadowbrook (P)

Sharon's by the Sea (P,W)
Shoopra (P)
Sierra Mar (T,W)
Skates on the Bay (W)
Sociale (P)
South Park Cafe (S)
Spago Palo Alto (G,P,T)
Spiedini (P)
Station Hse. Café (G,P)
Stinking Rose (P)
Stinson Beach (P)
St. Michael's Alley (S)
Straits Cafe†
Street Rest. (S)
Sushi Ran (P)
Tarpy's Roadhse. (P)
Tastings Rest. (P)
Taylor's Automatic (G,P)
Three Seasons (S)
Ti Couz (S)
Tomatina†
Townhouse B&G (P)
Town's End (P)
Trader Vic's†
Tra Vigne (G,T)
Tuscany (P)
Universal Cafe (P)
Valhalla (W)
Verbena (P)
Via Centro (S)
Viaggio Rist. (P)
Via Vai (P)
Vic Stewart's (P)
Villa Corona†
Village Pub (P)
Wappo Bar (G,P)
Waterfront Rest. (P,W)
Water St. Bistro (P)
Wente Vineyards (P)
Willow Wood (P)
Wine Spectator (T)
Yankee Pier (P)
Yank Sing†
Yianni's (P)
Yumma's (G)

Z (T)
Zao Noodle Bar†
Zazie (G,P)
Zibibbo (G,P)
Zinsvalley (P)
Zuni Cafe (S)

## People-Watching

Ace Wasabi's
Ana Mandara
Asia de Cuba
AsiaSF
Balboa Cafe
Betelnut Pejiu Wu
Bistro Don Giovanni
Bistro Jeanty
BIX
Black Cat
Blowfish, Sushi
Bouchon
Boulevard
Cafe Bastille
Café Claude
Cafe Flore
Caffe Centro
Caffè Greco
Carême Room
Cha Cha Cha†
Charlie's
Chaya Brasserie
Cozmo's
Dal Baffo
downtown
Downtown Bakery
Eastside West
El Palomar
Enrico's
Evvia
Flea St. Café
Foreign Cinema
Grasshopper
Jardinière
Julia's Kitchen
Left Bank†
Mario's Bohemian

Mas Sake
MatrixFillmore
Mecca
Moose's
Mustards Grill
Nola
Pasta Pomodoro†
Perry's
Postrio
Restaurant LuLu
Rose Pistola
Rose's Café
Sam's Anchor
Spago Palo Alto
Sushi Groove
Tin-Pan Asian
Tokyo Go Go
Tra Vigne
2223 Restaurant
Village Pub
Viognier
Wild Hare
Zao Noodle Bar†
Zibibbo
Zuni Cafe

## Power Scenes

Allegro
Ana Mandara
Aqua
Asia de Cuba
bacar
Big Four
Blackhawk Grille
Boulevard
Buck's
Charles Nob Hill
Dal Baffo
downtown
Evvia
Fifth Floor
Fleur de Lys
Fly Trap
Hawthorne Lane
Il Fornaio†

Jardinière
Jeanty at Jack's
Kokkari Estiatorio
Le Central Bistro
Le Colonial
Le Poisson Japonais
Lion & Compass
mc2
Mistral
Moose's
One Market
Park Grill
Pisces
Plumed Horse
Postrio
Redwood Park
Ritz-Carlton Din. Rm.
Rubicon
Spago Palo Alto
Tommy Toy's
Village Pub
Viognier
Wild Hare
Zuni Cafe

**Pre-Theater Menus**
(Call for prices and times)
Absinthe
Alamo Square
Anjou
Anzu
Bistro Aix
Caffe Delle Stelle
Campton Place
Chapeau!
Christophe
Clémentine
First Crush
Garibaldis†
Hyde St. Bistro
Indigo
Jardinière
Juban†
La Scene Café
Millennium

paul K
Postrio
Stars
Suppenküche

**Private Rooms**
(Restaurants charge less at
off times; call for capacity)
Acme Chop Hse.
Acquerello
Ahwahnee Din. Rm.
Alegrias
Alfred's Steak
Alioto's
Alma
Ana Mandara
Andalu
Angkor Wat
Anton & Michel
Anzu
A.P. Stump's
A. Sabella's
Asia de Cuba
A Tavola
Auberge du Soleil
Autumn Moon
Avenue 9
Aziza
Balboa Cafe
Baldoria
Basin
Basque Cultural Ctr.
Bay Wolf
Beach Chalet
Bella Vista
Betelnut Pejiu Wu
Big Four
Blackhawk Grille
Blue Nile
Blue Plate
Boonville Hotel
Boulevard
Brandy Ho's
Brava Terrace
Bridges

Brix
Bruno's
Buca di Beppo†
Buca Giovanni
Buckeye Roadhse.
butterfly
Cafe Bastille
Cafe Beaujolais
Cafe Kati
Cafe Lolo
Cafe Prima
Cafe Riggio
Café Rouge
Café Tiramisu
Caffe Delle Stelle
Calistoga Inn
Capellini
Caprice
Carême Room
Carnelian Room
Carneros
Carrara's
Casanova
Casa Orinda
Catahoula Rest.
Central Park
Cetrella Bistro
Cha Cha Cha†
Chantilly
Charles Nob Hill
Chaz Rest.
Chef Chu's
Chenery Park
Chez Papa
Chez Spencer
Chez TJ
Citron
Cliff House
Club XIX
Cosmopolitan Cafe
Cozmo's
Daily Grill
Dal Baffo
Della Santina's
Deuce

Doña Tomás
downtown
Dry Creek Kitchen
Duarte's Tavern
Duck Club†
E&O Trading Co.†
Eastside West
El Paseo
Emile's
Eos Rest.
Erna's Elderberry
Eulipia
Fandango
Farallon
Farmhouse Inn
Faz
Felix & Louie's
Fifth Floor
F.I.G.S.
Fior d'Italia
First Crush
FlatIron Grill
Flea St. Café
Fook Yuen
Fournou's Ovens
Frantoio
Frascati
French Laundry
Fresh Cream
Fuki Sushi
Gabriella Café
Garibaldis†
Gary Chu
Gary Danko
Gaylord India†
General's Daughter
Gervais Rest.
Ginger Island
Glen Ellen Inn
Globe
Gordon Biersch†
Gordon's Hse./Fine Eats
Grand Cafe
Grasing's Coastal
Great Eastern

Guaymas
Guernica
Harbor Village
Harris'
Hawthorne Lane
Hong Kong Flower†
House of Prime Rib
Hunan†
Hunan Home's†
Iberia
I Fratelli
Il Davide
Il Fornaio
Incanto
Indian Oven
Indigo
Insalata's
Izzy's Steak
Jade Villa
Jardinière
Jeanty at Jack's
John Ash & Co.
John Bentley's
John's Grill
Jordan's
Julius' Castle
Kelly's Mission Rock
Kenwood
Khan Toke
Kingfish
King of Thai†
Koi Palace
Kokkari Estiatorio
Kuleto's
La Folie
La Forêt
Lark Creek†
Lark Creek Inn
La Scene Café
La Toque
Le Bistrot
Le Central Bistro
Le Colonial
Ledford House
Left Bank

Le Papillon
Le Poisson Japonais
Liberty Cafe
Lion & Compass
Lisa Hemenway's
Little River Inn
L'Olivier
Lorca
MacCallum Hse.
Maddalena's/Café Fino
Madrona Manor
Maharani
Mandarin
Manzanita
Marché
Marinus
Martini Hse.
Masa's
Max's Diamond
Maya (SF)
McCormick & Kuleto's
mc$^2$
Meadowood Grill
Mel Hollen's Bar
Mendo Bistro
Mezza Luna
Mikayla/Casa Madrona
Millennium
Miramonte
Miss Millie's
Mistral
Mixx Rest.
MoMo's
Montrio
Moose's
Morton's
Moss Beach
Nan Yang Rockridge
Napa Valley Grille
Navio
Nepenthe
Nola
North Beach Rest.
Olema Inn
Oliveto Cafe

# Special Feature Index

One Market
Osake
Ozumo
Pacific's Edge
Pairs
Palio d'Asti
Pangaea
Paragon
Paragon Bar
Parcel 104
Park Grill
Passionfish
Pasta Moon
Pauline's Pizza
Pelican Inn
Perlot
Perry's†
Piatti
Piazza D'Angelo
Picante Cocina
Pinot Blanc
PJ's Oyster
Plearn Thai
Plumed Horse
PlumpJack Cafe
Ponzu
Postino
Postrio
Prima
R & G Lounge
Ravens
Red Herring
Redwood Park
Rest. at Meadowood
Restaurant LuLu
Restaurant Peony
Restaurant 301
Rick's
Rio Grill
Ritz-Carlton Din. Rm.
Ross Valley Brew.
Rotunda
Rubicon
Ruth's Chris
Salute Rist.

Sam's Grill
Sanraku Four Seasons†
Santé
Sardine Factory
Sassafras
Scala's Bistro
Schroeder's
Sea Ranch Lodge
Seasons
Sent Sovi
71 Saint Peter
Shadowbrook
Shalimar†
Shanghai 1930
Silks
Soizic
Soléa
Spago Palo Alto
Spenger's
Spiedini
Stars
Station Hse. Café
Stinking Rose
Stokes Rest.
Suppenküche
Taiwan†
Takara
Tarpy's Roadhse.
Terra
Thanh Long
Thirsty Bear
Ti Couz
Tommy Toy's
Ton Kiang
Trader Vic's
Tra Vigne
2223 Restaurant
231 Ellsworth
Uva Trattoria
Uzen
Valhalla
Venezia
Verbena
Viaggio Rist.

Vic Stewart's
Village Pub
Viognier
Wappo Bar
Wasabi & Ginger
Waterfront Rest.
Wente Vineyards
Wild Hare
Wine Spectator
Woodward's Garden
Yank Sing†
Yoshi's
Z
Zao Noodle Bar†
Zibibbo
Zinsvalley

## Prix Fixe Menus

(Call for prices and times)
Ajanta
Alamo Square
Anjou
Anzu
Aqua
Asia de Cuba
AsiaSF
Auberge du Soleil
Avenue 9
Aziza
Baker St. Bistro
Bistro Elan
BIX
Bizou
Black Cat
Café Tiramisu
Campton Place
Capp's Corner
Carême Room
Carnelian Room
Carta
Chapeau!
Charles Nob Hill
Chaya Brasserie
Chez Panisse
Chez TJ

Christophe
Citron
Cityscape
Clémentine
Cliff House
Coriya Hot Pot City
Della Santina's
Domaine Chandon
Elisabeth Daniel
Emile's
Erna's Elderberry
First Crush
Fleur de Lys
French Laundry
Grasing's Coastal
Greens
Hyde St. Bistro
I Fratelli†
Indigo
Jordan's
Juban†
Julia's Kitchen
Kyo-Ya
La Felce
La Folie
La Note
Lark Creek Inn
La Scene Café
La Toque
Le Charm
Ledford House
Le Papillon
Le Soleil
L'Olivier
Lotus Cuisine
Lovejoy's Tea Rm.
Madrona Manor
Maharani
Mandarin
Manka's Inverness
Marché aux Fleurs
Martini Hse.
Masa's
Maya (SF)
Merenda

North Beach Pizza†
Ozumo
Pacific
Pacific's Edge
Passage to India
Pastis
Pinot Blanc
Redwood Park
Rest. at Meadowood
Restaurant 301
Rice Table
Ristorante Bacco
Ritz-Carlton Din. Rm.
Robert's Bistro
Rubicon
Sanraku Four Seasons†
Sea Ranch Lodge
Seasons
Sierra Mar
Tastings Rest.
Tonga Room
2223 Restaurant
231 Ellsworth
Victorian Gardens
Viognier
Watergate
We Be Sushi†
Zaré
Zucca

## Quiet Conversation
Acquerello
Applewood Inn
Auberge du Soleil
Bella Vista
Britt-Marie's
Cafe Jacqueline
Campton Place
Casanova
Chantilly
Charles Nob Hill
Chaz Rest.
Chenery Park
Chez Panisse
Chez TJ

Duck Club†
Elisabeth Daniel
El Paseo
Fifth Floor
Fournou's Ovens
Gary Danko
Iberia
Julius' Castle
Lalime's
La Toque
L'Olivier
Madrona Manor
Masa's
Ma Tante Sumi
O Chamé
Oswald's
Pacific's Edge
Park Grill
Pelican Inn
Postino
Redwood Park
Silks
St. Orres
Uzen
XYZ
Zaré
Zax

## Raw Bars
Absinthe
Ace Wasabi's
Acme Chop Hse.
bacar
Bistro Vida
Black Cat
Blowfish, Sushi
Bouchon
Café Rouge
Cetrella Bistro
Deep Sushi
Eastside West
Elite Cafe
Faz†
Fog City Diner
Foreign Cinema
Fuki Sushi
Globe

Grandeho's Kamekyo†
Grasshopper
Hamano Sushi
Hana Japanese
Higashi West
Jeanty at Jack's
Jianna
Kabuto Sushi
Kingfish
Kirala
Kyo-Ya
Le Bistrot
Le Poisson Japonais
McCormick & Kuleto's
Navio
Olema Inn
Osake
Ozumo
Pesce
Pisces
Plouf
Red Herring
Restaurant LuLu
Stinson Beach
Sushi Groove†
Swan Oyster Depot
Takara
Ten-Ichi
Ti Couz
Tokyo Go Go
Wasabi & Ginger
We Be Sushi†
Yabbies
Yankee Pier
Yoshi's
Zibibbo
Zuni Cafe

### Romantic Places

Acquerello
Ahwahnee Din. Rm.
Anton & Michel
Applewood Inn
Auberge du Soleil
Aziza
Bella Vista

Big Four
Bistro Clovis
Bistro Elan
Bistro Vida
Britt-Marie's
Buca Giovanni
Cafe Beaujolais
Cafe Jacqueline
Caprice
Carnelian Room
Casanova
Chantilly
Chapeau!
Charles Nob Hill
Chateau Souverain
Chez Panisse
Chez TJ
Christophe
Citron
Compass Rose
Cool Café
Dal Baffo
Della Santina's
Domaine Chandon
Duck Club†
Elisabeth Daniel
El Paseo
Emile's
Erna's Elderberry
Evvia
Fandango
Fifth Floor
Flea St. Café
Fleur de Lys
Foreign Cinema
French Laundry
Fresh Cream
Gabriella Café
Gary Danko
General's Daughter
Glen Ellen Inn
Greens
Guernica
Hyde St. Bistro
Iberia

Il Davide
Indigo
Jardinière
Jianna
John Ash & Co.
John Bentley's
Julius' Castle
Katia's Russian Tea
Kenwood
Khan Toke
La Folie
La Forêt
Lalime's
L'Amie Donia
La Note
La Toque
Le Papillon
L'Olivier
MacCallum Hse.
Maddalena's/Café Fino
Madrona Manor
Maharani
Manka's Inverness
Marché
Marché aux Fleurs
Marinus
Martini Hse.
Masa's
Matterhorn Swiss
Meetinghouse
Mikayla/Casa Madrona
Moosse Cafe
Napa Valley Wine
O Chamé
Olema Inn
Oliveto Cafe
Ondine
Pacific's Edge
Perlot
Postino
Redwood Park
Rest. at Meadowood
Rest. at Stevenswood
Ritz-Carlton Din. Rm.
Ritz-Carlton Terrace

Robert's Bistro
Roy's at Pebble Beach
Salute Rist.†
Sent Sovi
71 Saint Peter
Sierra Mar
Silks
Slow Club
Soizic
St. Michael's Alley
St. Orres
Terra
Venticello
Victorian Gardens
Viognier
Waterfront Rest.
Wente Vineyards
Woodward's Garden
Zaré
Zarzuela
Zax

**Senior Appeal**
Acme Chop Hse.
Acquerello
Alfred's Steak
Alioto's
Anton & Michel
Bella Vista
Big Four
Buca Giovanni
Cafe For All Seasons
Caprice
Chantilly
Charles Nob Hill
Christophe
Cole's Chop Hse.
Compass Rose
Dal Baffo
Duck Club†
Emile's
Eulipia
FatApple's
Fior d'Italia
Fleur de Lys
Fly Trap

Fournou's Ovens
Garden Court
Harris'
Hayes St. Grill
House of Prime Rib
Izzy's Steak†
John's Grill
La Felce
La Ginestra
Lalime's
Le Bistrot
L'Olivier
Marin Joe's
Masa's
Mixx Rest.
Morton's
North Beach Rest.
Plumed Horse
Robert's Bistro
Rotunda
Sardine Factory
Scoma's†
Sears Fine Food
Tadich Grill
Vic Stewart's

### Singles Scenes
Ace Wasabi's
Alma
Andalu
Asia de Cuba
Balboa Cafe
Beach Chalet
Betelnut Pejiu Wu
Bissap Baobab
BIX
Blowfish, Sushi
Blue Plate
Bruno's
butterfly
Cafe Bastille
Café Claude
Cafe Flore
Cafe Marimba†
Cha Cha Cha
Charlie's

Cosmopolitan Cafe
Cozmo's
Curve Bar
Deep Sushi
Dine
E&O Trading Co.
Eastside West
Elite Cafe
El Palomar
Emmy's
Firecracker
Foreign Cinema
42 Degrees
Frjtz Fries†
Gordon Biersch†
Gordon's Hse./Fine Eats
Guaymas
Home
Infusion Bar
Kan Zaman
Kingfish
La Mooné
La Rondalla
Le Krewe
Luna Park
MatrixFillmore
Mecca
MoMo's
Nola
Ozumo
Palomino
Paragon
Pearl Alley Bistro
Perry's
Pier 23 Cafe
PJ's Oyster
Ponzu
Puerto Alegre
Ramblas
RoHan Lounge
Rose Pistola
Sake Tini
Sam's Anchor
Slow Club
Spoon

Sushi Groove
Thanya & Salee
Thirsty Bear
Ti Couz
Timo's
Tokyo Go Go
Townhouse B&G
2223 Restaurant
Universal Cafe
Zibibbo

## Sleepers
(Good to excellent food, but little known)
Alcatraces
Anton & Michel
Basque Cultural Ctr.
Boonville Hotel
Cafe Gibraltar
Cafe Lucy
Caffè Greco
Cambodiana
Carneros
Chantilly
Chaz Rest.
Cityscape
Cool Café
Costeaux Bakery
Cucina Paradiso
Deuce
Dusit Thai
Farmhouse Inn
Gabriella Café
Gervais Rest.
Geyserville Smokehse.
girl & the gaucho
Glen Ellen Inn
Gordon's
Grasing's Coastal
Graziano's
Green Valley Cafe
JoAnn's Cafe
John's Grill
K&L Bistro
La Felce

La Ginestra
La Mooné
LaSalette
La Scene Café
Lauren's
Mandalay
Marché
Marché aux Fleurs
Marinus
Massawa
Mescolanza
Model Bakery
Omei
Osake
Oswald's
Pangaea
Parcel 104
Park Grill
Pearl
Pho Vietnam
Pizza Azzurro
Pizzetta 211
Red Rock Cafe
Restaurant 301
Rice Table
Robert's Bistro
Rosamunde Sausage
Rotunda
Roux
Sassafras
Seasons
Sharon's by the Sea
Verbena
Victorian Gardens
Villa Corona
Vi's
Wasabi & Ginger
Yumma's
Zucca

## Tasting Menus
Acquerello
Ahwahnee Din. Rm.
All Season's Cafe
Applewood Inn
Aqua
Auberge du Soleil

Aziza
Blackhawk Grille
Bridges
Cafe Kati
Café Tiramisu
Campton Place
Charles Nob Hill
Chez Spencer
Citron
Domaine Chandon
Dry Creek Kitchen
Duck Club†
Elisabeth Daniel
Erna's Elderberry
Fifth Floor
First Crush
Flour do Lye
French Laundry
Gary Danko
Greens
Jardinière
Julia's Kitchen
Kingfish
La Folie
La Forêt
Lalime's
La Mooné
Lark Creek Inn
La Toque
Le Papillon
Le Poisson Japonais
Little Shin Shin
Madrona Manor
Maharani
Manka's Inverness
Marché
Masa's
mc$^2$
Mirepoix
Navio
Oliveto Cafe
Ondine
Pacific's Edge
Pinot Blanc
Pisces

Redwood Park
Rest. at Meadowood
Restaurant 301
Ritz-Carlton Din. Rm.
Roux
Roy's
Rubicon
Santé
Sea Ranch Lodge
Silks
Soléa
Spiedini
Tastings Rest.
Tommy Toy's
Tratt. La Siciliana
231 Ellsworth
Victorian Gardens
Wine Spectator
Zaré

### Tea Service

(See also Hotel Dining; the following are highly touted)
Citizen Cake
Dragon Well
Garden Court
Katia's Russian Tea
Lovejoy's Tea Rm.
O Chamé
Rotunda
Watergate
Yank Sing

### Teen Appeal

Barney's
Fog City Diner
Geyserville Smokehse.
Hard Rock Cafe
Max's†
Mel's Drive-In†
Mo's Grill
Peninsula Fountain
Rutherford Grill
Sardine Factory
Spenger's
Stinking Rose

Taylor's Automatic
Tonga Room

## Theme Restaurants
Hard Rock Cafe
Maharani
Martini Hse.
Max's
Mel Hollen's Bar
Napa Valley Wine
Sardine Factory
Spenger's
Stinking Rose

## Valet Parking
Absinthe
Albona Rist.
Alfred's Steak
Ana Mandara
Antica Trattoria
Anzu
Aqua
Asia de Cuba
Auberge du Soleil
Azie
Aziza
bacar
Balboa Cafe
Big Four
BIX
Black Cat
Boulevard
Bridges
Buckeye Roadhse.
Campton Place
Capellini
Caprice
Casa Orinda
Chantilly
Charles Nob Hill
Chaya Brasserie
Cityscape
Club XIX
Cosmopolitan Cafe
Crustacean
Duck Club†

Eastside West
Emile's
Enrico's
Evvia
Farallon
Fifth Floor
Fior d'Italia
Fleur de Lys
Foreign Cinema
Fournou's Ovens
Frantoio
Garibaldis†
Gervais Rest.
Golden Turtle
Grand Cafe
Harbor Village
Hard Rock Cafe
Harris'
Hawthorne Lane
Home
House of Prime Rib
I Fratelli†
Il Fornaio†
Indigo
Insalata's
Jardinière
Jianna
Jordan's
Julius' Castle
Kokkari Estiatorio
Kuleto's†
Kyo-Ya
La Felce
La Folie
Lapis Rest.
Lark Creek†
Lark Creek Inn
La Scene Café
Le Colonial
Left Bank†
Lion & Compass
Little Joe's†
L'Olivier
Maddalena's/Café Fino
Marin Joe's

Marinus
Masa's
Matterhorn Swiss
Maykedah
mc$^2$
Mecca
Meetinghouse
Mel Hollen's Bar
Mikayla/Casa Madrona
Millennium
MoMo's
Moose's
Morton's
Navio
Nob Hill Café
North Beach Rest.
Ondine
One Market
Original Joe's†
Pacific
Pacific's Edge
Pane e Vino
Paragon
Perlot
Piatti†
Piazza D'Angelo
Plumed Horse
PlumpJack Cafe†
Ponzu
Postrio
Prima
Red Herring
Restaurant LuLu
Ristorante Ideale
Ritz-Carlton Din. Rm.
Ritz-Carlton Terrace
Rose Pistola
Rose's Café
Roy's
Roy's at Pebble Beach
Rubicon
Ruth's Chris
Salute Rist.†
Santé
Scoma's†

Shanghai 1930
Sierra Mar
Silks
Slanted Door
Spago Palo Alto
Spiedini
Stars
Suppenküche
Sushi Groove†
Tommy Toy's
Trader Vic's
Valhalla
Venticello
Viaggio Rist.
Wasabi & Ginger
Waterfront Rest.
Wente Vineyards
Wild Hare
Wine Spectator
XYZ
Z
Zibibbo

## Views

Ahwahnee Din. Rm.
Albion River Inn
A. Sabella's
Auberge du Soleil
Barbara's Fishtrap
Beach Chalet
Bella Vista
Bistro at Glen Ellen
Bistro Don Giovanni
Blackhawk Grille
Brix
Caprice
Carnelian Room
Chateau Souverain
Chaya Brasserie
Cityscape
Cliff House
Club XIX
Cool Café
Delancey St.
Domaine Chandon

Duck Club†
42 Degrees
Fresh Cream
Gaylord India†
Greens
Guaymas
Harbor Village
John Ash & Co.
Jordan's
Julia's Kitchen
Julius' Castle
Kelly's Mission Rock
Lapis Rest.
Ledford House
Liberty Cafe
Little River Inn
Mandarin
Marinus
McCormick & Kuleto's
Meadowood Grill
Mikayla/Casa Madrona
Mistral
Moosse Cafe
Moss Beach
Napa Valley Wine
Navio
Nepenthe
Ondine
Pacific's Edge
Palomino
Paragon Bar
Ravens
Red Herring
Rest. at Meadowood
Rotunda
Roy's at Pebble Beach
Salute Rist.†
Sam's Anchor
Scoma's
Sea Ranch Lodge
Seasons
Shadowbrook
Sharon's by the Sea
Sierra Mar
Skates on the Bay

Tarpy's Roadhse.
Trader Vic's
Valhalla
Waterfront Rest.
Wente Vineyards
Wine Spectator
Zinsvalley

## Visitors on Expense Account

Acquerello
Aqua
Auberge du Soleil
Azie
Black Cat
Boulevard
Campton Place
Carnelian Room
Charles Nob Hill
Chateau Souverain
Chez Panisse
Chez TJ
Club XIX
Dal Baffo
Elisabeth Daniel
Erna's Elderberry
Eulipia
Evvia
Fifth Floor
Flea St. Café
Fleur de Lys
French Laundry
Fresh Cream
Gary Danko
Gervais Rest.
Greens
Harris'
Jardinière
John Ash & Co.
Julius' Castle
Kyo-Ya
La Folie
La Forêt
Lark Creek†
La Toque

Le Poisson Japonais
Mandarin
Marinus
Masa's
McCormick & Kuleto's
$mc^2$
Morton's
Napa Valley Wine
Pacific's Edge
Park Grill
Perlot
Plumed Horse
Redwood Park
Ritz-Carlton Din. Rm.
Ritz-Carlton Terrace
Roy's
Roy's at Pebble Beach
Santé
Sea Ranch Lodge
Sent Sovi
71 Saint Peter
Shanghai 1930
Sierra Mar
Silks
Soléa
Spago Palo Alto
Tommy Toy's
Village Pub
Wild Hare

**Wine Bars**

All Season's Cafe
bacar
Bistro Aix
Café Niebaum-Coppola
César
Cetrella Bistro
Cucina Viansa
Eos Rest.
First Crush
Frascati
girl & the fig
girl & the gaucho
Gordon's
Hayes & Vine Wine

Incanto
Kuleto's
Le Zinc
Liberty Cafe
Merenda
Pairs
Pearl Alley Bistro
Plouf
Prima
Restaurant LuLu
Sassafras
Sociale
Sushi Groove
Sushi Ran
Uva Trattoria
Zibibbo

**Winning Wine Lists**

Absınthe
Acme Chop Hse.
À Côté
Acquerello
Ahwahnee Din. Rm.
Albion River Inn
Alioto's
All Season's Cafe
Alma
Anton & Michel
A.P. Stump's
Aqua
Auberge du Soleil
Azie
bacar
Balboa Cafe
Bay Wolf
Bella Vista
Bistro Aix
Bistro Clovis
Bistro Don Giovanni
Bistro Elan
Bistro Vida
Blackhawk Grille
Bouchon
Boulevard
Brannan's Grill

# Special Feature Index

Bridges
Brix
Cafe Kati
Cafe La Haye
Cafe Lolo
Café Marcella
Calistoga Inn
Campton Place
Carnelian Room
Carneros
Casanova
César
Cetrella Bistro
Chapeau!
Charles Nob Hill
Chateau Souverain
Chez Panisse
Chez Panisse Café
Chez TJ
Citron
Club XIX
Cole's Chop Hse.
Cosmopolitan Cafe
Dal Baffo
Deuce
Domaine Chandon
downtown
Dry Creek Kitchen
Elisabeth Daniel
El Paseo
Emile's
Eos Rest.
Erna's Elderberry
Fandango
Farallon
Fifth Floor
First Crush
Flea St. Café
Fleur de Lys
Fournou's Ovens
French Laundry
Gabriella Café
Gary Danko
General's Daughter
girl & the fig

girl & the gaucho
Glen Ellen Inn
Gordon's
Greens
Hawthorne Lane
Hayes & Vine Wine
Iberia
Il Davide
Incanto
Indigo
Jardinière
Jianna
John Ash & Co.
Jojo
Joubert's
Julia's Kitchen
Julius' Castle
Kenwood
Kuleto's
La Folie
La Forêt
L'Amie Donia
Lark Creek Inn
La Toque
Le Papillon
Liberty Cafe
Madrona Manor
Manzanita
Marché
Marinus
Martini Hse.
Masa's
mc$^2$
Meadowood Grill
Mecca
Meetinghouse
Merenda
Mikayla/Casa Madrona
Millennium
Miramonte
Moose's
Mustards Grill
Napa Valley Grille
Napa Valley Wine
955 Ukiah

North Beach Rest.
Oliveto Cafe
Ondine
One Market
Pacific's Edge
Pairs
Pangaea
Park Grill
Passionfish
Pearl Alley Bistro
Pinot Blanc
Pisces
Plumed Horse
PlumpJack Cafe
Postrio
Prima
Red Herring
Redwood Park
Rest. at Meadowood
Restaurant LuLu
Restaurant 301
Restaurant Umunhum
Rio Grill
Ritz-Carlton Din. Rm.
Rivoli
Rose Pistola
Roux
Roxanne's
Roy's
Rubicon
Santé
Santi
Sardine Factory
Sassafras
Sea Ranch Lodge
Sent Sovi
Sierra Mar
Silks
Slanted Door
Spago Palo Alto
Stars
St. Michael's Alley
St. Orres
Sushi Groove
Sushi Ran

Syrah
Tastings Rest.
Terra
Tra Vigne
231 Ellsworth
Valhalla
Verbena
Vic Stewart's
Village Pub
Viognier
Wappo Bar
Waterfront Rest.
Wente Vineyards
Wild Hare
Wine Spectator
Yabbies
Zibibbo

**Worth a Trip**
EAST
Berkeley
    César
    Chez Panisse
    Chez Panisse Café
    downtown
    O Chamé
    Rivoli
    Zachary's Chicago
Livermore
    Wente Vineyards
Oakhurst
    Erna's Elderberry
Oakland
    À Côté
    Bay Wolf
    Oliveto Cafe
    Zachary's Chicago
Yosemite Nat'l Park
    Ahwahnee Din. Rm.
NORTH
Albion
    Albion River Inn
    Ledford House
Boonville
    Boonville Hotel

Eureka
  Restaurant 301
Geyserville
  Chateau Souverain
  Santi
Glen Ellen
  girl & the gaucho
Gualala
  St. Orres
Healdsburg
  Dry Creek Kitchen
  Madrona Manor
  Manzanita
  Tastings Rest.
Inverness
  Manka's Inverness
Kenwood
  Kenwood
Larkspur
  Emporio Rulli
  Left Bank
Manchester
  Victorian Gardens
Mendocino
  Cafe Beaujolais
  MacCallum Hse.
Napa
  Celadon
  Julia's Kitchen
  Mustards Grill
  Napa Valley Wine
Rutherford
  Auberge du Soleil
  La Toque
San Anselmo
  Insalata's
Santa Rosa
  John Ash & Co.
Sausalito
  Ondine
  Sushi Ran
Sonoma
  Cafe La Haye
  Carneros

Della Santina's
girl & the fig
St. Helena
  Martini Hse.
  Meadowood Grill
  Miramonte
  Pinot Blanc
  Rest. at Meadowood
  Roux
  Terra
  Tra Vigne
Yountville
  Bistro Jeanty
  Bouchon
  Domaine Chandon
  French Laundry
SOUTH
Big Sur
  Sierra Mar
Carmel
  Grasing's Coastal
  Marinus
  Pacific's Edge
Half Moon Bay
  Cetrella Bistro
  Navio
  Pasta Moon
Montara
  Cafe Gibraltar
Monterey
  Fresh Cream
  Montrio
  Stokes Rest.
  Tarpy's Roadhse.
Pacific Grove
  Fandango
Pebble Beach
  Club XIX
  Roy's at Pebble Beach
Pescadero
  Duarte's Tavern
SILICON VALLEY/PENINSULA
Burlingame
  Pisces

## Special Feature Index

Menlo Park
   Dal Baffo
   Flea St. Café
   Marché
   Wild Hare
Mountain View
   Chez TJ
Palo Alto
   Cool Café
   Evvia
   L'Amie Donia
   Le Poisson Japonais
   Spago Palo Alto

San Jose
   A.P. Stump's
   Emile's
   La Forêt
   Le Papillon
San Mateo
   Viognier
Saratoga
   Sent Sovi
Woodside
   Bella Vista
   John Bentley's
   Village Pub

# Wine Vintage Chart 1985–2001

This chart is designed to help you select wine to go with your meal. It is based on the same 0 to 30 scale used throughout this *Survey*. The ratings (prepared by our friend **Howard Stravitz**, a law professor at the University of South Carolina) reflect both the quality of the vintage and the wine's readiness for present consumption. We do not include 1987, 1991–1993 vintages because they are not especially recommended for most areas.

| | '85 | '86 | '88 | '89 | '90 | '94 | '95 | '96 | '97 | '98 | '99 | '00 | '01 |
|---|---|---|---|---|---|---|---|---|---|---|---|---|---|
| **WHITES** | | | | | | | | | | | | | |
| **French:** | | | | | | | | | | | | | |
| Alsace | 24 | 18 | 22 | 28 | 28 | 26 | 25 | 23 | 23 | 25 | 23 | 25 | 26 |
| Burgundy | 26 | 25 | 17 | 25 | 24 | 15 | 29 | 28 | 25 | 24 | 25 | 22 | 20 |
| Loire Valley | – | – | – | – | 25 | 23 | 24 | 26 | 24 | 23 | 24 | 25 | 23 |
| Champagne | 28 | 25 | 24 | 26 | 29 | – | 26 | 27 | 24 | 24 | 25 | 25 | – |
| Sauternes | 21 | 28 | 29 | 25 | 27 | – | 20 | 23 | 27 | 22 | 22 | 22 | 28 |
| **California (Napa, Sonoma, Mendocino):** | | | | | | | | | | | | | |
| Chardonnay | – | – | – | – | – | 22 | 27 | 23 | 27 | 25 | 25 | 23 | 26 |
| Sauvignon Blanc/Semillon | – | – | – | – | – | – | – | – | 24 | 24 | 25 | 22 | 26 |
| **REDS** | | | | | | | | | | | | | |
| **French:** | | | | | | | | | | | | | |
| Bordeaux | 25 | 26 | 24 | 27 | 29 | 22 | 26 | 25 | 23 | 24 | 23 | 25 | 23 |
| Burgundy | 23 | – | 21 | 25 | 28 | – | 26 | 27 | 25 | 22 | 27 | 22 | 20 |
| Rhône | 25 | 19 | 27 | 29 | 29 | 24 | 25 | 23 | 25 | 28 | 26 | 27 | 24 |
| Beaujolais | – | – | – | – | – | – | – | – | 23 | 22 | 25 | 25 | 18 |
| **California (Napa, Sonoma, Mendocino):** | | | | | | | | | | | | | |
| Cab./Merlot | 26 | 26 | – | 21 | 28 | 29 | 27 | 25 | 28 | 23 | 26 | 23 | 26 |
| Pinot Noir | – | – | – | – | – | 27 | 24 | 24 | 26 | 25 | 26 | 25 | 27 |
| Zinfandel | – | – | – | – | – | 26 | 24 | 25 | 23 | 24 | 25 | – | 24 |
| **Italian:** | | | | | | | | | | | | | |
| Tuscany | 26 | – | 24 | – | 26 | 22 | 25 | 20 | 28 | 24 | 27 | 26 | 25 |
| Piedmont | 25 | – | 25 | 28 | 28 | – | 24 | 26 | 28 | 26 | 25 | – | – |